The
OUTSIDER'S GUIDE
to UFOs

VOLUME 1: MYSTERY AND SCIENCE

The OUTSIDER'S GUIDE to UFOs

JAMES T. ABBOTT

 ARCHWAY
PUBLISHING

Archway Publishing books may be ordered through booksellers or by contacting:

Archway Publishing
1663 Liberty Drive
Bloomington, IN 47403
www.archwaypublishing.com
1 (888) 242-5904

ISBN: 978-1-4808-5455-0 (sc)
ISBN: 978-1-4808-5456-7 (hc)
ISBN: 978-1-4808-5457-4 (e)

Library of Congress Control Number: 2017917107

Print information available on the last page.

Archway Publishing rev. date: 12/4/2017

And ye shall know the truth and the truth shall make you free.
CIA Motto

Semper Occultus (Always Secret)
MI6 Motto

For Miranda:
the sort of human being who puts most of the rest of us to shame.

Acknowledgements

Sir Isaac Newton said, way back in the seventeenth century, "If I have seen further, it is by standing on the shoulders of giants". It's a sentiment which applies very much to anyone writing books on the UFO phenomenon.

Thank you, therefore, to all the authors, investigators, and organisations mentioned in the text; to the late Edward Ruppelt, Donald Keyhoe, J Allen Hynek, and James MacDonald; to Bruce Maccabee, Richard Haines, Robert Dolan, Stanton Friedman, Nick Pope, and David Clarke; and to all of the others whose expert and considered views illuminate the complexities of this fascinating subject.

And finally, thank you to my wife, who listened to my diatribes, contributed ideas, questioned my more excessive conclusions, and kept faith with me throughout.

It only remains to say that the views expressed are my own and that any and all errors and omissions are unintentional and entirely my own responsibility.

Yorkshire, England, 2017

Contents

PART 1

PART 2

PART 3

PART 1

Introduction

THE TRUTH MAY, OR may not, be out there, but one thing is absolutely certain: In order to get the most from this book, you will need to have – and maintain – an open mind.

That's impossible, of course. We all have our preconceptions and prejudices, and the subject of UFOs attracts prejudice like a summer picnic entices wasps. Some people scoff at the very idea of strange, non-earthly machines, while others are attracted and a little scared by the idea of us being visited by weird objects. The subject is one of the most convoluted and confusing anyone can ever try to tackle. It extends from simple sightings of things in the sky to the most outlandish and challenging events and theories.

This book is about those strange things in the sky. Its central thesis is that the UFO phenomenon remains unproven but is sufficiently well-evidenced to require much more serious investigation. As such, my book is for people who aren't wedded to either side of the debate. It's for those of you who are neither believers nor non-believers: people who are curious, are open-minded, and would like to know more.

What you are about to read has been restricted, as far as possible, to the simplest end of the subject's spectrum, which extends from fairly straightforward things in the sky, to weird and scary stuff like abductions, animal mutilations and dark conspiracies. Yet, even so, you'll find the material incredibly challenging: a mental conundrum of multidimensional proportions. You will find it hard to cope with the detail and the tortuous chains of logic and even tougher having to constantly resist every fibre of your being shying away from, or laughing at, the terminology or the exotic concepts.

I've done my best to make it easy for all of us outsiders by using the word "objects" for "flying saucers" and "UFOs" wherever possible and by using the neutral terms "event", "sighting", or "incident" for that which some of the more extreme ufologists, in their traditionally loaded way, call "encounters" or "close encounters". The book tries to focus on the very simplest of our UFO problems: the UFOs themselves. Aliens, abductions, "missing time" events, conspiracies, cover-ups, and the Disclosure movement – while all mentioned and even discussed in passing – are very much treated as side issues for the time being.

Furthermore, you should be clear that, in this book, "UFO" is used literally to mean *unidentified flying object* (sometimes, in these euphemistic days, called a UAP: unidentified aerial phenomenon). The emphasis is on *unidentified*. That is, the term UFO is not used in this book to mean anything more exotic than a thing which is seen in the air which is not immediately identifiable. This means that, right now, I can answer the question you're all dying to ask at this very moment: Do UFOs exist? Of course they do. We frequently see things in the sky that we cannot immediately identify, but we have got so used to seeing the acronym widely used as shorthand for "little green men from outer space" that it has been thoroughly debased, to the extent that many people are afraid to use it at all, in case they are regarded as kooks and weirdoes.

There are strong arguments on both sides of the UFO debate, and we'll look at most of them in the course of this book. The extreme sceptics generally decide that all UFO sightings are either hoaxes or natural phenomena which people have misconstrued. The ufologists take the same cases and come to entirely different conclusions. The key aim of this book is to examine the subject as impartially as possible and to consider both sides of the debate.

It's now been seventy years since, way back in 1947, journalists reacted to Kenneth Arnold's sighting by inventing the term "flying saucer" for the first time. If one thing is very, very certain about those seventy years and hundreds of thousands of sightings of unidentified objects in the United

States, Europe, the UK, and most other countries around the world, it is the amazing similarity of descriptions over both time and geography. In the same sense, and contradicting many sceptical authors who argue the power of myth, it is noteworthy that the sightings bear very little resemblance to the space ships of popular culture. We will revisit these important issues later in the book.

Consistency is one of the most surprising things about the UFO phenomenon, but its other defining characteristic is probably the degree to which it is subjected to scorn and derision by officials, the media and, indeed, the general public.

Under these circumstances, you will probably experience the full gamut of being excited, offended, attracted, appalled, fascinated, repulsed, revolted, and possibly much else as the book progresses. This is why, even when your first instinct is to scream your disbelief or to burst out laughing, I ask you to try to meet every step of the story with an open mind. You may, however, need to keep close to you a cup (or glass) of whatever soothes your turbulent spirit. Believe me, you'll need it.

Just a word about the strategy of this book. As a fully-paid-up non-ufologist, who has never seen a UFO, never met a ufologist, and never belonged to a single UFO study group, I have nevertheless always been fascinated by the idea of UFOs and what they might mean. Equally, I have always been more than a little repulsed by some of the weirder extensions of the debate, the hoaxes, the insane arguments, and the extremes to which some websites are prepared to go to titillate and attract visitors (and advertisers).

There is a certain amount of reasonably credible evidence for UFOs having been seen well before the beginning of the nineteenth century, but what one might call the modern era of sightings began in the late nineteenth century and the first half of the twentieth century. H G Wells may have been a major mover in all this, but he wrote *War of the Worlds* at a time when people on several continents were already seeing strange things in their skies. At the time they called them airships. In 1938, Orson Welles (no relation) staged his famous radio broadcast of *War of the Worlds*, which set off a national panic in the United States and probably sparked the avalanche of science fiction movies which have entertained us right up to the present time.

But no one has yet convincingly connected H G Wells, Jules Verne, or any of the other early science fiction writers to the earliest recorded sightings of things in the sky. The sceptics believe that these early sightings were suspiciously coincidental, but I have yet to see any proof of the alleged connection.

If there were a link between H G Wells and people seeing things in the sky in Edwardian times, surely the things they would see would be objects shaped like artillery shells, not the massive, lighted airships which were reported. World War II saw a tremendous increase in sightings of strange objects following, or interacting with, bomber formations and military aircraft generally. More on these fascinating subjects later.

And it did not begin with Erich von Däniken and his *Chariots of the Gods* book. There were plenty of stranger theories before him, but the idea of spacemen visiting the Earth really took off after that book was published in 1968. Alleged abductions of humans by UFOs, and animal mutilations performed by their crews, have been staple fare ever since. There are some famous and fascinating cases, but they are not the core subject of this volume.

Allegations of cover-ups by the FBI, the CIA, the US Air Force, MI6, the British government, and many other official bodies have increased over the years. The United States introduced its Freedom of Information and Privacy Act (FOIPA) in the 1960s, and UFO files have been released into the public realm in many countries, including France, Britain, and America. Some documents were redacted, and there is evidence that many relevant documents were held back by various official agencies. For example, the files of the FBI from the early years, and of the CIA well into the twenty-first century, have only now been released (many still heavily redacted). Consequently, the US and European Disclosure movements have become stronger and more active in recent decades.

One of the most hilarious quotes I have found illustrates the Machiavellian levels of complexity in the ongoing battles between governments and ufologists. It is from an FBI response to a request for documents from Major Donald Keyhoe in 1958 and its core philosophy appears to be followed by most governments to this day. In its response, the FBI said:

> "This Bureau does not have information on unidentified flying objects which can be released. This does not mean that this Bureau has information concerning unidentified flying objects which cannot be released."[1]

And if you persist, it gets even weirder. According to many ufologists, aliens are already here on Earth, in bases under the sea or the Antarctic (take your pick) and our planet is simply a battleground on which conflicts of different alien races are being played out in sinister secret.

However, the whole circus with which we have become familiar really kicked off in the years immediately following the war. As you will see later, the key initial events – that is, the most highly publicised ones – occurred in the United States in the year 1947, when the term "flying saucer" was aired for the very first time. That year also saw the incident at Roswell (see chapter 2). Whatever happened near that New Mexico town in 1947 spawned a raging controversy from about the mid-1970s which has never flagged. The sceptics regard that year as a prime example of mass psychosis, of a war-weary nation adjusting to peace after a very nasty conflict. They argue that the US population did this by inventing strange and wonderful objects. But the British, French, Dutch, Belgian, Italian, and German populations (not to mention the Japanese among many others) had experienced considerably more death and devastation on their own soil, so why was the UFO craze of '47 not duplicated (to the same extent, anyway) in any of those nations?

The term flying saucer has since had a long and chequered history. Very quickly, the subject of flying saucers, in itself pretty strange, was expanded to include visitations from other planets. George Adamski was among the first to claim to have met aliens.[2] Adamski (born 1891) was a

---

[1] Maccabee, 2014.

[2] His book *Flying Saucers Have Landed* was published in 1953 (Desmond Leslie and George Adamski), and *Inside the Space Ships* was published in 1955.

Polish-American occultist who was the first widely publicised person to claim they had seen and photographed alien spaceships, met aliens, and travelled to other planets. In the famous year of 1947, he claimed to have counted 184 UFOs as they travelled over his home on Palomar Mountain in California. Adamski's life was filled with controversy. He claimed to have met and travelled with a Venusian named Orthon and to have attended an interplanetary conference on Saturn. See, I told you you'd want to laugh out loud.

Over the years, the strange claims have been extended to include alien autopsies, animal mutilations, abductions, so-called "missing time" incidents, electromagnetic interference with vehicles and power supplies, the existence of multiple extraterrestrial races with different agendas, infiltration of certain governments by aliens, Earth-built UFOs, government cover-ups, and even the complete but secret mastery of the planet by races from other worlds.

The arguments in this book certainly do not mean that any of these out-there theories are necessarily wrong. Anyone with an open mind has to accept that we humans do not know everything. The sad fact is that we do not know very much at all. So all of those ideas *could* be possible. But in the overheated intellectual stew that is the UFO phenomenon – one that has been simmering nicely over a seventy-year period – ideas become myths, and myths become reality, arguments become circular without anyone noticing, and rationality becomes another word for cover-up.

The reader should also resist the temptation to believe that all ufologists are simply ordinary people who've found a new hobby to replace pigeon-racing, stamp collecting, or going to *Twin Peaks* conventions. The image of people who study UFOs as being cranks or nutters is, unfortunately, commonly held. But like most generalisations, it is only true in parts. There most definitely are a good many UFO-nutters, but there is also a strong core of very intelligent, very experienced, and cool-headed ufologists throughout the world, who work very hard to explore the subject in a balanced manner. As we will see, that core includes scientists, government officials, astronauts, US military officers, at least one former governor, an ex-Canadian defence minister, and senior British military officers.

There will be points in this book when elements of the weirder side of the debate will have to be introduced, but the central premise is that it's the UFO sightings that are the key to the whole issue. They form the logic gate for everything else, and we can effectively ignore all the froth until the yes/no challenge has been settled, until the sightings are proven to be either total nonsense or the most profound thing that has happened to the planet since opposable digits. The prime object is to keep the argument focused on the vital prerequisite for all the other flimflam: Are *any* UFOs inexplicable in conventional terms, or are they all perfectly susceptible to scientific explanation within our scientific paradigm? It's that approach that makes this book unique in the UFO arena.

The true sceptic and, to a large extent the true ufologist, is someone who is agnostic on the subject: neither a believer nor a nonbeliever. You will find, however, that there are also pseudo-sceptics and pseudo-ufologists: those who pretend to be neutral but actually start from a position of either rabid, irrational disbelief or hysterical conviction. They can be spotted, quite easily, by their use of absolutes and their ill-justified leaps of logic. When describing sightings, the immovably convinced ufologist tends to slip in words like "craft" and "intelligent movement," where they really should be talking about "objects" and "unpredictable or unnatural movement". The pseudo-sceptic often uses words like "impossible" and similar absolutes when describing features of sightings. They may also arrive at conclusions of mass hysteria or delusion without the slightest proof of such statements.

As this book was being finalised, NASA announced that no fewer than seven Earth-sized planets had been identified and measured as they rapidly rotated around a dwarf star which, hitherto, had been at the bottom of the list of possible life-bearing star systems. The planets of the Trappist-1 system are almost certainly far too problematic in their orbits for humanoid life but there is a chance that somewhere, on one of those very strange worlds, life will exist. Humanity is constantly being surprised by totally unexpected and unpredicted discoveries.

In the early 1960s, chemist Stephanie Kwolek discovered Kevlar when she was looking for a new polymer for car tyres. In 1928, the Scot,

Alexander Fleming, then working at St Mary's Hospital, London, discovered penicillin in a culture dish of a bacterium that had been accidentally left uncovered near a window. And equally unexpected was the discovery, in 1965, of the radio energy left over from the Big Bang. It was made by two engineers at Bell Labs – Arno Penzias and Bob Wilson – who were actually trying to reduce electrical noise in their latest radio antenna.

It's just too easy for humans to decide that something is impossible. For many hundreds of years, the thought of rocks falling from the sky, particularly burning ones, was derided by mainstream science in much the same way that UFOs have been over the past seventy years.

Although falling rocks were well-known as a phenomenon by the ancients, often worshipped as gifts or threats from the gods, the notion of rocks falling from the skies had, by Christian times, become heresy. The Christian faith believed that the Earth had been created by God some four thousand years ago as the centre of the universe. The sun and a few planets circled us for company, and there was a canopy of stars to amuse and distract. To that core Christian doctrine, there really could be nothing else beyond the Earth.

Even to those with slightly freer minds, the issue of falling rocks was a bit baffling. How would huge lumps of rock get up into the sky in the first place? What was it that could possibly set them on fire? The whole notion reeked of witchcraft. How could any sensible person imagine that a piece of rock could burn? For goodness sake, we use rocks to put around a fire to *stop* other things from setting themselves alight. If you listened to stories of burning rocks tumbling out of the sky, you'd be forgiven for suspecting that the people who were telling such tales were, at best, malicious pranksters and, at worst, part of a group seeking to destabilise the entire foundations of the established church and state.

Yet ordinary people had always known that falling rocks existed. When they were working outdoors, they saw them streaking across the skies and found bits of charred rock lying on the ground. But they tended not to tell their priests. You could be burned at the stake for less.

Even after the Renaissance had begun to loosen things up a bit, and well into the seventeenth and eighteenth centuries, the whole idea remained scientifically impossible. The scientists asked – quite reasonably in terms of their existing understanding and knowledge – how would the rocks have got up there? They had identified all the planets and most of the moons of the solar system. How could rocks be levitated from them, up into their skies, out into space, across whatever unimaginable distances separate us, and then fall onto the Earth? And what could then set alight those pieces of solid, inert rock? The notion simply did not make sense. "Modern science" did not accept that these falling rocks were possible. So the natural philosophers of the day scoffed and jeered and called them figments of people's inflamed imaginations. They might even have labelled them a myth, although I can't be sure!

But ever-so-slowly, science began to experiment and to undertake research, to create a basis on which different ideas could be tested and sometimes proved. First we accepted, after much argument, that the Earth was not the centre of the universe, and, an even bigger shock for some, it wasn't even the centre of the solar system. Think about it: Those two apparently simple facts represented an earthquake for people's world views. Absolutely everything that everyone had believed as true prior to that point suddenly became untrue and irrelevant. It took a very long time for some to accept it, but eventually, discoveries followed about the planets, about gravity, and more, until scientists began to wonder about other strange things – like whether it was possible, after all, that rocks could fall in a burning streak from the sky.

It was Ernst Chladni in Germany who, in 1764, first put forward the astounding idea that the rocks came from space. But, even in the mid-eighteenth century, his ideas were generally ignored or derided. That is, until forty years later, in April 1803, a fall of literally thousands of meteorites occurred near the French town of L'Aigle in Normandy. This mass fall, unlike individual meteorites, could not be ignored, and it caused the French Academy of Sciences and the British chemist Edward Howard to begin the work which eventually proved the existence and origin of meteors and meteorites.

Although they had been seen and experienced for millenia, it still took a very long time for the phenomenon of meteors and meteorites to be proved beyond reasonable doubt and, more to the point, to be accepted by mainstream scientists. Nowadays, the patently ridiculous idea of large chunks of heavy rock falling in flames from the sky is an accepted fact, and we go out at night to marvel at the fiery trails as the known showers intercept the Earth's orbit. We now understand that rocks can be present in interplanetary space for many reasons: rocks left over when proto-planets broke up, rocks blasted into space by huge asteroid or meteor impacts, rocks created by collisions between asteroids, and so on. Furthermore, we now also understand that friction in the Earth's atmosphere can create such intense heat that the rocks do, indeed, burn.

Chladni's theory ended up being part of a small shift in the overall paradigm of what we know about our solar system and the way it works. The impossible had become not only possible but an accepted and valuable fact.

Modern scientists are widely respected and admired for their mind-boggling inventions. From stunning advances in life-saving drugs and gene therapy to communications satellites, from the Large Hadron Collider to theoretical quantum physics, scientists constantly change the world we live in.

But the outsider has to understand some fundamental facts about scientists: They are human, they are not always right, and they can be as jealous and protective as the rest of us. They possess just as much stubbornness and blind prejudice as the ordinary person in the street and they are every bit as prone to bring those unattractive characteristics to bear on those whose ideas threaten them and their livelihoods.

The tendency for established engineers and scientists to pooh-pooh new ideas is well documented. Heavier-than-air flight was demonstrated several times throughout the nineteenth century in glider form[3]. Manned,

---

[3] A balloon – which is usually filled with a hot air or certain gases – is made lighter than the air around it and therefore floats up into the air just like a bubble floats upward in a bottle of fizzy drink. Any machine that does not use this approach is known as a heavier-than-air machine. It relies on a cambered wing or rotor and its speed through the air (provided by powerful engines) to enable it to fly. Cayley understood these forces and invented the cambered wing.

heavier-than-air flight is much older than we usually believe. Around 1849, Sir George Cayley (the father of flight) flew a small boy in a glider across Brompton Dale, Yorkshire, and in 1853, he flew a man (we do not know precisely who he was, but it is said to have been his coachman) across the same dale in a biplane glider. Cayley worked out the mechanics of flight (including cambered wings) and also predicted that powered flight would only be possible once engines had become light enough. In spite of this and other experiments, the established engineers and scientists clung to their belief that heavier-than-air flight was impossible. In the 1890s, Baron Kelvin of the Royal Society is reputed to have been somewhat sceptical about heavier-than-air flight, and other scientists and engineers in both the US and the UK took the same line.

Dr Simon Newcomb, the famous Canadian-American scientist, pronounced in 1903 that heavier-than-air flight was impossible without someone discovering a new "force in nature". That was fifty years after Cayley's flights, twenty years after the gasoline engine had been fully developed, and ten years after the Duryea brothers had launched their first horseless buggy onto the market.

Francis Crick and James Watson were heavily scorned for their DNA theories, but Albert Einstein was in a different league. He set off a world-shattering avalanche of criticism when he published his *General Theory of Relativity*[4]. Scientists queued up to lambast him, and hundreds of doctors, engineers, and others did their best to undermine the theory. It just could not be right, they argued; it was impossible.

We now know that rocks can fall from the sky, and most of us accept other ridiculous ideas like the sun being the centre of the solar system, people being able to travel at more than 30 mph, the existence of black holes, evolution, continental drift, exo-planets, symbiogenesis,[5] heavier-than-air flight, prions, and the power of nuclear reactions.

As outsiders, therefore, it is vital that we try never to use the word

---

[4] See the interesting commentary by a staffer at the Max Planck Institute: https://www.mpiwg-berlin.mpg.de/en/news/features/features-feature7
[5] The once-revolutionary theory that bacteria and viruses contributed symbiotically to the development of the human genome. In more recent times, scientists have found that

"impossible". If rocks can fall from the sky and particles can communicate at immense distances faster than light,[6] who are we to set absolute limits on what might or might not be possible? One could only wish that scientists could set aside their prejudices against the UFO phenomenon and accept that we have yet to meet much that is absolutely and provably impossible.

This book argues that the most pressing need is for us to scientifically investigate the UFOs themselves. In a very real sense, the logic for the human race is simple: prove beyond doubt that a *single* unidentified flying object is from somewhere other than this planet or time, and we will have changed the world forever in the most profound way. Only then will we need to go into the motives and mechanisms of whoever or whatever might be travelling in them, or whoever or whatever sends them to whiz around our backyard.

Equally, prove that *every single* UFO can be scientifically explained, and the whole issue can safely be consigned to the bookstore shelves marked "Weird Things and Silly Theories," and we can all go home and watch some football (or whatever).

Okay, so we're all agreed:

1. There's been something called a UFO phenomenon for at least the past seventy years;
2. We all have to keep an open mind;
3. We are going to avoid the weird stuff as much as possible; and
4. Nothing is impossible unless proven so in a scientifically replicable fashion.

Heads Up

Towards the end of the book you can find a glossary of most of the acronyms used in the text. There are also two full bibliographies: One is chronological, and the other is in the traditional author-surname order.

so-called retro-viruses also contributed (to about 8 percent of the human genome) and that almost half of the human genome developed from viruses.
[6] The proven phenomenon of quantum-entanglement.

CHAPTER 1
Early UFO Sightings

THE SUBJECT OF UFOS is like a battleground. The metaphorical and actual bodies of ufologists and sceptics are scattered across it like cherry-blossom after a gale. After so many years, both sides have dug themselves into positions which make the Maginot Line look like a Japanese paper screen. Each set of zealots has convinced themselves that they, and only they, are in the right. The exchanges, especially between the more extreme ends of the spectrum, are bitter indeed. And that's not the end of the conflict. Even within the individual UFO groups, there are factions and jealousies which in some cases have riven the organisations so deeply that they have collapsed. Some believe that governments have despatched agents-provocateurs to foster and encourage this sort of internecine warfare and destroy certain active UFO groups (e.g. the 1950s to 1980s NICAP).

If you want to understand how bitter and enduring the battles can be, take a look at the latest book by the eminent UFO researcher Stanton Freidman and, particularly, the chapter in which he describes his long-running disputes with the late-arch-sceptic Philip Klass[7] (the chapters on Menzel and Condon are also instructive). If a novelist constructed a plot along those lines, it would be rejected by publishing houses as being too far-fetched.

---

[7] Stanton Friedman and Kathleen Marden. *Fact, Fiction and Flying Saucers*. New Page Books, 2016; see, particularly, chapter 4.

UFO has become a term of fascination and sometimes of humour over the past seventy years, but the outsider is often more amazed at the subject's complexity and depth. At one extreme, we find the cartoonists depicting transparent-domed saucers with cheeky little green men inside, while, at the other, we find sinister stories of black-suited men, evil aliens, death threats, and even allegations of assassinations.

There are people who claim to have found evidence of UFOs in ancient texts, in ancient murals, and even in ancient statues. For the most part, these are references to wheels in the sky, or fiery globes, or bars. In all honesty, they could be about anything. The visual evidence from murals and stonework is pretty equivocal at best. A search on the Internet for "ancient ufos" will reveal scores of such possibilities, but as they are so old, and as the evidence is somewhat limited and ambiguous, it is impossible to give them too much credence. We have to be very careful not to use our current culture to interpret what ancient cultures drew or carved. Just because a carving *looks* like a modern jet fighter does not mean the artist saw a jet fighter a thousand years ago, any more than someone looking at a Picasso in two thousand years' time should conclude that we all looked like that.

Several purported early sightings of objects, such as the alleged sightings by monks at St Albans in 1254 and at Byland Abbey in Yorkshire in 1290, are quoted in books such as Jim Marrs' *Alien Agenda* but are difficult to substantiate. Marrs says, for example, that on New Year's Day, 1254, the monks at St Albans Abbey saw "a kind of ship flying in the sky that was 'large, elegantly shaped and of a marvellous colour'". This example has been quoted by numerous websites and in several other books without question but with nothing in the way of cross-checking references.

There are paintings, too, of strange objects. For example, there is the famous *Battle of Nuremburg*, which is supposed have occurred on April 14, 1561, and the equivalent woodcut of similar alleged mass sightings over Basel in 1566. The witnesses describe disks and rods and triangular objects, which sound very similar to what modern UFO witnesses see, except in Nuremburg and Basel, they saw a great many objects in the sky at once.[8]

---

[8] https://en.wikipedia.org/wiki/1561_celestial_phenomenon_over_Nuremberg

A contemporary impression of objects which appeared in the sky over Basel in 1566. (Charles Walker/Topfoto.co.uk)

There is little in the way of hard evidence and a great deal of doubt, but the UFO issue almost certainly extends back quite a few years. So if you're sitting comfortably, let's begin with a brief overview of the most fascinating events leading up to the end of World War II.

Windsor Castle, 1783

A number of UFO websites make a great deal of the records of a sighting in 1783 which was made from the terrace of Windsor Castle, to the west of London, England. In August of that year, a number of eminent members of the Royal Society were standing out on the terrace, presumably getting some air after dinner and some highly energetic academic discussions, when they witnessed an object streak across the sky. Being a scientist, one of those present, an Italian named Tiberius Cavallo, wrote the sighting up and read his account to the assembled members of the Royal Society in January of 1784. The account was also published in the *London Magazine* of August 13, 1784, and two artists who were present at the sighting later produced an engraving of the event.[9]

For the outsider, the Windsor Castle "UFO" illustrates an important aspect of the UFO phenomenon: the tendency for modern UFO websites to simply copy each other and thereby extend and reinforce the chain of error and misinformation.

In this case, the following quote appears on several UFO websites:[10]

> "An oblong cloud moving ... parallel to the horizon. Under this cloud could be seen a luminous object ... which came to a halt ... soon it set off again towards the East."

The quote goes on to say that the object changed direction and moved parallel to the horizon before disappearing to the southeast.

A luminous object which stops in mid-air, which "sets off again", and which changes direction: This is truly the stuff of UFO mysteries. But don't get too excited. The quote is deceptively similar to Signor Cavallo's genuine account, but differs in a few vital elements and is, therefore, misleading. The case underlines the essential need for the outsider to check sources and, wherever possible, to cross-check and confirm the details with primary sources.

Luckily for us, the Royal Society's archives are open to the public, and you can easily locate the original account, which was presented to the assembled members on January 15, 1784. In it, Signor Tiberius Cavallo specifically does *not* say that the oblong cloud moved. Instead, he describes a normal cloud in order to distinguish between it and the haze which he said dominated the horizon:

> "A narrow, ragged and oblong cloud stood on the north-west side of the heavens ... stretching itself for several

---

[9] Thomas and Paul Sandby; see below.
[10] See, for example, the websites UFOEvidence.org and ufology.patrickgross/htm/windsor1783.htm

degrees towards the east, in a direction nearly parallel to the horizon."[11]

"Stretching itself" did not mean moving. The phrase is clearly used figuratively to describe the way in which the cloud was stretched across the sky.

In the warmth and calm of a summer's evening, at about 9.25 p.m., the group was standing at the north-east corner of the castle's terrace, which runs above a good part of the northern walls and looks out over Windsor Great Park and the countryside to the north of the castle. They first saw lights which, to them, appeared like the northern lights (aurora borealis) and then an object glowing with a bluish light. It was "roundish" and appeared to be about half the size of the moon.

Cavallo goes on to report that, at first, the object appeared "almost stationary," but that it

> "... soon began to move, at first ascending ... after which
> it turned itself towards the east, and moving ... nearly
> parallel to the horizon, reached ... S. E. by E. where it
> finally disappeared."

The object appeared to break up before it, and some smaller objects, then displayed "tails". The entire incident lasted about thirty seconds, and as the group were about to go back inside the castle, they heard a loud rumble, as if the object had exploded.

Although the calculations made by the scientists at the time may be in error – they were, after all, based on imprecise visual data for size, speed, distance, and so on – there seems little doubt that the August 18, 1783, sighting was not of a sinister spacecraft but of a meteorite or bolide.[12] Some ufologists, however, have taken a slightly ambiguous account, written in

---

[11] "Description of a Meteor, Observed Aug. 18, 1783. By Mr. Tiberius Cavallo, F. R. S." *Phil. Trans. R. Soc. Lond.* January 1, 1784, 74 108-111; doi:10.1098/rstl.1784.0010.
[12] They estimated that the object was about 1,000 yards in diameter, 56.5 miles high, and 130 miles from Windsor.

eighteenth-century language, to create a UFO sighting in which a cloud moved and the object "came to a halt" (Cavallo merely said that it *appeared* stationary at first) and then changed direction. The witnesses were reporting the *apparent* movement from their own vantage point, so the object may not have actually changed direction).

In reality, the whole ufologist case has been built on a lack of understanding of the way language was used two hundred and fifty years ago, together with some poor research and crafty toying with the original account.

And just in case you are still unsure as to whether this was a meteorite or not, Signor Cavallo's account to the Royal Society prompted other papers at the same meeting. Three other people submitted papers or letters about the event, and none were present on the terrace of Windsor Castle: Alexander Aubert, William Cooper, and Richard Lovell Edgeworth.[13] Their accounts are all available in the Royal Society's archives.[14]

Aubert was an eminent amateur astronomer who possessed an excellent observatory at his home in Deptford, Kent. His account, published in November 1783, is very similar to that of the observers at Windsor Castle. Although witnessed from a separate vantage point (his horse as he was riding home), the details corroborate the Cavallo account. He places the occurrence at about 9.17 p.m. on that same evening. He reported the object as being extremely bright and that it seemed very near, although he estimates a height of forty to fifty miles from the surface. In his account in the Royal Society Archives is a diagram of the sighting which is virtually identical to the Thomas and Paul Sandby engraving of the Windsor Castle sighting, in that it displays three separate phases of the occurrence. In all likelihood, the Sandbys adopted this diagram as the basis for their own engraving.

William Cooper's sighting was a valuable addition to the data on the August 18 meteorite, for he witnessed it well to the north of the other observers. Cooper was archdeacon of York (two hundred miles north

---

[13] Edgeworth (who had four wives and twenty-two children) was a landowner and inventor. He wrote a short letter in September of 1783

[14] http://rstl.royalsocietypublishing.org/content/74.toc

of London) and had been to the seaside that hot and sultry day. He was returning to the city on horseback, accompanied by his attendants, when they saw the object at about 9 p.m.. It appeared from the north-west and disappeared to the south-east, travelling directly over the heads of Cooper's party. At the end of his account, he reported two loud explosions. He likened them to the reports of a nine-pounder cannon.[15]

He wrote:

> "The horses on which we rode shrunk with fear; and some
> people whom we met upon the road declared their con-
> sternation in the most expressive terms."

And wouldn't we all.

And yet the Internet still carries a good many seriously phrased assertions that the Windsor Castle event of 1783 shows that a UFO (meaning an interplanetary craft) was observed in Georgian times and that it performed some fairly dramatic feats.

Hatton Gardens, 1809

Another reasonably well-documented sighting, this time from the early nineteenth century, is also worth a little detail. It allows a possibly different conclusion to the Windsor Castle affair. In his 1966 book, *Challenge to Science: The UFO Enigma*, Jacques Vallée discussed a sighting which was made in August 1809 by someone he named as John Staveley. The quotation Vallée cited is as follows:

> "I saw many meteors moving around the edge of a black
> cloud from which lightnings flashed. They were like
> dazzling specks of light, dancing and traipsing thro' the
> clouds. One of them increased in size until it became of

---

[15] "Observations on a Remarkable Meteor Seen on the 18th of August, 1783. Communicated in a Letter to Sir Joseph Banks, Bart. P. R. S." By William Cooper, D.D., F.R.S. Archdeacon of York.

the brilliance and magnitude of Venus, on a clear evening. But I could see no body in the light. It moved with
great rapidity, and pasted on the edge of the cloud. Then
it became stationary, dimmed its splendor, and vanished.
I saw these strange lights for minutes, not seconds. For at
least an hour, these lights, so strange, played in and out
of the black cloud. No lightning came from the clouds
where these lights were playing. As the meteors increased
in size, they seemed to descend."

The observation was actually made by a chap named James (often reported as John) Staveley, at Hatton Gardens, London, on August 10, 1809.
It was reported in the *Journal of Natural Philosophy, Chemistry and the Arts*
(Vol. 24, 1809, pages 161–163[16]). What he said, in reality, was even more
fascinating than the Vallée quote (slightly misquoted as it is). Staveley was
up late that night and, at about 1.30 a.m., was watching a thunderstorm
through a window of his home. He noted a very dark, black cloud in the
higher sky and some internally lit lower clouds. He said that the clouds

"... seemed full of little dazzling and dancing specks of
light, that sometimes shone as stars peeping through a
misty cloud ... One in particular became more and more
distinctly visible, and increased in size, till it reached the
brilliancy and magnitude of Venus, as she shines in a clear
evening: and yet, there seemed no body of the light ... I
observed it coast, if I may use the expression, round the
edge of that mass in which it appeared, and, having again
become stationary, diminish from its full splendour till it
disappeared ... Its duration must have been of minutes.

P. S. As these meteors increased in size, they seemed to
descend, and had much of that semblance, which the

---

[16] The edition is online and available for inspection by anyone who cares to locate it.

phantasmagorial spectres have, as they seem to approach the spectator."

Although he calls them "meteors", Staveley could not have seriously believed that these lights were caused by meteors. One can see what attracted the famous scientist Jacques Vallée to this report. At first consideration, it might well have been some form of ball lightning (and that could well be the explanation, though ball lightning is not well understood even now[17]) but it is interesting that Staveley, who watched the storm and these lights for a long time that night, particularly mentions that the object "coasted" around the edge of the cloud but that at other times, the movements were extremely rapid. The length of time that the object was in view might also tend to work against the possibility of ball lightning.

It may also be worth noting that there is a known and fascinating relationship between UFOs and thunderstorms. Many ufologists believe that the storms provide power in some way to whatever UFOs are. Sceptics believe of course that what people are seeing is some form a very long-lived plasma event.

There is no way of being sure at this distance in time, but the Hatton Gardens event remains of considerable interest to ufologists, astronomers, physicists, and meteorologists.

Airships, 1890s

Airship-shaped objects were seen all across England during the 1890s and the early years of the twentieth century. In the United States, there was a wave of such sightings from San Francisco and Sacramento (nocturnal lights in November 1896) to Chicago, Texas, and New England in the years after 1896. Astoundingly, Captain Edward Ruppelt (who in 1956 wrote one of the best books about the UFO phenomenon) wrote in

---

[17] Even today, scientists do not fully understand what causes lightning to apparently form a bright sphere of various sizes and appear to float through the air. Stories of ball lightning are many and go back several hundred years, but in spite of a host of theories, science has yet to explain the phenomenon – or even prove that it is possible in nature.

1952, that he actually spoke to a man who had seen an "airship" in 1897. The man had been employed as a copy-boy for the *San Francisco Chronicle*. The witness was unable to remember details but did recall the "airship" in the sky. He told Ruppelt that others had seen it, too, but that the editor and staff of the paper did not say anything to anyone in case they were labelled "crazy". Even in 1897, you were risking scorn and derision if you saw unusual things in the sky.

In July 1907, an extremely indistinct photograph of the harbour at Drøbak (to the south of Oslo, Norway) caught a strange object in the sky near two sailing vessels. (Fortean/Topfoto.co.uk)

Equally, there was a growing interest in "outer space" (meaning the moon and the nearest planets, Mars and Venus). Many of the ideas which later became the foundation of much science fiction were being introduced and honed. Jules Verne's brilliant techno-adventures which began with *From the Earth to the Moon* in 1865 had laid the seeds of massive public interest in all things technical and a number of British writers began to pen interplanetary and extraterrestrial ideas during the last years of the century. H G Wells' story of the invasion of Earth by Martians was by no means the first time writers had speculated upon and depicted Martians. Wells was interviewed by the *Daily News* for its January 28, 1898, edition. In it, he said that he had taken the idea of "interplanetary cylinders" from Jules Verne and that he could see that humans might one day evolve into "big brained, big headed, small bodied people".

England, 1909

It is possible to find numerous references to strange flying objects in the newspapers during the period leading up to World War II. In 1934, for example, there was evidently a suspected UFO crash near Milan. According to Timothy Good, the Italians suspected British or French advanced aircraft, and there was a rumour that material and technology had been removed from whatever crashed (Good, 1988).

Another excellent and fascinating resource is that provided by Patrick Gross, the French ufologist. He has created an incredibly detailed database of newspaper and media reports of UFOs since about the start of the twentieth century.[18] In that valuable database, he lists some of the articles produced in 1909 about various sightings in England and many other countries. One, in particular, is worth airing here.

"Aerial Mystery

There is ... after two months ... not the faintest clue to an elucidation of the mystery.

There seems little doubt that something has been seen, for ... witnesses living many miles from one another agree on certain vital points ... the airship travels very swiftly and is held ... in complete control."

---

[18] http://ufologie.patrickgross.org/htm/newspapers1900.htm; *The Standard*, May 17, 1909, page 7.

The article, in the May 17, 1909, edition of the British newspaper *The Standard*, says that the War Office and the Aeronautical Society had made enquiries but without success. The journalist explained that the idea of it being German was considered but discounted in favour of the object being the product of an English inventor (highly unlikely at that time for a number of reasons, not the least of which were the speed and the use of searchlights). However, these fascinating 1909 incidents appear to have begun with a sighting by a policeman.

At about five in the morning on March 23, 1909, a police constable in Peterborough witnessed a cigar-shaped object travel across the city. PC Kettle made no formal report but did tell his friends, who were understandably sceptical. Over the next couple of months, however, this object – or something similar – was seen at night by many independent people across the east Midlands and East Anglia. Several of them reported lights in front and behind, generally reported as "searchlights", and the fact that it travelled swiftly.

The article – which can be seen in full on Patrick Gross's excellent website – listed twenty different sightings between PC Kettle's on March 23 and one on May 13th of the same year. The strange objects were seen in numerous locations, stretching from Peterborough and March in Cambridgeshire, to the city of Coventry, and including Ipswich, Bury St Edmonds, Market Harborough, Kings Lynn, Stamford, St Neots, Northampton, and even Sandringham (the summer residence of the Royal family).

It's an intriguing story for a number of reasons. At the time, everyone assumed that this object must have been an airship of sorts (the artist who tried to draw a visual impression of it naturally used the known shape of airships for inspiration). However, to the modern observer, with knowledge of the scientific and engineering developments of the time, some of the details do not chime with the technology of airships. Note that it was said to move swiftly and in complete control, and to have two searchlights, front and rear.

Airships do not fly swiftly. A more apt adverb would be "ponderously," and one would dearly love to be able to question the witnesses more closely as to what they meant by "in complete control". One assumes that it meant that the witnesses noted definite changes of course and speed. What would an aerial object have to do to appear to an Edwardian witness as being under complete control? But the most perplexing feature of this object was the lights.

An artist's impression of the airship sighted by Police Constable Kettle over Peterborough, England, on March 23, 1909. (Fortean/Topfoto.co.uk)

Modern readers might not question this because everything has lights these days. But more than a century ago, a "powerful searchlight" was a very heavy and energy-hungry piece of equipment, requiring an equally heavy gasoline generator plus its fuel and a small crew to manage and direct it. In those pre-WWI times, searchlights were operated by very high voltage power through the carbon arc process. Although some later airships did carry searchlights, the fire risk alone, should a hydrogen leak occur, would have made them anathema to German Zeppelin designers before the craft became large enough for protective screens and specially sealed systems.

In the year 1909, the small, early Zeppelins were still in the flight-test phase prior to their introduction into service in 1910. But not even the larger M-class Zeppelins of the beginning of World War I (1914-15) carried even a single searchlight.

As for it moving "swiftly", there is no reliable way of understanding what witnesses in 1909 perceived as swift. The early Zeppelins could manage about 30 mph[19] (much slower than a passenger express train of the era). Assuming, not unjustifiably, that most of the witnesses had seen an express train in full flight, one might be safe in assuming that it would have required a speed considerably over 30 mph for it to have been regarded by them as "swift". Incidentally, there were no British airships in the air in 1909.

So was this object a German Zeppelin airship? Almost certainly not. Apart from everything said above, Count von Zeppelin had experienced massive problems in creating successful prototypes of the Zeppelin and would not have risked early versions over England under any circumstances. British designs were nowhere near as far advanced as the Zeppelins and they did not begin test flights until 1911 . The objections to searchlights (on the grounds of weight and danger) have been discussed and the speed discounts all other lighter-than-air craft (particularly as the objects were generally seen moving from east to west against the prevailing winds.

So what was it that a police constable and a good many civilian witnesses saw in the air over a large swathe of central England in 1909?

---

[19] Even five years after these sightings, the Zeppelins of 1914 could only manage a little over 50 mph flat out

Clapham, 1914

This is a very intriguing case which is included here partly because of its obvious sincerity but also because it illustrates, in the exact words of the witness, the fact that inexplicable things have been sighted in the skies of England for at least the past century. The object was not sighted amidst mass flying-saucer hysteria; there was no hype about abductions by Martians. Instead, the object was reported in a cool, detached manner just in case it might be of value to the authorities. [20]

The incident happened on August 26, 1914, a hot summer's night in the early weeks of World War I. A gentleman named Henry White was staying for a few days at an address in Clapham, south-west London. The house he was visiting was in Offerton Road, a wide street flanked by terraces of four-storey Victorian town-houses. From his bedroom in number 4, Mr White saw a lighted object or objects moving around in the distance. Being a patriot, he reported the matter to the authorities.

Britain had been at war for three weeks, and the population was worried about raids by German airships, as well as the usual concerns about spies flashing messages with torches to their collaborators. So Mr White was extremely suspicious of the lights he saw, although the powers-that-be decided no action was required.

It must have been a very warm night, for Mr White had drawn back the curtains of his front-of-house room (as a guest room, it was likely to have been on the third floor) and had the window wide open to admit whatever breeze was available. He had retired at 10 p.m. but, perhaps because of the heat, woke up at just after 1 a.m. and was then awake for several hours. As he explained in his letter, he noticed a very bright star-like light in the sky through the window and was surprised that he had not noticed it immediately upon waking (the implication being that it had appeared suddenly while he was initially looking out of the window). He said the light was in a south-easterly direction and

---

[20] A manner and a motivation which are replicated by most witnesses to this day.

that it faded after some minutes. It came back again after about twenty minutes.[21] This time, it was close to the tall, elegant spire of the nearby Congregational church.

Puzzled, he got out of bed and observed that the light was larger and brighter than the stars and that occasionally, a light came upwards or downwards from the object. Then, after about fifteen minutes, this light too began to fade. Finally, at about two thirty, it appeared again but, this time, to the right of the church steeple and lower down. It was visible for some time before fading again. To assist the authorities Mr White kindly drew a sketch of the various positions of this bright light.

Number 4 is on the eastern side of Offerton Road, which runs roughly north-south at this point. The front of the house therefore faces roughly west, and from the vantage point of an upper-floor front bedroom, Mr White would have been able to clearly see the steeple of the church slightly off-centre to his window (which is the way he drew it in his diagram).

The Congregational church was a magnificent edifice with an extremely tall spire. Unfortunately, the church was hit by one of seventeen V1 flying bombs which struck Clapham during 1944. The beautiful building was damaged so badly that it was demolished in 1954. Today the site is still a Christian centre, but the buildings are considerably less imposing.

The Congregational church was located, from the vantage point of number 4, Offerton Road, beyond a small open square called Grafton Square, and in the direction of Clapham Common. It is conceivable that the lights Mr White saw moving around so much that night, were, therefore, actually over the large open area of the Common. But we will never know.

---

[21] Although he reported it as such, it could not have been in a south-easterly direction because the church was to the south-west of Offerton Road, but that's an easy mistake to make. (See Charles Booth's map of London on the London School of Economics' website.) Booth considered Offerton Road at that time to be "middle class, well to do".

GROSVENOR HOTEL
LONDON
S.W.

Aug. 27. 1914.

Sir,

I am staying for a few days at Clapham; and last night, having retired about ten o'cl, woke up shortly after one, and remained awake for several hours; the window in my room being wide open, and the curtains fully drawn aside.

To my surprise, I presently saw, - (the bed directly facing the window,-) what appeared to be a very brilliant star, and wondered I had not observed it immediately on waking up. It was in a south easterly direction. After gazing at it intently for some minutes, it gradually faded, and I supposed that a cloud was hiding it from my sight.

Window.
See figure 1.

After about 20 minutes or so, it gradually came into view once more. Had I been walking in the street, I should probably not have observed the change in its location; but the spire of a Congregational chapel is seen from the window in my room, and I was not a little surprised to see the star - or whatever it was, appear this time close to the steeple (see fig 2.)

I jumped out of bed; and going over to the window, observed that although many stars were to be seen, this object greatly surpassed them in size and brilliancy. It seemed, too, that light darted upwards and downwards occasionally from it.

After about a quarter of an hour, this strange object began to fade as before. About half past two it again appeared, this time on the right side of the steeple. (See figure 3.)

I was greatly puzzled; & after waiting some time it disappeared. I am perfectly sure that I was fully awake; & though I should have liked to call some of the others, in order that they might substantiate what I have said, feared to do so, as one of my friends is in an extremely nervous condition. But when I related this to some other acquaintances this morning, we concluded it might be as well to speak of it elsewhere. I am dining with some friends here this evening; but should you desire any further information, kindly address - 4 Offerton Rd. Clapham.

Your obedient servant, Henry White.

The letter written by Mr Henry White from the Grosvenor Hotel, London, concerning his strange sighting of moving lights seen from his bedroom in Clapham in August 1914. The British War Ministry appears to have taken no action (The National Archives, UK).

Foo-Fighters, 1939–45

It was during the global conflict of World War II that UFOs really began to make a name for themselves, and with that inimitable talent that Americans always display of coming up with great titles for things, the name adopted at the time was "foo-fighters".

Whatever they actually were, a great many aircrew on both sides, right across the globe, saw some very strange objects. They were seen by many nations' air-crews but especially by US, British, German, and Japanese military aircraft. The Americans dubbed them "foo-fighters", and that name has stuck.[22] Most of the sightings (but by no means all) were of bright globes or slivers of light, some of which seemed to pass through aircraft. Others flew alongside or darted in front of and behind allied bomber formations. In at least one case, the object was reported as being tubular. The Allies thought that these objects were German secret weapons, and the Germans and Japanese believed them to be the latest inventions of the Allies.

One fascinating sighting occurred on the night of May 26–27, 1943, during an RAF raid on Essen. It was not the standard foo-fighter type, but something even stranger.

The captain of an RAF Halifax bomber, Flight Sergeant Cockcroft, together with most of his crew, saw a large object to one side of them, which Cockcroft described as being tubular: the shape of a "king-size cigarette". I had not known that king-sized cigarettes were available as early as 1943 and that misapprehension cast some doubt on the pilot's statement as reported. However, a quick check showed that, while Chesterfield cigarettes did not introduce a king-sized cigarette until 1952,

---

[22] The best story explaining the name starts with the fact that a Chicago cartoonist in the 1930s used a character called "Smokey Stover" – a fireman – who had a favourite catchphrase: "Where there's foo there's fire". The tale goes that an American airman who was reporting being buzzed by fiery globes of light lost his temper with the debriefing officer and told him that it was "those f***ing foo fighters". According to the Wikipedia account, that first word remained with the phrase for much of the rest of the war but was understandably dropped in official histories and subsequent newspaper accounts.

British-American Tobacco's Pall Mall brand of king-sized cigarettes was launched in the United States in 1939 . It's likely therefore that British aircrew were made aware of these new-fangled, king-sized cigarettes by their USAAF allies.

The Halifax, of 77 Squadron, was based at RAF Elvington near York – which is now a wonderful time capsule. This museum of a wartime RAF base preserves a Halifax in splendid condition. Cockcroft's sighting is well-documented but still totally unexplained.

Foo-fighters photographed from a Japanese bomber in flight. The aircraft may well be Mitsubishi Ki-51 dive bombers. (Fortean/Topfoto.co.uk)

There are several fascinating accounts of foo-fighter encounters with both RAF and USAAF aircraft, but perhaps the most interesting fact about the accounts is that some report fiery balls with some sort of exhaust of "black smoke".

On both sides of the war, and within all of the major air-forces involved – Japanese, German, Russian, British, and US – the debriefing intelligence officers simply recorded what the aircrews said they had seen and moved on. There were almost no reports of the objects attacking or damaging aircraft,[23] and although they certainly scared a few pilots and gunners, there were far more important things to worry about. So, as long as none of the objects actually fired on an aircraft, there was nothing to be done. Foo-fighters were an amusing side issue in a very serious war.

---

[23] I have been able to find only a single report of an Allied aircraft's wing being allegedly set on fire by a foo-fighter.

CHAPTER 2

It Gets Hotter

DUE TO THE SHEER volume of recorded sightings, the timeline from 1945 onwards is impossibly crowded. Therefore, I've been forced to leave out a large number of what a knowledgeable person would regard as significant sightings. Quite a few of these happened in the early 1950s, including many encounters between unidentified objects and both USAF and RAF fighter aircraft and civilian airliners. There were also the cases of the famous Lubbock Lights and the sightings at Terre Haute, Indiana. Captain Edward Ruppelt's account of those years is very well worth reading. His book is one of the most balanced and detailed in the long history of UFO literature (Ruppelt, 1956).

It is fair to say that the year 1947 marks the true beginning of the UFO story in post-war times. As we've seen, it's not that UFOs suddenly appeared for the first time in that year. There had been a great many sightings of objects before then[24] and a good many in the years 1945 and 1946 in the United States and in the UK.

The really important thing about 1947 is that it marks the first time a government got really upset about, and involved in, the "flying saucer" issue. The younger modern reader needs to understand that those post-war years were incredibly strained. The greatest and most destructive war ever fought had ended, but another, potentially much more devastating, was

---

[24] The British broadsheet newspaper *The Daily Telegraph* has published eighty-four very interesting photos of UFOs taken over the past 140 years. See Bibliography.

lurking menacingly in the background. Espionage and military sparring were endemic in Europe, in Asia, and in the United States itself, and a lot of the suspicion on both sides of the Iron Curtain was founded on astoundingly few facts. Both sides knew the other had grabbed a number of very good German rocket scientists and engineers in the closing months of the war, and it was very easy for them to imagine that the other side had got the best of the bunch and had quickly developed super-aircraft in addition to thermo-nuclear bombs.[25]

But to return to the central issue: It all really began with Kenneth Arnold and the global publicity resulting from his sighting of nine unidentified objects. Millions of words have been written about the Arnold sighting (Arnold even wrote his own book about it: *The Coming of the Saucers*, in 1952). It wasn't by any means the first-ever sighting of a UFO, but for a long list of reasons, the Arnold sighting ignited the UFO craze, like a match in a pool of gas.

Why? One reason that has been proposed by sceptics is that the Western world, especially the people of the United States and the United Kingdom, had suffered three and five years, respectively, of the most gut-wrenching war. Not just any war but one which threatened their very existence as nations. The two peoples had fought, side by side, against the Germans, Italians, and Japanese (among many others). The British, surviving by the skin of their teeth for more than two years (from late 1939 to the end of 1941), had lived through some truly terrible times which impacted directly on their everyday lives. For much of that time the British fought alone against a Germany which had conquered most of Europe. The civilian population of the UK had suffered years of bombing, hardship, hunger, privation, and the constant early fear of invasion. Rationing of food in Britain did not end until the mid-1950s; the shortages of food and the derelict bomb sites in London and other cities impacted well into that

---

[25] The purloining of German scientists and engineers went on for some time after the war, with many being forced to leave Germany and work for one of the victorious nations. Werner von Braun is perhaps the best known German scientist who voluntarily worked for the United States, but Russian, American, and British snatch squads operated well into 1946 and possibly beyond.

decade and beyond. In the United States, fears of a Japanese invasion and of the consequences of losing the war in Europe and the Far East were what people lived with on an everyday basis. And if that were not enough, the two nations now bore the responsibility for defending Europe and several other regions of the world against the threat of renewed war, this time potentially nuclear, from the Soviet Union.

Flying saucers came, say the sceptics, as a little light relief in the midst of all that. Perhaps the ordinary people of the Western world, and by that, in 1947, is meant only the United States and the UK, needed an exciting diversion (because France, Germany, Italy, and Japan had many other, more pressing day-to-day issues to worry about).

For the governments, it was different, and it is important for the modern reader to understand the feelings and the attitudes of senior government and military figures at that time. Only by doing so can one truly understand why things probably happened the way they did.

As we've seen, it was a time of profound fear and confusion. The Soviet Union had switched from theoretical ally to very real enemy. The powerful armies of the Soviet state had pushed across Europe and had taken Berlin and many other parts of the continent, including all of what we today call Eastern Europe, plus half of Germany and parts of Austria. From their desks in Washington and London, it did not seem at all inconceivable to politicians and civil servants that the Soviets would rest a while and then renew the push, with the serious intent of taking the rest of Germany and Austria, perhaps Denmark and Scandinavia, and maybe even more.

The fact that Soviet Russia had grabbed a goodly bunch of top German scientists and plans for new aircraft and missiles caused the US and UK authorities to be very focused on how those acquisitions would leverage the already-frightening Soviet capability. We should not forget that the Germans had perfected drone bombs and long-range missiles in the form of V1 and V2 weapons; they had used them in waves on London and other British and European cities. They had developed and deployed stand-off anti-ship missiles, and there were rumours that they were also experimenting with the anti-missile-missile concept.

So when multiple reports of flying saucers began to be publicised by the press in the middle of 1947, the US and British governments went into urgent research and espionage mode. Were they real objects or just hallucinations? If they were real, where did they come from? The strongest theories at that time were that the Soviets had somehow developed, and possibly improved on, German technology to produce very high performance aircraft, which they were using to test out US and British air defences and, perhaps, to spy on highly secret bases such as those responsible for the development of nuclear weapons in the US Southwest.

Conspiracy theorists often see sinister purpose and clinical organisation behind the US and UK reactions to the flying saucer sightings. A different, and no less plausible, view was put forward by Edward Ruppelt – that of ignorance, confusion, and, not to put too fine a point on it, near panic (Ruppelt, 1952).

While the more publicised UFO sightings were occurring in the United States, the British had their own problems: with "ghost rockets" and with strange radar contacts over the North Sea. The ghost rockets began to be seen in Scandinavia in 1946 and were widely believed, even to this day, to be Soviet rocket tests. Between 1945 and 1946, the UK radar network (called Chain Home and top secret during the war) picked up very high flying and very fast contacts on an intermittent basis.[26] In January 1947, six months before Kenneth Arnold's sightings, radar operators in southern England were plotting a training mission, when they spotted a very high stationary target which then darted around erratically, making astounding (at that time) speeds of an estimated 1,000 mph. The plotting went on for around an hour, with the target moving towards the UK coast and away again.[27]

In the same month, at the start of the worst winter in modern British history, British radar operators again picked up strange contacts on their screens. An object over the North Sea was tracked at wildly varying speeds (from over 400 mph to 120 mph), and the operators said that it climbed

---

[26] "Over 35,000 feet" was extremely high – close to impossible for most aircraft at the time.
[27] See Dr David Clarke's very detailed accounts at http://www.project1947.com/1947/opcharlie.html

and descended at a rapid rate. A Mosquito night fighter was tasked to try to intercept the object, which it eventually did, but its two airborne radar contacts faded quickly. An Air Ministry note to the Americans stated that the contact "appeared to take efficient, controlled, evasive action".

Contacts with such objects continued during the month of January; weather balloons and atmospheric inversions were mooted as possible causes of the contacts (for explanations of these possible causes, see chapter 7). But those explanations did not convince many.

The ghost rockets were reported again in many countries in early 1948 and one is forced to wonder why the Soviet Union (if, indeed, the rockets were theirs) should test such advanced equipment over what they would see as enemy territory.

The bottom line is that, by the end of 1947, both the British and the American governments were extremely concerned at the spate of flying saucer reports and, one might guess, at the high level of credibility of many of them. It's important not to forget though, that at that time, although the clever money was still on earthbound causes, the major objective was to try to find out what these objects were – and fast.

Let's take a look at some of the most famous cases between 1947 and 2014. Later, we'll go into some in-depth case studies to give you a more comprehensive understanding, but for now, we'll scan a tiny sample of the rock stars of UFO lore.

Kenneth Arnold, 1947

June 24, 1947, was a momentous day. For on that bright, sunny day, an American aviator named Kenneth Arnold launched the whole crazy, modern love affair with flying saucers.

Arnold, an experienced pilot, was flying his small plane (an A-class Callair, registration 33355) in the Cascade Range in Washington State, when he saw a group of nine delta-shaped objects flying in a reverse wedge formation. They were flying much faster than aircraft, he told reporters, and they were doing it like saucers skipping over a pond. His report was extremely detailed; he watched them flying at pretty high speeds and timed them, roughly, between and behind mountain peaks. He estimated their speed at 1,700 mph, much faster than any aircraft of that day. This wasn't the first US sighting of strange objects by a long chalk, but it was the first to receive massive global publicity and was the one which gave us the term "flying saucer". The outsider should note that the term actually refers to the mode of flight, skipping or bouncing up and down as they flew, rather than them having a saucer shape (although that's what caught on). What Arnold saw were not discs but open delta-shaped objects.

Some have said that he was actually seeing a flight of geese, but in that case, those geese fooled an experienced aviation observer and another, totally unconnected chap who viewed them from the ground on the same day. But we did not know that until thirty years later. When FBI files were released to Dr Bruce Maccabee in the late 1970s, they showed that Arnold's objects were almost certainly also seen by a prospector named Fred Johnson. On that same afternoon, Johnson was near Mount Adams and saw the objects overhead. His sighting matched Arnold's for number, speed, and shape. He told the FBI that these objects "tilted back and forth as they flew" and stood on edge before climbing out of sight.[28]

Three points: firstly do geese "skip" up and down as they fly? Secondly, what aircraft tilts on its edge to climb? And thirdly, why did the FBI keep secret that second, corroborating sighting?

Whatever Arnold and Johnson saw, there were several other fairly credible sightings in the following weeks and months (Ruppelt, 1952). Those reports set off the flying saucer phenomenon, but they also established some key things about the objects which have endured over the intervening seventy years. Some UFOs are still reported as boomerang-shaped, they still travel at very high speeds, they still seem to be able to stand on their edges (in fact, some are photographed titling as they hover or fly), and they are still sometimes reported as oscillating in flight.

---

[28] Maccabee, 2014.

Mr Kenneth Arnold pictured with an artist's impression of the objects he saw in 1947. Note that they were delta/wedge/boomerang shaped, very much like those still being reported in the United States, Britain and Europe today. (Fortean/Topfoto.co.uk)

Roswell, 1947

This single incident, whatever it was, has spawned a veritable industry of UFO books, films, souvenirs, and memorabilia. To many people, Roswell was the beginning of the entire UFO extravaganza – but that, as we've seen, was not so.

What Roswell almost certainly was, though, was the beginning of the "UFO cover-up" theory, the very foundation of the modern Disclosure movement. But it did not become that until the mid-1970s. There were also rumours of another one or possibly two crashes in the Roswell area around that time.

The incident is now so shrouded in claim and counterclaim, so distorted with commercial interests, so confused as to what is fact and what is not, that a final answer is probably not going to be possible unless someone pops up one day with a frozen alien body on a bench for the world's press and doctors to prod and poke.

The story is probably the most famous of all UFO tales, but it may well also be the greatest UFO non-event as well. As an outsider I have to say that my researches lead me to believe that there may be something to the incident. Too many witnesses have come forward and too many of them have maintained their stories to their death beds. One, very important, witness even wrote a stunning legal affidavit which could only be opened after his death. Coming from one of the central characters in the original incident, it revealed further evidence of a very strange set of events.

The bare bones of what is supposed to have happened are as follows:

Sometime on a night in early July 1947 (the date is disputed), near the town of Roswell, New Mexico, *something* apparently crashed.

Roswell Army Air Force base as it was then, was a major facility in the US programme to develop and deploy nuclear weapons. It also lay quite close to several highly classified US bases (including Holloman AFB, Alamogordo, and the White Sands missile testing area, as well as the famous Los Alamos facility).

Strange objects had been seen in the sky in the area for weeks prior to the Roswell crash. On that day in early July a local foreman, Mack Brazel, reported debris on the Foster ranch on which he worked. It seems that debris was scattered over a wide area and some accounts say that Brazel also saw small bodies. The occurrence eventually reached ears at the local airbase at Roswell, and a small team was despatched to see what was going on. It seems that the team returned with "material" from the crash site.

Donald R Schmitt alleges, in his book *Cover-Up at Roswell*, that in the days and weeks following this incident local people were intimidated and even falsely imprisoned for short periods by the military, aided and abetted (under duress) by the local Sheriff. Brazel, the man who found whatever it was, had a remarkable change of heart. He told the *Roswell Daily Record* on the day *after* their story (July 9) that he'd simply found "debris".

Rumours in the area then prompted the Roswell base commander to order the preparation and issuance of a press release, and on July 8, 1947, the local paper published a stunning story about a crashed "saucer" under the earth-shattering headline "RAAF Captures Flying Saucer on Ranch in Roswell Region".[29] This article was based on the Air Force press release which said that a "disc" had been recovered.

The stunning Roswell newspaper headline the day following the release of the USAAF press statement in July 1947. (Topfoto.co.uk/Fortean)

Then, almost as quickly, the US Army Air Force (USAAF) released a second press statement which said that the item was actually a weather balloon. The RAAF Intelligence Major, Jesse Marcel, posed for photographs with parts of what was supposed to be the weather balloon and the fuss died down. After that, nothing was heard about the Roswell incident until

---

[29] *Roswell Daily Record*, July 8, 1947. Note that RAAF stands for Roswell Army Air Field. In 1947, the United States Air Force was still part of the army: the United States Army Air Force (USAAF).

the 1970s, when a witness came forward to reignite the story like someone throwing a stick of TNT into a paint store.[30]

The *official* explanation boils down to this (but this has only come to light in recent times): The USAAF was, it is claimed, actually testing a secret balloon and instrument package designed to monitor Soviet rocket and nuclear activity. This so-called Mogul balloon had crashed, and rather than admit that they were testing such a monitoring device, they made up the story about the weather balloon. It was this reason, they argued, that accounted for the initial conflicting press releases, both of which were said to have been attempts to avoid letting the Soviets know what the Americans were developing and testing. From the general public's standpoint, the US Air Force had settled on the story that a weather balloon had come down and had been misidentified by local yokels as a flying saucer (chortle, chortle).

The first RAAF press release, issued from Roswell base on Tuesday, July 8, is extremely interesting when set against subsequent official claims. On that day, the base commander at RAAF dictated and authorised the issue of the following release:

> "The many rumors regarding the flying disc became a reality yesterday when the intelligence office of the 509th Bomb group of the Eighth Air Force, Roswell Army Air Field, was fortunate enough to gain possession of a disc through the cooperation of one of the local ranchers and the sheriff's office of Chaves County. The flying object landed on a ranch near Roswell sometime last week. Not having phone facilities, the rancher stored the disc until such time as he was able to contact the sheriff's office, who in turn notified Maj. Jesse A. Marcel of the 509th Bomb Group Intelligence Office. Action was immediately taken and the disc was picked up at the rancher's

---

[30] Roswell was, at the time, a forgotten story. Edward Ruppelt, the ex-head of Project Blue Book, did not mention Roswell a single time in his 1956 book on flying saucers. Neither did Major Donald Keyhoe nor J Allen Hynek in their own early books on the subject of UFOs.

home. It was inspected at the Roswell Army Air Field and subsequently loaned by Major Marcel to higher headquarters." (see Ruppelt, 1956).

We will return to this simply amazing press release, but the name of Major Jesse Marcel is also a crucial element of the emerging tale.

Based on a great deal of research from about the 1970s onward, the UFO community now believes that an alien spaceship crashed near Roswell, and that one or more craft and the bodies of aliens were recovered. The two sides, the modern USAF and sceptics on the one hand and the ufologists on the other, could simply not be further apart. There are some heavy guns on both sides of the issue.

Lt Col Philip Corso is just one of those who have written detailed books claiming that the USAAF took away the "saucer" and several "alien" bodies, and the continuous arguments have fed forty years of intense activity by publishers, film-makers, and conference organisers. Clarity has not been aided by the fact that many records, alleged photographs, and reports appear to have been lost or destroyed over the years and many of the prime witnesses have passed away.

In 1995, for example, Congressman Steven Schiff of New Mexico managed to get a formal General Accounting Office (GAO) investigation launched. It was designed to finally track down some of the key records relating to Roswell. Among other things, Schiff eventually announced that the "GAO report states that the outgoing messages from Roswell Army Air Field (RAAF) for this period of time were destroyed without proper authority".

Around the same time, the USAF (which had claimed for almost fifty years that the crashed object was a weather balloon) announced that the debris was actually from a classified detection device designed to spot Soviet nuclear testing. That revelation brought renewed sighs and knowing winks from the UFO fraternity. The new information had only become necessary, they argued, because the UFO network had gradually gnawed away at the weather-balloon explanation for decades, and it was not holding up well. One reason was that witnesses had testified that the "debris" was actually situated in a large gash in the desert which appeared as though an object had landed or crashed.

The Roswell incident has never been completely cleared up (and in all probability never will be), but it has certainly produced some very interesting books, not the least of which was *The Day after Roswell* (Corso, 1997), by the above-mentioned Philip Corso.

Lieutenant Colonel Corse is now dead, but his legacy of accusations and evidence lives on. You can read his book and watch the man himself in James Fox's DVD documentaries (see Bibliography) to judge his credibility for yourself and, by extension, the credibility of an incredible story.[31] You should note that, although the story involved a huge amount of very weird stuff, there are a good number of otherwise highly credible researchers who don't just believe in Roswell, they say they know for sure that it happened (e.g. the aforementioned Don Schmitt and Robert Salas, an ex-USAF captain, in his 2014 book, *Unidentified: The UFO Phenomenon*).

Strangely enough, although that very first press release was the first shot in the Roswell war, it also forms an excellent place to leave things for now. It's an accepted fact that a USAAF major had been dispatched to find out what a local farmer had found on his land. Major Marcel collected whatever the rancher had found and, given that many excited rumours were circulating in the Roswell locality, the commander of the Roswell airbase, Colonel William Blanchard,[32] issued a press release.

In that very first published account (see above), the word "disc" appears four times; at other points, it was called a "flying disc" and a "flying object". And this official USAAF press release most specifically does *not* speak of thousands of bits of debris – it speaks of "it".

Any sort of balloon in those days was a mixture of rubber and aluminium foil with some metallic elements (such as a radar reflector) and, of course, an instrument package (which is in a box suspended below

---

[31] In common with all things "Roswell" controversy also bedevils Lt Col Corso. There is a pretty comprehensive discussion of him and his role – and the accusations levelled at him by the sceptics – on http://www.bibliotecapleyades.net/exopolitica/esp_exopolitics_ZZO.htm . The discussion is in two parts on the same site.

[32] By the mid-1960s, he was a four-star general.

the balloon which eventually floats to earth on a parachute when its job is done). When the balloon bursts, which they all do when they reach extreme altitudes, we get large chunks of rubber and tin foil falling to earth – usually across a very wide area. Okay. Now here we have a USAAF Intelligence major and his men (albeit Marcel's character has been called into question by sceptics over the years). They travel out to look at whatever the farmer has to show them and they see ... well, according to the US Air Force, they see shards of rubber and some tin foil and a few bits of metal. It is pretty safe to say the US Air Force specialises in knowing what these things are, and even if an officer like Major Marcel was a UFO nut and was determined to turn some shards of rubber into a flying saucer, there were a great many other people on the base who might easily have spotted that the wreckage was actually that of a balloon (including Col Blanchard himself). And if the balloon had actually been an unusual and much larger surveillance balloon, one has to imagine that the materials would still have been pretty similar.

So let's assume the USAAF was right and that the debris was from a weather or surveillance balloon; why did Blanchard phrase his press release in that way? Why not just say that the debris was from a weather balloon?

Nevertheless, the base commander sanctioned his press office to write and distribute a press release which talked of a flying object, a "flying disc" being recovered, and whatever *it* was, it then being "loaned" (another strange word) to higher headquarters. The release actually specifically alludes to the rumours that had been circulating and says they "became a reality".

If one assumes that what was found was genuinely a weather or surveillance balloon, it does not take a genius to see that a press release worded in that way might well stir up a hornets' nest of excited conjecture. In fact, Blanchard should have known that a release saying that flying discs were a reality was of global importance. If the wreckage of a balloon had been found, what Blanchard did was tantamount to lunacy. Yet his career was unblemished and his promotions kept coming.

But they released it anyway. It was only later that the Air Force hastily released a second statement saying the object was a weather balloon.

The outsider is left with a puzzled expression on their face. Why did

Colonel Blanchard not calm down all the wild rumours? After all, he'd seen the stuff brought back from the hinterlands, and presumably, between all those senior Air Force officers and non-comms, there was someone who could recognise the debris from a balloon when they saw it. Why not just say, in that very first official statement, that after all the rumours, what Major Marcel had found were some strips of rubber, some bits of tinfoil, and some chunks of twisted metal from a weather balloon? Most journalists would have thrown in the towel at that point, and even if they had printed a story, the description would not have made many readers think of bright, silver saucers with little green men inside. The *Roswell Daily Record* would certainly not have been able to print a headline like "RAAF Captures Flying Saucer," and the story would have died an instant death right there.

Technically, a balloon is a "flying object", but it certainly is not a "flying disc". And why use that term disc so often? Fallen segments of a rubber and metal balloon are "debris" – even the radar reflector would not be called a "disc"; it would be recognised by USAAF officers as such and would be called a radar reflector. I'd hazard a guess it would even have carried USAAF markings somewhere. No one in their right mind would take a look at a pile of twisted and torn bits of rubber and foil and call it a "disc", especially if one wanted to calm the hysterical rumours about flying saucers being seen in the area.

But then there's also Nick Redfern's theory: that what crashed at Roswell was more to do with nasty experiments than aliens:

> "There is, of course, another theory. It's a far more probable one. Aliens didn't try and recover the Roswell wreckage because...what happened at Roswell didn't involve aliens..."[33]

Just a thought or two to keep the old brain cells firing on all cylinders.

[33] Nick Redfern, The Roswell UFO Conspiracy: Exposing A Shocking And Sinister Secret; Lisa Hagan Books. 2017.

Farnborough, 1950

The steady stream of UFO sightings was by no means restricted to the United States. On a bright, clear summer's day (August 15, 1950), Wing Commander Stan Hubbard,[34] a test pilot based at the Royal Aircraft Establishment at Farnborough, saw an object in the sky which, he said, looked:

> "... for all the world like the edge-on view of a discus, the sort of discus we used to throw at sports day in school ... and it was rocking from side to side very slightly ... but maintaining a very straight approach." (Clarke, 2009).

It emitted what he likened to an electrical hum and had small lights along its edge. The object passed overhead, Hubbard estimated, at about a thousand feet. He gave its size at around a hundred feet in diameter, and its speed between 500 mph and 900 mph. In later years, he told David Clarke that his estimates were "best guesses" because there was nothing to help him to judge exact distance and speed. But, then again, he was a very experienced test pilot.

On September 5, another clear and bright day, Hubbard and five other airmen saw another disc in the distance over the Farnham area. This time, the disc "fluttered" and descended, and then rose again several times. In the end, about a dozen people witnessed this latter event. All concerned were interviewed by the Flying Saucer Working Party on both occasions. The Flying Saucer Working Party (great name, eh?) was the British government's secret committee looking into sightings of strange objects in and around the UK; we'll learn more about it later.

What is perhaps most interesting about these reports is not only that those concerned were told not to speak about the sightings, even among themselves, but that the investigation's conclusions (made public only in

---

[34] He flew Halifaxes during the war and was a very distinguished test pilot. He tutored at the Empire Test Pilots School and flew the famed Fairy-Delta 2 at speeds over 1,000 mph.

2001) were that Hubbard had experienced an optical illusion and that the larger group on September 5 had watched an aircraft but had been influenced to see something else by the first sighting.

Really? An experienced test pilot suffers one optical illusion and one mistaken identification – the first of which flew right over him, and the other was described in some detail by a number of people as "fluttering": not a word one would readily apply to the movements of an aircraft unless it was in severe trouble. One has to ask, also, whether optical illusions can make a sound like an electrical hum?

An optical illusion is usually something one sees in a single direction due to atmospherics such as heat haze or cloud formations. This "optical illusion" not only made a slight noise, it also sported lights, changed direction, and flew right over the head of the observer.

In his retirement, Hubbard, who had had spells with the USAF and with McDonnell Douglas, was told of the then-derestricted Flying Saucer Working Party's conclusions. His response: "Absolute rubbish. My engineering experience convinced me it was not of this earth".[35]

The 1952 Show

This year was one of the most momentous years for UFO sightings around the world. Interest in the subject was high, and even prestigious magazines like *Life* were not afraid to get their hands dirty. In April, *Life* ran an article entitled "Have we visitors from space?"[36] It caused an uproar in the United States, highlighting support for the UFO concept from some eminent scientists. The reason it is important is not so much what the article said, as that it was only written because several high-ranking military officers believed in the extraterrestrial hypothesis (ETH), as it is now known (Ruppelt, 1956). Captain Ruppelt also showed how that year had been a major one for Project Blue Book: the US equivalent of the British Flying Saucer Working Party.

[35] Quoted from his obituary in the *Daily Telegraph*, dated January 1, 2015. He died in 2014 aged 93.
[36] *Life* magazine. "Have we visitors from space?" April 7, 1952.

> "In 1948, 167 UFO reports had come into ATIC [Project Blue Book]; this was considered a big year. In June 1952 we received 149. During the four years the Air Force had been in the UFO business, 615 reports had been collected. During the "Big Flap" (lasting a few months of 1952) our incoming-message log showed 717 reports." (Ruppelt, 1956)

Ruppelt said that the tempo of UFO reports appeared to be speeding up, especially in the eastern States. US sightings increased during the first part of the year and peaked in the period June to August. One might be tempted to make a connection between the sightings and the summer vacation window, but some of the most important were made by professionals, military and civil pilots, and air traffic controllers, who were very much at work. That year also saw one of the very first major multiple sightings where objects were seen by radar, sometimes more than one radar set, as well as by USAF fighter pilots who had been sent up to investigate. In the United States, the 1952 UFO Flap included the Carson Sink sighting and the Washington National wave (see chapter 16).

In the UK, the most spectacular sightings of that year occurred during Operation Mainbrace and at RAF Little Rissington. Just as in the United States, these sightings were so impressive that the Ministry of Defence (MoD) reconstituted the Flying Saucer Working Party, this time under the chairmanship of the eminent scientist Dr R V Jones. These are also discussed in more detail later.

London, 1953

In the autumn of 1953, radar and visual sightings were made near London. In September, objects were picked up at high speeds at high altitudes (forty-four thousand to sixty-eight thousand feet), and in October, the crew of a British European Airways (BEA) Elizabethan passenger plane said that an object flew alongside the aircraft for about half an hour.[37]

---

[37] See Ruppelt, 1956.

Then, on November 3, 1953, anti-aircraft radar near London picked up two objects which ground observers said were circular, or spherical, and white in colour. Ruppelt says that Vampire jet fighters were scrambled and that the pilots saw "a strange aerial object". Men at a radar site watched the object through a telescope and described it as a "flat, white coloured tennis ball" (Ruppelt, 1956).

According to Ruppelt, the flap in Europe carried on into 1954 and included a visual sighting by a Swedish airliner and a sighting by just about everyone aboard a Dutch ocean liner of a greenish object which swept across the sky (July 3, 1954).

Edward Ruppelt also discussed the reactions of the Soviet bloc and their accusations that all UFOs were the nasty inventions of the bourgeois capitalists desperate to destabilise the Warsaw Pact. This notion was, of course, remarkably similar to the contrary suspicions of the United States and Britain in the early 1950s. He also stated that the equivalent flap in the USSR received no press or TV coverage, a fact which, he shrewdly pointed out, tended to undermine the argument that UFO flaps were simply the result of hysterical people being encouraged by the press and incited to see things by publicity.

Childerhose, 1956

On August 27, 1956, a Royal Canadian Air Force pilot, R J Childerhose, was flying an F-86 Sabre at thirty-seven thousand feet over the Rockies when he saw a glowing object. The importance of this sighting lies in the photo taken by the pilot that day.[38]

It was about 7.20 p.m., and the flight of four Royal Canadian Air Force F-86s was heading west near Fort MacCleod, Alberta. Childerhose saw, below him and almost at the top of a thundercloud, a stationary glowing object which he said looked "like a shiny silver dollar tipped horizontal". He pointed out the object to his flight leader, who said it must be a reflection, but Childerhose also took a colour photo, which remains impressive even though it has been subjected to considerable scrutiny.

---

[38] Read the report at http://brumac.8k.com/RJC/RJC.html

Philip Klass believed it was ball lightning or a "plasma" (that is a natural aggregation of high energy suspended in the air – something which, like ball lightning, is still not fully or convincingly explained), but the reader should take at least a quick look at Dr Bruce Maccabee's scientific study of the photo and the statements from the pilot quoted towards the end. Childerhose remained very sure that what he saw was not natural.[39]

Lonnie Zamora, 1964

Apart from Roswell, this is the first case in this book in which we encounter a report of alien beings. It was April 24, 1964, and a police officer, based in the town of Socorro, New Mexico, was dutifully chasing a speeding motorist. As he was doing so, he noticed a flash in the distance to one side of the road and immediately wondered whether it might be a serious incident at a dynamite shack that was located in that area. Patrolman Lonnie Zamora broke off the chase (lucky speeder) and drove off the main road and into the hills where, on coming over a rise, he saw what he first thought was an overturned car and two small adults or young people standing beside it. On foot, he approached through some gullies, thinking to help, and briefly lost sight of the "car". When it came into view again, the people had disappeared, and the machine took off slowly with flames and a roar. Once it reached a reasonable height, it sped off.

Zamora was interviewed several times by the FBI and by Air Force investigators from Project Blue Book. He had been badly frightened by the incident, but he stuck to his story until his dying day.

The event remains unexplained.

---

[39] Bruce Maccabee. "Optical Power Output of an Unidentified High Altitude Light Source." *Journal of Scientific Exploration*, 13, 2, 1999, p. 199.

One of several drawings which Police Officer Lonnie Zamora provided of what he witnessed in Socorro in 1964. The drawing is a rough one of the "footprints" he found. (Fortean/Topfoto.co.uk)

Pilot Sightings This Century

There are those who believe that the UFO craze is over and that – in modern times – people have better things to do than to spot and report things in the sky. Not only did I find no sign of a waning in UFO interest and sightings, but reports from highly credible witnesses are regularly submitted. I have to say that the professionalism and credibility of some of these witnesses makes you think. Here are just three of the recent ones, but they should be read against other important pilot sightings, such as the TWA and JAL ones in the United States, the Aurigny incident in the UK, and the Air France Flight 3532 sighting.

On December 2, 2012, an Airbus A320 reported a narrow miss at four thousand feet on final approach to Glasgow Airport. An object was alleged to have passed four hundred to five hundred feet below the aircraft. The object, according to the UK Airprox Board, was not seen on radar. Both pilots saw an object loom ahead of them, but it passed before they could react. No warning was received by the aircraft's traffic collision avoidance system (TCAS).[40] The pilots said the object was either blue and yellow or silver in colour. It had a small frontal area but was bigger than a balloon. Radar at nearby Prestwick Airport had tracked an unidentified object 1.3 nautical miles east of the Airbus' position and twenty-eight seconds earlier.

The pilot of the A320 wasn't sure but thought that it might perhaps have been a microlight aircraft, but the board could find no evidence to pin down the cause. Microlights, paragliders, and several other sorts of air vehicle were ruled out by the board as being "radar significant" (that is, they would have been seen by radar stations).

The final verdict of the Airprox Board was "insufficient evidence".

On July 13, 2013, an Airbus A320 was at thirty-four thousand feet over Berkshire when the pilot reported that an object, bright silver metallic and shaped like a rugby ball, narrowly missed his aircraft. Coming so close that the captain instinctively ducked, it moved so quickly from a left-hand side cockpit window and across the aircraft that the crew had no time to react or evade.

Again the UK Airprox Board could find no answer but ruled out meteorological conditions and balloons. At that height, drones, paragliders, and microlights could also be ignored. Military radars had, apparently, not picked up anything.[41]

Another interesting near-miss occurred on March 19, 2014, near Perth, Western Australia. At about thirty-eight hundred feet on the approach

---

[40] TCAS systems only work between aircraft fitted with transponders. If the other object does not have a transponder (and that can include business jets, small aircraft, ultralights, and drones), the TCAS system is of no use.

[41] See http://www.independent.co.uk/news/weird-news/airbus-pilot-reveals-near-miss-with-ufo-over-berkshire-countryside-9040010.html

to Perth Airport, a DHC-8 aircraft carrying fifty-three passengers en-countered a dark-green, cylindrical object which passed at speed about a hundred feet below the aircraft. The pilots first saw it as a white flashing light and took evasive action. The object passed them about a hundred feet below and only sixty feet to the side, which was why the Australian Transport Safety Board (ATSB) classified it as a serious incident.

The ATSB investigated the event (case AO-2014-052) but was unable to explain it, even after researching all possible unmanned aerial vehicle (UAV) possibilities. Two NARCAP investigators interviewed the captain (with permission from the airline) and concluded that the object was not a weather balloon and that it was not floating or hovering but travelling in the opposite direction to the aircraft.[42] Both pilots were shocked by the event. The final word of the ATSB was that the incident "should be regarded as an example of an unidentified aerial object".

[42] Keith Basterfield and Paul Dean. "Near-miss between an Australia [sic] Airplane and an 'Unknown Object' near Perth, Western Australia, on 19th March 2014." NARCAP IR-7; January 2015.

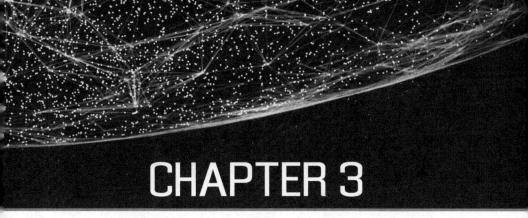

CHAPTER 3

US Government Investigations

IN THIS CHAPTER, WE'LL take a look at how the US government reacted to the sightings of UFOs from the earliest modern sightings to the late 1960s.

Project Sign

As a result of the furore over Arnold and Roswell in 1947 and a swathe of other sightings of UFOs, the US Air Force established the first of a series of investigative projects aimed at working out what flying saucers were all about. They began with Project Sign in 1948 and went on through Projects Grudge and Blue Book to 1969, when that final project was closed and all its UFO files (in theory) were released to the American public.

Project Sign began operation in early 1948 at Wright Field in Ohio (now called Wright-Patterson Air Force Base). It was tasked with collecting information on UFO sightings, evaluating those data, and then assessing whether UFOs constituted a threat to national security. This is a theme which crops up in the UFO investigations of virtually every nation one studies. It's not surprising that any object which appears in national airspace which cannot be immediately identified should be considered a threat until proven otherwise. If there is a mystery it is why the United States and Great Britain are so certain that UFOs do *not* present a threat to national security.

In post-war America and Britain, in the Soviet Union, and later in such countries as France, Belgium, and China, UFOs have been primarily investigated by governments for their potential to offer a threat.

Nick Pope, the former UK Ministry of Defence official, explained how nations define "threat" in the form of a formula (Pope, 2014):

Threat = Capability + Intent.

In other words, it is not sufficient for one nation to have the *capability* to harm another for it to be regarded as a threat, which would then necessitate some sort of protective or retaliatory action. Simply because the United States has sufficient nuclear weapons, and certainly conventional forces, to overwhelm the UK does not make it a threat. For the United States to become a threat to Britain, there would have to be proven *intent* to cause harm or to invade UK sovereign territory. That intent does not have to be made public, of course, but it generally presents itself, even in the public arena, as an attitude or a predisposition, or it may be evident in the predominant political culture. So, was Nick Pope also sending a message? That the United States and Great Britain know full well that UFOs exist and have the capability to be a threat but that they are absolutely certain that intent is absent. Or is it merely that both governments are certain that there is no such thing as UFOs and that they can therefore be ignored?

When the UK closed its MoD UFO desk in 2009, it did so on the basis that UFOs were of no defence significance. Note, not that they did not exist, but that they were not considered to be a threat. The wording was very precise.

There is alleged to have been a report by the Project Sign group called "An Estimate of the Situation". It was said to have been presented to USAF General Hoyt Vandenberg and summarily rejected. No evidence of such a report has been forthcoming, except for a number of references to it by officers from that period, references which have remained largely unverified (mainly because the alleged Estimate has never been found). The reason that the Estimate is regarded as important by the UFO community is that it is alleged to have included the conclusion that UFOs were real, probably extraterrestrial, and that further investigations were warranted. But even if the Estimate did so conclude, that does not make it necessarily of earth-shattering importance. It could have been wrong.

"Estimates of the Situation" are produced by a great many military officers in response to requests from their superiors. They are what it says on the tin: an *estimation* of what is going on in the eyes of whoever is writing it. They are the weather forecasts of the military world. It is entirely likely that this one, like many others, was simply destroyed when its recipient (General Vandenberg) decided that its conclusions were unjustified.

A document entitled "Analysis of Flying Object Incidents in the US" is, however, on public record. Dated December 1948 (Analysis, 1948), it reviewed twenty significant US sightings of UFOs during 1947 and 1948. The analysis, which appears to have been pretty balanced, also highlighted and discussed a number of aircraft which had either been developed or were being tested by various nations at the time and which, if spotted over the territory of the United States, could potentially be mistaken for flying saucers. These included a number of revolutionary designs for what are called flying wings.

One very relevant design had been produced during the war in Germany by the Horten brothers (Reimar and Walther). A flying wing design is one in which there is no separate fuselage and wings (sometimes, not even any tailplane). The whole single body of the aircraft acts as the wing for lift purposes; the final product can be wedge shaped or even circular. The Ho229, as the 1944 Horten design was styled, was a revolutionary jet-engined fighter aircraft with a wedge-shaped configuration which looked very similar to the B-2 and F-117 stealth aircraft of today. The Allies were worried that the Soviets had acquired the design and had created a capable airframe which was now being tested over the continental United States and over Britain.

The detailed analysis came to two interesting conclusions where the UFO debate is concerned:

> "11. Since the Air Force is responsible for control of the air in the defense of the U.S., it is imperative that all other

agencies cooperate in confirming or denying the possibility that these objects have a domestic origin. Otherwise,
if it is firmly indicated that there is no domestic explanation, the objects are a threat and warrant more active
efforts of identification and interception.

12. It must be accepted that some type of flying objects
have been observed, although their identification and origin are not discernible. In the interest of national defense
it would be unwise to overlook the possibility that some
of these objects may be of foreign origin."

The conclusions highlight the fact that the authors were not permitted to know whether or not these objects were of US manufacture; they
boil down to "further investigation is necessary". Following this analysis,
the USAF research project was renamed Project Grudge and eventually
became Project Blue Book in 1951.

The UFO fraternity has always asserted that none of these projects
were genuinely focused on objectively examining the UFO phenomenon
but that, instead, they'd been tasked to debunk it. But the actual situation,
as usual, is less black-and-white. Real life is never so clear-cut or starkly
defined.

On the surface, that is, as far as most researchers have been able to
ascertain, the attitude of the US authorities changed quite a bit between
about 1947 and the mid-to-late 1950s. In the early years, the memos and
reports behind the closed doors of the military establishment seem pretty
balanced and the research very open-minded. Investigations were targeted
mainly towards trying to find out if the UFOs were actually of Soviet, or
other earth-bound construction and whether they constituted a threat to
the United States. In Britain, the Flying Saucer Working Party carried out
the same type of study. The tone of these confidential or secret documents
tended towards bafflement. Macho military officers could never admit to
being baffled, but they certainly used phrases like "identities not discernible" and "further research is necessary".

Somehow, though, as the 1950s progressed, and not too far at that, the tone of US documents on the subject became highly secretive, and there was much more of a feeling that the authorities wanted the population to accept that there was nothing to UFOs except mass hysteria and people misinterpreting perfectly normal things. The ufologists immediately yelled, "Cover-up", but it is just as likely that this change occurred because the US authorities got mightily scared by the UFO waves of 1952 and genuinely believed that, if not squashed, such events might see the Soviets given a massive strategic weapon to use against the US populace, its armed forces, and its government: that of panic.

This is where the conspiracy theories started. Between the first press release after whatever happened in Roswell, New Mexico (the one which announced that a "flying disc" had crashed) and around 1949, a great deal changed in the way the US Air Force and the military in general handled the UFO phenomenon. In the UK the authorities' reaction to Stan Hubbard's sightings at Farnborough showed that the British government, too, was being strangely dismissive of pretty credible reports of weird things in their skies.

In the United States much of the response to strange objects seems to have been compartmentalised, with the left hand never quite understanding what was going on with the right. For example, the people who wrote the "Analysis" found it impossible to know enough about secret US aircraft programs in order to rule them out as a possible cause. This is common in military organisations, and it is important for the outsider to recognise that individual elements of the US armed forces and security service almost never knew what was going on in other elements. It's the same today and is the way the military works in all nations. All have secrets that they do not want their enemies (and sometimes their friends) to know. These are most commonly about new weapons or tactics or battle plans or strategy. Whatever the peaceniks argue, there is no point in having any armed services at all unless their developments and plans can be kept secret. Otherwise, it's a bit like a boxer shouting to his opponent what punch he is going to throw next. Those sort of bouts would not last long, and you have just one guess as to which boxer will win. In any large organisation, secrets can only be kept if they are shared by as few people as possible. Hence the famed "need to know" principle: If your job means that you do not need to know something, then you will not be told it.

It was precisely these issues which caused Project Sign to experience unresolvable problems in assessing the sightings from 1947 and 1948. Formally established in December 1947, the officers of Project Sign did their best to evaluate the objects and to rule out most of the common explanations. In the end, they were left with them being:

a) foreign advanced aircraft (ie, Soviet);
b) secret US advanced aircraft; or
c) something else, for example, extraterrestrial.

They came to be fairly sure that whatever was being seen was not Soviet. This for two reasons: Firstly, they calculated that the Soviets could not have technically developed such highly advanced craft in the short space of time since the end of the war, even with their acquisition of some German engineers and scientists, and secondly, that even if they had managed to develop the craft, they would most certainly not test them over the United States or the UK, because there was too much of a risk that these advanced aircraft would crash and thereby allow all that advanced engineering to fall into Allied hands.

When Project Sign staff attempted to investigate option (b), they came up against the inherent secrecy and complexity of the US armed forces and security services. They made valiant efforts to get information on the latest US secret aircraft but ran into the oldest conundrum: If the aircraft were not highly secret and therefore not technologically advanced, they were never going to be the answer to the flying saucers; if they *were* US projects and were advanced enough to be seen as flying saucers, they would be so highly classified that no one would tell them. And that's what happened. Project Sign could be pretty sure that the objects were not Soviet, but they failed to rule out the possibility that they might be super-advanced US aircraft (Maccabee, 2014).

The pooh-poohing of sightings in public, and the secret studies going on in the background, could possibly be explained by a conflicted government wary of public panic and the opportunity that might give to an enemy to destabilise the country before a pre-emptive strike or invasion. At the same time, they were frantically trying to get to the bottom of all those sightings.

However, the way that the US government elected to deal with UFOs raises a number of questions. In the early stages of cold war paranoia, the authorities were worried about the Soviet Union using flying saucer hysteria for nefarious purposes. But even if the concern carried any genuine threat, it was soon discounted. Even as early as Project Sign (between around 1947 and 1948), the Air Force was certain the flying objects were not Soviet. They were also pretty sure – given the numbers and spread of sightings – that they were not highly secret US prototype aircraft.

So that leaves a straightforward question as to exactly why, after 1948, the US authorities should take the approach of ridiculing and playing down UFO sightings. If UFOs were simply a function of social or psychological delusions, or were manifestations of everyday phenomena such as the weather, why did the authorities not just say so, produce a detailed booklet with all the various silly reasons, and then forget the matter? If people continue to see the objects, just point them to the book. Why the derision?

Probably for two reasons: In the first place, there was always the possibility that the Soviet Union could use UFO panic to destabilise US defences at a vital time. Therefore, if the public laughed at UFOs, they were less likely to run around screaming if the newspapers announced one. In the second place, the US authorities were, perhaps, concerned that they still did not have an answer to what the objects were. Governments hate their voters to see that the emperor is naked.

And there was also the not-insignificant problem that, even within the US military, there were officers who did not feel that the phenomenon had been completely explained, and others who privately believed that the objects *were* extraterrestrial. Some kept their views inside the military establishment; others published books when they retired from active service – most notably Lt Col Corso, Major Donald Keyhoe, and Captain Edward Ruppelt.

Even Project Sign's demise was a little mysterious. As mentioned above, the staff were rumoured to have produced an "Estimate of the Situation" in the summer of 1948. No one is absolutely sure what the estimate concluded[43] (because all copies were apparently destroyed), but its conclusions were allegedly rejected by General Hoyt S Vandenberg. Captain Ruppelt said that he, himself, had read it. Shortly afterwards, Project Sign was replaced by Project Grudge. People in the UFO community have speculated that Grudge replaced Sign so that the staff could be changed and its procedures made less assiduous. But the fact is that no one knows for sure.

However, it is certainly clear that the newly formed US Air Force[44] had changed direction insofar as UFOs were concerned. Such documents as have survived seem to indicate a far more sceptical public approach to the subject, with the default position being that UFOs were either imaginary or due to natural phenomena. Subsequent documents released by the FBI and CIA tend to show that, whatever the public explanations, the authorities, behind closed doors, took a different view.

Project Grudge

By January 1949, Captain Edward Ruppelt says that the US military had "decided" that UFOs did not exist; that is, they were all explicable in normal terms. It was the first policy change of what was to be a series over the coming decades – first blowing hot, then blowing cold (sometimes, as with Project Grudge and its transformation into Project Blue Book, in very quick succession). Ruppelt described Grudge's approach as follows:

"Project Grudge had a two-phase program of UFO annihilation. The first phase consisted of explaining every

---

[43] Edward Ruppelt said that he read a copy and that it concluded that the "extraterrestrial" explanation was the most likely one (Ruppelt, 1956).

[44] Up to the summer of 1948, the US Air Force had been part of the Army, known as the United States Army Air Force (USAAF).

UFO report. The second phase was to tell the public how the Air Force had solved all the sightings. This, Project Grudge reasoned, would put an end to UFO reports." (Ruppelt, 1956)

The message, as Project Sign morphed into Project Grudge in 1949, seemed to be that "UFOs were on their way out". Ruppelt calls this period "the Dark Ages", saying that Project Grudge was tasked simply to refute UFO sightings and find ways of explaining them in ordinary terms. Whether or not project members were specifically instructed to do so, Grudge came to detailed conclusions on the whole issue uncannily quickly.

The project was closed down shortly after the publication of Major Donald Keyhoe's famous article in *True* magazine. In late December 1949, the article, in one of America's most popular men's magazines, was entitled "*The Flying Saucers Are Real*". It caused a storm of debate and controversy.

Project Grudge's secret report was also dated December 1949, but its conclusions were contrary to Keyhoe's:

"A. There is no evidence that objects reported upon are the result of an advanced scientific foreign development; and, therefore they constitute no direct threat to the national security. In view of this, it is recommended that the investigation and study of reports of unidentified flying objects be reduced in scope. Headquarters AMC [Air Material Command] will continue to investigate reports in which realistic technical applications are clearly indicated.

NOTE: It is apparent that further study along present lines would only confirm the findings presented herein. It is further recommended that pertinent collection directives be revised to reflect the contemplated change in policy.

B.   All evidence and analyses indicate that reports of unidentified flying objects are the result of:

    1. Misinterpretation of various conventional objects.
    2. A mild form of mass hysteria and war nerves.
    3. Individuals who fabricate such reports to perpetrate a hoax or to seek publicity.
    4. Psychopathological persons."

Conclusion B placed anyone who reported a UFO into a pretty awkward situation. Furthermore, it set an official tone which was passed down through the ranks of the US armed services and has coloured the official reaction to UFOs ever since. Project Grudge rubbished virtually all sightings and made fools of those who reported them and, even to this day people in the armed forces and commercial aviation are extremely wary of admitting that they have seen a "UFO".

According to conclusion B, if you tell someone you've seen a UFO, you must either be seeing things, be suffering from hysteria, be a malicious self-publicist, or be a psycho. Take your pick. It's not difficult to imagine how pilots and police officers would feel after that damning verdict had filtered down to them. If they saw something which they could not immediately explain, it was clearly far better to keep quiet about it. Conclusion B2 was interesting primarily because no evidence was provided that such a condition could exist or, if it could, why the public got themselves into a state about flying saucers and not ghosts, goblins, fairies, Big Foot, or, indeed, the far more scary threat of nuclear war. The Cuba missile crisis of 1962 and the Soviet invasion of Czechoslovakia in 1968 showed that neither the American nor the British publics were easily thrown into hysterical panic.

Ruppelt also discusses the strange final appendix to the report: the "Summary of the Evaluation of Remaining Reports" (Ruppelt, 1956). He says that Grudge's report admitted that no less than 23 percent of all sightings could not be explained in conventional terms in spite of evidence being available. They were listed in that final appendix. Yet the report itself still concluded that *all* UFO reports were misinterpretations, misidentifications, or hoaxes.

However, no matter what Project Grudge said, UFOs continued to be reported. After some interesting and controversial sightings in 1950-1951, the US Air Force effectively ignored the Grudge findings and replaced Project Grudge with a slightly upgraded version under Captain Ruppelt. Project Blue Book continued to investigate and report on US UFO sightings through to 1969. The best account of the Sign, Grudge, and early Blue Book years was Captain Ruppelt's book, *Report on Unidentified Flying Objects*. The book is an intelligent, balanced and thoughtful insight into the phenomenon, a book which should always appear on the UFOs 101 reading list. Unlike many books on the subject it is also well-written.

Project Blue Book

On October 27, 1951, Project Grudge was relaunched as the "new Project Grudge" before eventually getting more people and more support and becoming Project Blue Book in early 1952. But one has to ask, if the conclusions of Project Grudge were correct, why launch another expensive research project? The answer appears to be that many senior officers simply did not accept the Grudge conclusions.

Captain Ruppelt, as the head of Grudge and then Blue Book, was one of the more balanced players in America's on-and-off, hot-and-cold history of UFO investigations. He says in his book that he wanted only open-minded people on the team and that, during his time, he had to let three people go for being either too pro-UFO or too biased against the UFO subject.

At this time, Ruppelt was also given funds to commission an outside research agency (called Project Bear) to provide scientific consultancy, to design a better witness-interrogation form, and to conduct a statistical analysis of sightings based on the 650+ cases already on file and on new ones as they came in.[45] In the mid-1970s, Dr Bruce Maccabee gained access to FBI files from the period. He highlighted the fact that the FBI

---

[45] Although classified at the time, Project Bear was actually performed by the Battelle Memorial Institute of Columbus, Ohio (Bennett, 2010).

files contained a few sightings that were different from Blue Book, which is a little strange because Blue Book was supposed to be the official UFO investigative body (Maccabee, 2014).

According to Ruppelt, the external research agency was going to punch the data onto IBM cards (one hundred items of information and one case per card) and then machine-sort and analyse them. The technology was highly advanced for the time, but it looks positively archaic in modern terms. If we assume that one piece of information is represented by perhaps five bytes (forty characters or bits), then a thousand cases, each comprising a hundred pieces of information, would have taken about five hundred thousand bytes on a modern computer. That's 500k or about 0.008 percent of one of today's 64-gigabyte thumb drives.

Any detailed analysis which Project Bear came up with, along with its database, has yet to see the light of day (in public, at least).

The Robertson Panel

In January of 1953, in parallel to Project Blue Book, a secret CIA report prompted the US authorities to set up a review committee which became known as the Robertson Panel, after its chairman, the eminent physicist Howard P Robertson. The group comprised a stellar array of physicists, with a CIA secretary (Mr F C Durant). It was given top-level briefings by the military and then held just twelve hours of formal meetings over a four-day period.

Ruppelt confirmed that it reviewed two highly regarded UFO-sighting films and twenty-three of Blue Book's most convincing cases (that is, 1 percent of the 2,331 then on file). The report's conclusions and recommendations, which are available on Wikipedia,[46] stated essentially that UFOs do not offer a direct threat to US national security but that they pose an indirect threat through public interest "overwhelming standard military communications".

The panel's members were unconvinced by the two film clips of UFOs

---

[46] https://en.wikipedia.org/wiki/Robertson_Panel

and stated that most UFO sightings could be explained as misidentifications of ordinary things in the sky. They felt that even the unexplained ones would "in all likelihood" just need some further study to explain them in the same manner.

In an edited form, the conclusions were:

> "That the evidence ... shows no indication that these phenomena constitute a direct physical threat to national security. That the continued emphasis on the reporting of these phenomena does, in these parlous times, result in a threat to the orderly functioning of the protective organs of the body politic."

In other words, the Robertson Panel was saying that allowing or encouraging people to report UFOs was a threat to national security because the mass sightings and reports might overwhelm the communications systems (mainly landline telephone and radio) and stop the "protective organs" from functioning in an orderly and effective manner in an emergency. This is a return to the fear that an enemy could create a mass "UFO scare" and use the resulting communications chaos to launch an attack. No one had forgotten the panic caused by Orson Welles's radio adaptation of H G Wells's *War of the Worlds* in October 1938. Superficially, this theory sounds feasible, but a little calm thought reveals that it is perilously close to nonsense.

In order to create such a situation, an enemy would need to do the following:

1. Manufacture enough "UFOs" of sufficient credibility to fool a great many people across a continental-sized nation. They'd need to be fast, high-flying, covered in lights, and totally silent.
2. Make them appear in lots of militarily critical locations, because even if they could manufacture sufficient UFOs to fool an entire region, this would still not be enough to cripple a country the size of the United States.

3. Hope that the apparitions actually succeeded in creating panic sufficient to snarl up police and military communications for a fair amount of time while they got their "invasion" act together or flew in enough atomic bombers to cripple a score or more of vital US cities and facilities (there were no such things as ICBMs in those days).

The fear of such a possibility is, in itself, somewhat difficult to understand even in terms of 1953 politics and society, but I suppose it is no stranger than the domino theory of the 1960s, which had the whole world falling to Communist revolutions if South Vietnam was to fall. The point is that governments are not omniscient, and neither are they always right. Even the US government can get things wrong from time to time.

The Robertson Panel recommended:

> "That the national security agencies take immediate steps to strip the Unidentified Flying Objects of the special status they have been given and the aura of mystery they have unfortunately acquired;
>
> That the national security agencies institute policies on intelligence, training, and public education designed to prepare the material defenses and the morale of the country to recognize most promptly and to react most effectively to true indications of hostile intent or action.
>
> We suggest that these aims may be achieved by an integrated program designed to reassure the public of the total lack of evidence of Inimical forces behind the phenomenon, to train personnel to recognize and reject false indications quickly and effectively, and to strengthen regular channels for the evaluation of and prompt reaction to true indications of hostile measures."

So there is a strong sense from the fact that the CIA pushed for the Robertson Panel, and then banned any mention of a link between the CIA and its work, that the concern in government was to keep the subject of UFOs as low key as possible. Cold War paranoia ruled. On the surface, it appears that this was due to quite serious worries that the subject could be used as "psychological warfare" by an enemy creating mass panic, but also that it could be used to distract the armed forces from a genuine enemy attack:

> "We cite as examples the clogging of channels of com-munication by irrelevant reports, the danger of being led by continued false alarms to ignore real indications of hostile action, and the cultivation of a morbid national psychology in which skilful hostile propaganda could induce hysterical behavior and harmful distrust of duly constituted authority."

This report, to the extent that it set a very specific tone within the government, appears to have severely curtailed, for a long time, any open-minded investigations of the phenomenon. The message was very clear: Anyone who took the issue seriously was effectively aiding the enemies of the United States by making it easier for them to fool the US public with false UFO sightings. Once you had bought into the idea that UFOs could panic the US public and undermine the defences of an entire nation, taking UFOs seriously in an open-minded way became not far short of treason.

The Condon Report, 1968

After Edward Ruppelt's tenure, Project Blue Book came under increasing criticism as the years went by. One of its later heads, Major (later Lt Col) Hector Quintanilla, came in for particular criticism for allegedly delib-erately driving down the unexplained proportion of UFOs to less than 1 percent during his period in office between 1963 and 1969. Following the passing of the Freedom of Information and Privacy Act (FOIPA) in 1966, a decision was taken to launch another major review of the UFO issue.

The Project Blue Book team with its then boss, Major Hector Quintanilla (seated). (Fortean/Topfoto.co.uk)

It appears that even the US Air Force, long accused of covering up UFOs, wanted this review done properly. It wanted two or more universities to study the subject in parallel. Apparently, however, it experienced extreme difficulty finding even a single university willing to stick its neck under the UFO guillotine. The subject of UFOs had been publicly rubbished and derided for thirteen years since the Robertson Panel, with the result that government and media always treated the subject with patronising and derisive humour. It was unfortunate that a few misguided or insane people should think they saw things in the sky, but here's a nice cartoon of a happy alien in a bright blue flying saucer to cheer you all up.

Under those circumstances, it proved incredibly difficult for the USAF to persuade academics of sufficient standing to pin their names to the study. Who can blame them?

In the end, the review was commissioned to the University of Colorado and was chaired by Edward U Condon, a distinguished physicist with a lengthy history of work for the US government on nuclear issues. Condon later said that he'd had his arm twisted a little and that "duty to country" had been implied if not overtly mentioned.

After a two-year study between 1966 and 1968, the final report of the Condon group was published. It was called "A Scientific Study of Unidentified Flying Objects" and was a schizophrenic affair if ever there was one, its conclusions bearing little resemblance to the body of findings from its expert investigators.

One has to remember, though, that during those years, the United States had much more pressing things on its collective mind. At the start of 1966, around 185,000 US military personnel had been sent to South Vietnam. By the middle of 1968, that total had increased to 550,000, the war had grown incredibly expensive (in lots of ways), and the issue of the draft had bitterly divided the entire nation. The war in Vietnam was a huge psychological blow for the United States and its people, which is still being analysed by scholars. Against that backdrop, the issue of flying saucers must have seemed a little less than pressing.

The Condon committee was made up of some very eminent scientists. It was given full access to the reports of Project Blue Book and its predecessors as well as considerable help (initially) from two civilian UFO bodies: the National Investigations Committee on Aerial Phenomena (NICAP) and the now-defunct Aerial Phenomena Research Organization (APRO).[47]

Needless to say, the report remains highly contested. From the point of view of a great many scientists, it is the last word, the report which put the final nail into the coffin of alien UFOs. From the UFO enthusiast side of the debate (and many middle-of-the-road observers too), the conclusions were biased and weirdly unrelated to the scientific findings. The fact that it had to be separately validated indicates how little faith even the USAF had in its credibility.

---

[47] NICAP boasted military officers among its members, including Major Donald Keyhoe, USMC (Ret.), D S Fahrney USN (Ret.), and Vice Admiral R H Hillenkoetter. The organisation finally folded in about 1980. APRO seems to have been wound up some eight years later but at one time listed the atmospheric physicist Dr James McDonald of the University of Arizona and engineering professor Dr James Harder of the University of California, Berkeley, among its leading lights.

At one point, and well before the report was complete, Condon an-nounced in a public speech that the whole issue of UFOs was "nonsense". It was later revealed that in 1966 (that is, before the study commenced), Robert Low, an assistant dean of the university, had written to faculty se-niors at Colorado saying that the study could be expected to demonstrate that UFO observations had no basis in reality.

The committee's work descended into farce when, in May 1968, *Look* magazine revealed Low's prejudicial letter and labelled the Condon Committee a "Flying Saucer Fiasco". Low resigned later that month.

The chairman wrote the report's conclusions and recommendations, and some say that he didn't read the full report before doing so. There is certainly strong reason to believe so, because his conclusions contradict many of the findings in the body of the document. In the conclusions, Condon wrote:

> "Our general conclusion is that nothing has come from the study of UFOs in the past 21 years that has added to scientific knowledge. Careful consideration of the record as it is available to us leads us to conclude that further extensive study of UFOs probably cannot be justified in the expectation that science will be advanced thereby."

He also recommended against the creation of a government program to investigate UFO reports but hedged his bets strangely by saying that the committee's findings against further research in the matter "may not be true for all time". The report also said that further research was justified in such areas as atmospheric optics, radio propagation, and atmospheric electricity. One oft-quoted finding concerned the 1956 UFO sightings from the USAF bases of Lakenheath and Bentwaters in the UK. Of that particular series of sightings, the report said:

> "In conclusion, although conventional or natural expla-nations certainly cannot be ruled out, the probability of such seems low in this case and the probability that at

least one genuine UFO was involved appears to be fairly high."

One is forced to ask how many "genuine UFO" sightings one has to accumulate before further research is urgently necessary.

Although the UFO fraternity generally disparages the Condon report, we should remember that the US Air Force spent a lot of money on it – probably up to half a million dollars in 1960s cash (around $3.5 million in 2016) – and then also asked the National Academy of Sciences to undertake an independent assessment of the committee's work. The outsider is probably forced to the conclusion that the *Look* article and the general publicity circus surrounding Condon's handling of the study forced the Air Force to find ways of underpinning the report's credibility. In order to be absolutely watertight, the Condon report required unassailable scientific assessment.

The panel, established by the National Academy of Sciences (NAS) under the eminent Yale astronomer Gerald Clemence, examined the report over a six-week period and concluded that

> "... on the basis of present knowledge the least likely explanation of UFOs is the hypothesis of extraterrestrial visitations by intelligent beings ... no high priority in UFO investigations is warranted by data of the past two decades."

They were, of course, examining the report itself and were not re-examining the evidence, but it was enough to seal Project Blue Book's fate. The USAF (and, behind them, the American government) had spent a great deal of effort and money to establish a watertight review of the UFO phenomenon and had then paid the NAS even more money to do a review of the final report. The prestigious National Academy of Sciences agreed with the main findings of the Condon group but did not point out the inconsistencies in the report's content and its findings. It was enough to settle Blue Book's hash but, even then, the issue did not die the sort of death the USAF had presumably hoped for.

In 1970, the American Institute of Aeronautics and Astronautics also examined the Condon report. They concluded that Condon's summary did not reflect the body of the report and that "a phenomenon with such a high ratio of unexplained cases should arouse sufficient curiosity to continue its study". Leslie Kean (Kean, 2010) says that the Condon report itself stated that 30 percent of sightings were unexplained (even Robertson found a lower proportion of inexplicable sightings - 23 percent).

One of the investigators on the report was William Hartman, an astronomer from the University of Arizona. He carried out investigations on two of the photos from an incident in McMinnville, Oregon (see chapter 6), and famously stated that the accounts of the witnesses showed that this was almost certainly an "extraordinary flying object" (for his exact words, see the commentary on the Trent photos in chapter 6).

The photographs, however, were heavily criticised by sceptics on the basis of a critique which questioned the time of day the photos were taken (using what they identified as shadows). After this, Hartman withdrew his conclusion. Dr Bruce Maccabee later conducted further detailed examinations and concluded that the photos were, indeed, genuine (Maccabee, 2014).

Based on the Condon report's conclusions, Project Blue Book was officially closed on December 17, 1969, and the United States began the process of declassifying and releasing Blue Book files.

Meanwhile, across the wild waters of the North Atlantic, the British were going through exactly the same process of sightings, debunkings by the authorities, investigative studies by eminent scientists, "definitive" reports, more sightings, more studies and more reports.

CHAPTER 4

British Government Investigations

INVESTIGATIONS OF UFOS BEGAN in the UK at pretty much the same time as those in the United States – that is, in the years immediately following World War II. As we will see in the next chapter, formal investigations in France began almost three decades later.

The Flying Saucer Working Party: 1950–1953

In conscious or unconscious emulation of the Americans, the British also launched an enquiry into UFOs in the early years. They had experienced their own sightings and scares and had taken particular note of those reported by British police and RAF officers as well as those which had plagued the Americans. In 1950, the Ministry of Defence (MoD) asked its chief scientific adviser, Sir Henry Tizard, to chair what was colourfully named the Flying Saucer Working Party. The working party's 1951 conclusions, which were heavily classified, were that UFOs were mainly delusions, hoaxes, or people misidentifying ordinary objects. Just like the US investigations, the Tizard group in the UK said that UFOs should not be investigated any further. The working party also dismissed radar sightings and those by serving RAF and civilian pilots including two separate sightings by one of its own most trusted and experienced test pilots – Stan Hubbard. Then, following Britain's own spate of UFO reports in 1952, the

UK government reinstated the working party under a different chairman, Dr R V Jones, with pretty much the same results.

And yet, just as in the United States, UFOs continued to be reported, and the MoD maintained its process of collecting and analysing UFO data for over fifty years. The issue simply refused to die. It completely disregarded the conclusions of eminent scientists. The British were also to launch another detailed scientific investigation in the 1990s.

Condign, 1996–2000

For reasons which will probably forever be hidden, these were the years during which the British government made its own highly detailed investigations into the UFO phenomenon. The last official consideration of the subject had been by the Tizard and Jones groups of the 1950s. Since then, the British had kept half an eye on the subject by maintaining a part-time desk within the Ministry of Defence. Why the British should suddenly decide to launch a major secret enquiry thirty years after Condon and roughly coincident with the private French COMETA Report (see Chapter 5) is unclear. But they did.

The researchers and authors of the Condign report are unknown to this day, and the report itself might not have been revealed for a long time to come were it not for the efforts of Dr David Clarke of Sheffield-Hallam University. The report of the Project Condign study was classified "Secret UK Eyes Only" but was released in 2006 after a successful Freedom of Information Act request by Dr Clarke.

The Condign report is among the most important UFO studies ever to have been conducted by any nation. With academic precision, it calls them unidentified aerial phenomena (UAP). It took between three and four years to complete, and its three volumes run to over 450 pages of very detailed scientific discussion and analysis of virtually every possible cause of the sightings.

Predictably, the UFO community tends to disparage the report on the basis that it is another cover-up (in which case, why did the British government undertake it in the first place, and then keep it secret?), but the independent reader is forced to conclude that Condign is an extremely detailed piece of scientific work and, though heavily flawed, a thorough study of an extremely wide variety of possible causes of UAPs. It discusses all the usual ones plus something called atmospheric plasma (this was also a favourite explanation of UFOs used by Philip Klass – see note below). The working papers in the report appear to be balanced, although some of the science is most certainly beyond the average reader.

A Note on Plasmas in Nature

At present we think there are four states of matter – solid, liquid, gas, and plasma. The latter can be produced artificially – for example in a florescent tube – and it can exist in nature in various forms including lightning, the rarely-seen St. Elmo's Fire, sprites, blue jets (upper atmosphere lightning), the aurorae which appear in the skies over the poles, and so on.

The immense power of lightning effectively ionises the air through which it passes and, very briefly, it creates a shaft of plasma which is seen as light. St Elmo's Fire is a form of plasma that lights up the ends of pointed objects – generally during a thunderstorm. It is a kind of neon glow – generally blue or violet. Upper atmospheric lightning is not like normal lightning. The scientists call it a Transient Luminous Event (TLE) and the similar "blue jets" are still only partially understood. Sprites are similar upper-atmospheric discharges – this time short-lived red or reddish orange lights.

Ball-lightning may or may not be a form of plasma. Unlike all of the above it is reputed to last longer than milliseconds and some reports have it wandering down chimneys and through houses.

For the outsider, the main issues with the Condign report are that (a) many of the proposed causes of UAPs are themselves incompletely understood by scientists, and (b) the report, even quite early on, frequently uses the words "could", "surmise", "possibility", and "suppose" with far too great a frequency for a "scientific" study. An early example of the report's thinking is given below from Volume 1:

> "8. From the written descriptive evidence there appeared to be the possibility, excluding those events that could be attributed to a known cause, that UAP, despite often appearing to be so, are not solid objects. Also, conventional science suggests that the energy required to support a solid object would be excessive (within our earthbound understanding of the problem). This, together with other evidence from the reports leads to the supposition that the objects might have little or no mass. One might further surmise that if the object had little or negligible mass, it could be buoyant or semi-buoyant and, importantly, that if it had electrical charge or magnetic properties it might be propelled by interaction with other charges present on the surface or in the atmospheric [sic]. Because of the absence of actual UAP field measurements the potential of these possibilities has been examined using the available theory."

There is a *possibility*, it remarks, that UAPs *might* not be solid objects. This line of argument is then supported by the allegation that "conventional science" thinks that the amount of energy needed to support a solid object would be excessive ("excessive" in relation to what? And why should such an extraordinary phenomenon necessarily be subject to "conventional science"?). Therefore, it goes on to say, we can *suppose* that the objects have negligible mass, and then we can further *surmise* that they *might* be "buoyant masses" which dart about the sky driven by some form of interaction with other charges.

"Buoyant mass" is a term which is sometimes bandied about but almost never defined. In this context, it is meant as a plasma of some sort which is suspended in the air by electromagnetic forces. No one has yet proved that such things exist and certainly not for the extended periods over which some UFOs are seen.

The whole line of argument in that passage is based on an initial possibility, which is then extrapolated through several further layers of supposition to the conclusion that UFOs are "buoyant masses". As a non-scientist, I bow to superior knowledge, but the whole report seems to assume that, by default, plasmas are the explanation for most, if not all, unexplained UAP, but without anyone fully understanding the subject of buoyant masses, or, indeed, plasmas.

Supposition and conjecture abound in the Condign report, albeit that they are dressed up in some pretty heavy science. What is even more worrying is that the word "plasma" appears very early on as an almost accepted explanation for all UFOs. Volume 1 speaks of multiple sightings of objects in 1988 and 1996 as supporting the idea that multiple plasmas can be seen in more than one location.

But, they could equally mean that alien spaceships have been seen in more than one location! The focus on plasmas, supported by some detailed scientific discussion (but not proof), seems to have been adopted as the explanation for UFOs in spite of the fact that science does not yet fully understand what atmospheric plasmas are, how they form, how long they can last, how they might "travel" from place to place, how they might interact, how they might appear to float in formation over people's heads, and how they might manage to appear to shoot beams of light to the surface. The report conjectures that this might be due to electrical charge leaking from the plasma – but, again, without any experimental proof. One fascinating section speaks of witnesses reporting objects as spinning. This, the report confidently assures us, is an illusion caused by the fields within the plasma. One could, of course, *surmise* that this might be possible, but is there not an equally valid conjecture that they *might* be solid objects which spin?

There's no doubt that, when the weather balloons, planets, satellites, strange aircraft, and all other common explanations are taken away and we are left with what I've called "the 5 percent" (that is the proportion of all UFO sightings which have not been explained in conventional terms), the Condign report offers some interesting possible explanations in terms of "near field effects",[48] electromagnetic phenomena, plasmas, sprites, blue jets, and such like (see explanation of such phenomena above). These may well be *possible* explanations, but at no point in the report do the authors cite experiments and demonstrations which conclusively prove even so much as that plasmas can duplicate some of the more credible sightings. Human witnesses are, yet again, almost totally ignored and are consigned, whatever their professions and abilities, to the status of confused, misguided, or mistaken observers (pretty much as ordinary mortals were disregarded with respect to rocks falling from the sky).

It's fascinating that witnesses to a bank robbery, a car accident, or an air crash are taken pretty seriously by the authorities. They may not be believed without question, but their testimony is weighed carefully. Where two independent witnesses agree on an event, the police are usually pretty safe in accepting what they saw as what happened. Humans are fallible, no doubt, but at least in such cases, their statements are considered extremely seriously. The Condign report does not give any human testimony the slightest credence, and this is not unusual with official investigations and reports in the United States too. Mrs Scroggins sees something hovering over a nearby field, Mr Bloggs sees a lighted object sweep through the sky over his head, young Master Jones tells of something rising out of a nearby lake, but none are afforded the compliment that they may be honest and genuine people whose sightings deserve proper investigation.

The recommendations of the Condign report were:

"Although the study cannot offer certainty of explanation of all UAP phenomena, the existing evidence is sufficiently persuasive to make one key and four subsidiary recommendations:

---

[48] Electromagnetic effects which are relatively short-range and which are caused by some kind of powerful electromagnetic phenomenon. Scientists understand these in many contexts, but the report only states that these may be a possible explanation, without being able to prove the contention.

It should no longer be a requirement for DI55 to monitor UAP reports as they do not demonstrably provide information useful to Defence Intelligence.

Therefore, Hd Sec (AS)[49] should be advised.

Subsidiary Recommendations

- Selection of a ten year UAP reporting period for detailed statistical studies, allowed material from both the Cold War and post-Cold War periods to be studied. No significant differences were discovered in the results from these two time periods. For this and other reasons it is not expected that further inputs to the database will significantly change the findings stated in this Executive Summary. Consequently, and in keeping with the key recommendation, it is recommended that there be no further requirement for maintaining the database.

  - The flight safety aspects of the findings should be made available to the appropriate RAF Air Defence and other military and civil authorities which operate aircraft, particularly those operating fast and at low altitude.

In so advising:

It should be stressed that, despite the recent increase in UAP events, the probability of encountering a UAP remains very low.

No attempt should be made to out-manoeuvre a UAP during interception."

---

[49] Head of the Secretariat to the Air Staff.

Yet again, an official report concludes that UFOs are of no defence significance.

Some writers have pointed to that final line as being an extremely strange recommendation in a report which, on the surface, concludes that UAP are purely natural phenomena. They see the recommendation not only as confirming that UFOs exist but that they are somehow under intelligent control and a potential danger to aircraft. The wording is certainly unfortunate, but it may not have meant "UFOs are real and dangerous, and you should not attempt to get into a dogfight with them". The statement could also be interpreted as "UAPs are natural phenomena which move their position much faster than an aircraft. So, if you encounter one, you are likely to endanger your own aircraft by attempting almost impossible manoeuvres". A bit like saying, Do not attempt to outrun a lightning bolt.

The report also states:

> "No artefacts of unknown or unexplained origin have been reported or handed to the UK authorities, despite thousands of UAP reports. There are no SIGINT, ELINT or radiation measurements and little useful video or still IMINT."[50]

In view of the numbers of times that UAP have been reported by radar operators, and the numbers of photographs and videos of alleged objects, the final sentence seems extremely disingenuous. There is a good deal of evidence, from as far back as the 1940s and the Washington National affair of 1952, that the objects have been tracked by radar on many occasions and that they have been seen by military and commercial pilots at the same time (and, indeed, by other radar operators on the ground and in the air). The French had several occasions to gather scientific evidence of alleged UFO landings and could presumably have provided at least basic radiation and biological details.

---

[50] SIGINT: signals intelligence; ELINT: electronic intelligence; IMINT: imagery intelligence.

It seems a little disappointing, therefore, that a lengthy, and presumably expensive, scientific study should not have at least attempted to come to terms with some of the combined visual-radar incidents and some of the best video and photographic evidence from around the world and over a greater time span than ten years. The study was very much focused on a database of sightings which has never seen the light of day, and critics have wondered how accurate and detailed the entries in that database were.

The Condign report says very clearly that UAPs exist but that there is no evidence that they are under control (in spite of mounds of witness testimony to the contrary). One has to also point out that much of the theory underpinning the report's highlighting of atmospheric plasmas, "buoyant charged masses", near field effects, and other electrical fields is still not conclusive or particularly well-understood in scientific terms. The report admits that

> "... the conditions for the initial formation and sustaining of what are apparently buoyant charged masses, which can form, separate, merge, hover, climb, dive and accelerate are not completely understood."

Probably a bit of an understatement, given what observers report UAPs as doing in real life. More like "not even beginning to be understood". So while the study is impressive and the conclusions fascinating, we are left with findings based on very weak scientific grounds and lines of argument supported only by a great deal of supposition and conjecture. It may well turn out to be the case that there are such things as sufficiently long-lived and mobile "buoyant charged masses" and atmospheric plasmas and that they can do all the things that people see UFOs doing, but the report's theories are actually as unproven as UFOs themselves.

By 2000, therefore, the UK had reached the same point in policy terms as the United States had in 1969. The reader should also remember that both reports, Condon and Condign, were intended to be secret.

Once again, a UK scientific study had decided that UFOs were perfectly explicable in terms which did not include non-earthly sources. Once again, the conclusions, when they eventually became known to the general public, were questioned by just about everyone. And once again, a government shut down its formal monitoring and databasing of UFO reports.

But the UFOs kept coming, and no one has tried to explain them except the independent, underfunded ufologists and their arch-rivals, the equally underfunded sceptics.

The full report is available online but in a large number of separate downloads. If you have the stamina, it is certainly worth perusing. There is a huge amount of scientific detail and argument explaining the various possible causes of UFO sightings but very little indeed which specifically addresses individual cases.

I have not found any trace of the database upon which the Condign author(s) based their ten-year span of study material (1987–1997), and the universal truth has to be restated: Just because something *could* cause an event does not mean that it actually did.

Condign was, and still is, the most detailed scientific report on the more esoteric possible causes of UFOs that is (now) in the public domain. But even the least scientific outsider is left feeling, after scanning its more than four hundred pages of argument and surmise, that the report is simply the modern equivalent of the "rocks in the sky are impossible" argument. All of its possible causes might turn out to be relevant, but there are three key flaws:

1. By focusing on current scientific knowledge, it cannot admit to such things being possible; therefore, they are impossible.
2. Insufficient weight is given to the human beings who see the things. As I've said, humans are possibly more fallible than scientific instruments, but there are some humans who have the training, the eyesight, and the experience of things in the air to justify us in taking their testimony very seriously indeed. If pilots, with all their experience, training, and 20:20 vision, report solid, metallic, spinning objects, or wedge-shaped objects, or things which shadow or circle their aircraft, shouldn't we take them just

as seriously as the musings and surmises of scientists in window-less laboratories? Condign does not.

3. And finally, the most important flaw is that the report's possible causes are, for the greatest part, just as unproven scientifically, in the contexts in which UFOs are supposed to be seen, as the UFOs themselves.

CHAPTER 5

French Investigations

THE FRENCH GOVERNMENT DID not become formally involved in UFO research until thirty years after the United States and Britain. In fact, to be precise, the French government has never really been involved, preferring instead to insulate itself by having a third-party organisation do the dirty work. As we'll see below, the organisation they established was kept well away from the government, as a largely hidden subsidiary of the nation's main aerospace agency.

A couple of things need to be stressed, though. Firstly, in fairness to the French, it must be said that today, of all major Western nations, only the French retain any form of official reporting and investigation of UFOs. Secondly, we must recognise that there remains a significant difference between the United States on the one part and Britain and France on the other, in that American sightings tend still to be greeted by the media with subtle ridicule, and there is still almost total reluctance among American pilots and other professionals to risk their careers by reporting UFOs. The media in Britain and France still take UFO reports with a pinch of salt and write about them with their tongues very much in their cheeks, but senior people are still able to talk publicly on the subject, and there is far less official derision and scorn.

GEPAN/GEIPAN, 1977

In 1977, the French government established a UFO study and monitoring agency as a division of CNES, its national space programme (the French equivalent of NASA). It was originally entitled GEPAN (*Groupe d'étude des phénomènes aérospatiaux non identifies*: Group for the Study of Unidentified Aerospace Phenomena) under its first chief, Claude Poher.

At first sight, this looks ideal: a UFO study based on a major scientific and engineering organisation with legislated links to the *gendarmerie* and aviation authorities. In reality, the relationship with CNES has always been somewhat tense, with the leaders of the space agency somewhat unwilling to be associated with anything as "nuts" as UFO studies. Apart from during its very first incarnation, the UFO agency has never been well resourced. For much of the time, it has managed with just a chief and a secretary, unable to run many full investigations each year. But this is far more than exists in most other nations.

Unfortunately, M Poher was regarded by the powers-that-be as having blotted his copybook by entering into communication with French UFO groups. He was replaced, after less than two years in office, by Alain Esterle, a mathematician. M Esterle ran GEPAN until 1983 when he, too, ran foul of those pesky powers-that-be and resigned. It seemed that he had been getting GEPAN involved in experiments with a propulsion system called magneto-hydrodynamics. MHD drives have been prototyped and used in ships, but GEPAN would probably have been interested in them as a potential propulsion system for spacecraft. MHD has no moving parts and operates with electricity and a magnetic field. After M Esterle resigned, the organisation was managed for the next five years by Jean-Jacques Velasco.

In 1988, GEPAN was transformed into SEPRA (*Service d'expertise des phénomènes de rentrée atmosphérique*[51]), still under the leadership of M Velasco, who was nothing if not a survivor. He led GEPAN/SEPRA for

---

[51] An indication of the thinking behind SEPRA was its focus on the study of "re-entry" phenomena. Around the year 2000 this was changed to "rare aerospace phenomena".

no less than seventeen years, skilfully navigating the treacherous shoals between CNES's fears of a UFO embarrassment in its public relations and the French UFO community's constant criticisms that things were being dealt with too conservatively.

Eventually, however, the inevitable happened. The Board of CNES got fed up with M Velasco's increasingly public declarations that there was a strong possibility that some UFOs were of extraterrestrial origin. Under the guise of an internal reorganisation, CNES abolished SEPRA (and M Velasco's job) and sat back to reconsider.

If it had been Britain or the United States, the government would almost certainly have left things there and abandoned the whole subject to the private UFO groups. In France, though, there has always been a significant underswell in the scientific community supporting further research into UFOs, and CNES eventually decided to reincarnate GEPAN, but under a slightly different name: GEIPAN (*Groupe d'Etudes et d'Informations sur les Phenomenes Aerospatiaux Non-Identifier*: Group for the Study of, and information on, Unidentified Aerospace Phenomena). Perhaps more importantly, it was to be constituted with a heavyweight steering committee to watch over its activities. The committee is chaired by an ex-head of CNES, Yves Sillard. Its members, fifteen of them, are from the science community, the gendarmerie, the military, meteorologists, the security services, the air force, the French equivalent of the FAA/CAA, and, of course, CNES.

Since 2005, GEIPAN has managed to undertake investigations and to issue information to the French public on a regular basis. The organisation keeps its nose clean but still manages to publish scientifically examined reports on a number of UFO sightings in France. GEIPAN takes a very neutral stance on UFOs. Its site is a mixture of features on up-to-date space exploration and discussions on the causes of UFO sightings. Nevertheless, nine percent of all UFO sightings in 2016 were classified as not susceptible to explanation under our current understanding (down from thirteen percent the previous year). It's a fascinating and unique website and is well worth a lengthy visit. If you do not speak French, the pages can be translated by online systems. The translations are not perfect, but they are good enough to provide a genuine sense of how the organisation works and thinks. To a large extent, it puts the United States and the UK to shame.

COMETA Report, 1999

While the Condign study was still in progress in the UK, a number of very senior people in France had come to the conclusion that CNES and SEPRA were not doing enough to investigate and report on the UFO phenomenon. In 1999, therefore, a small group got together privately and published the COMETA Report ("COMETA" stands for *Comité d'Études Approfondies:* the Committee for In-Depth Studies).

Their report, a private, three-year effort, was entitled *"Les Ovni Et La Defense: A quoi doit-on se préparer?"* ("UFOs and Defence: What must we be prepared for?"). The report was written by eminent military officers, scientists, and engineers from irreproachable backgrounds.

The study group was led by an ex-Air Force General, Denis Letty, and included highly qualified former members of the French Defence Institute (*Institut des Hautes Etudes de Defense Nationale,* or IHEDN). The nineteen people involved included some top names and an eclectic selection of highly experienced engineers, generals, a police chief, a weapon engineer, and others. Professor André Lebeau, a former chairman of CNES, wrote the foreword to the report. Other big names included General Bernard Norlain, former director of IHEDN, and Jean-Jacques Velasco, head of SEPRA at CNES.

The ninety-page COMETA Report is balanced and comprehensive, looking in some detail at the key French sightings as well as a few others. It also examined the investigations which had been conducted by GEIPAN and its predecessors over the years (which in themselves were more detailed than almost any other nation's – at least any that have been revealed). It examined almost all possible explanations and came to the conclusion that there was a proportion of sightings which simply could not be explained and that the extraterrestrial hypothesis was actually the *most* likely explanation for some UFO sightings.

Perhaps the most refreshing thing about the report from an outsider's viewpoint is the wonderfully relaxed and open way in which very senior French scientists and military officers researched and wrote about the subject. The French government seems to keep a good arm's length away from the subject, but there appears to be little or no derision, no public attempt to write everything off as misinterpreted natural phenomena, and no sense that the people who got involved in COMETA were penalised in any way for propounding exotic theories.

The COMETA group chastised the United States for what it called an "impressive repressive arsenal" of tactics protecting UFO information, including a policy of disinformation and military regulations prohibiting public disclosure of sightings. It cited, as one of the most repressive US rules, Air Force Regulation 200-2 (1954). The rule, entitled *Unidentified Flying Objects Reporting*, prohibits the release to the public and the media of any data about "those objects which are not explainable". An even more restrictive procedure is outlined in the Joint Army Navy Air Force Publication (JANAP) 146e,[52] which threatens to prosecute *anyone* under its jurisdiction—including pilots, civilian agencies, merchant marine captains, and even some fishing vessels— for disclosing reports of those sightings relevant to US security.

If you've been paying attention, you will know that the US authorities have, on several occasions, stated categorically that UFOs are of no defence significance and pose no threat to US national security. So how could there possibly be a sighting of one of these harmless UFOs which *did* threaten US security, and more to the point, how would the authorities prove that it did? Why does the United States need such a regulation?

---

[52] Canadian-United States Communications Instructions for Reporting Vital Intelligence Sightings; JANAP 146(e) March 1966.

CHAPTER 6

UFOs Everywhere

WE'VE EXAMINED JUST A few of the rock stars of UFO sightings and we've poked around in the debris of official investigations. Now it's time to look at some intriguing numbers. How are UFOs classified? How many sightings have there actually been? What are the reasons for choosing a particular proportion of "inexplicable" sightings? And what do all the statistics mean in terms of the overall phenomenon?

Classification Systems

Before we look at numbers, we should think about how all that mishmash of different UFO sightings is classified: not classifications of the UFOs themselves, just how the mass of sightings is segmented (sometimes after a little investigation, but mostly not).

Broadly speaking, a simple segmentation of sightings would use three categories (the French use five). As you'll have guessed, the bulk of sightings are explicable in everyday terms using conventional explanations such as aircraft, balloons, cloud formations, meteorites, satellites, and rocket launches. These are the "explained UFOs" – sometimes, because we just love acronyms, termed "IFOs" (identified flying objects). Into the second box get tossed the sightings for which there is simply not enough evidence to be certain. And in the third and final box, we place those sightings for which there is quite a bit of evidence but which we still cannot explain in any conventional way. These are the cases which baffle investigators. They are the "unexplained" or, if you'd prefer, "the inexplicable".

Over the years since 1945, every nation that has conducted any sort of analysis of UFO sightings has used a roughly similar segmentation. In 1952, the American authorities talked in terms of a two-class system: the mass of sightings being explained in conventional terms, leaving a small proportion unexplained. The unexplained proportion varied between 1952 and 1969 from about 30 percent to a publicised total of 0.4 percent (this last proportion has been widely criticised as rigged and it is certainly very different from the results of virtually every other nation).

In the UK, the MoD UFO desk (known under different departmental references over the years) recorded sightings under three broad categories. For the British, the unexplained generally totalled about 5 percent (alongside a pretty large box of "insufficient evidence" sightings). The French launched their own UFO investigations on a much more formal basis in 1977. They passed laws requiring the national gendarmerie to act as the formal conduit for public UFO reports. Members of the public can complete a "sighting" form and then hand it in to the local gendarmerie, who may or may not begin an investigation, but who forward the report on to a section of the French national space agency (CNES) known as GEIPAN (originally GEPAN). Their investigators evaluate as many sightings as they can within their limited budget. They originally categorised them under four headings, now expanded to the six as listed below.

GEIPAN Categories

The French investigative agency uses an alphanumeric code to categorise UFO sightings and the results thereof. The prefix "PAN" stands for *Phénomènes Aérospatiaux Non-identifiés* (unidentified aerospace phenomena). The system uses four main categories and two numeric subcategories:

> PAN A: a sighting which has been explained without any
> ambiguity (explained)

PAN B: a sighting for which an hypothesis adopted by GEIPAN is considered to be very likely (probably explained)

PAN C: a sighting which cannot be fully assessed and analysed due to a lack of information (insufficient information)

PAN D: a sighting which remains unexplained despite all the information in the possession of GEIPAN (unexplained)

PAN D1: a class D sighting which has consistent and reasonably solid evidence, e.g. a single witness, without a photograph or video

PAN D2: a class D sighting of a very strange phenomenon with strong evidence: e.g. several independent witnesses or one or more photographs or video or traces on the ground

The French have, therefore divided the top and bottom of the British classification each into two separate elements to create "explained", "probably explained", "insufficient evidence", "unexplained but just a single witness", and "totally inexplicable in spite of very good evidence".

To cut a complex story short, the main categorisations of UFO sightings, and the proportions falling into each category for each nation and at various times, can be seen in Table 1:

Table 1: UFO Classification Systems and Proportions

Category	Rough Percentage of Sightings		
	USA(i)	UK(ii)	France(iii)
Fully/Probably Explained	70%–99%	80%	50%
Insufficient Evidence		15%	37%
Unexplained	Between 30% and 0.4%	5%	13%

(i) These are the publicly-available percentages from the period during which formal records were kept by the various official UFO bodies (Projects Sign, Grudge, and Blue Book) between about 1947 and 1969. See below for further detail.

(ii) Proportions provided by Nick Pope in his written accounts (see Bibliography).

(iii) GEIPAN, combining PAN A and PAN B into "explained/probably explained" and D1 and D2 into "unexplained" (2016 figures from GEIPAN website)

There is more to be said about this subject, but for now it is sufficient to underline the fact that the most recent and perhaps best investigated formal process – that of GEIPAN – categorises around 1 in 10 of UFO sightings as remaining unexplained, even after pretty rigorous and skilled investigations (2016). It also finds that it can only thoroughly explain around half of all sightings.

Perhaps the most famous classification system of them all is that which was invented by J Allen Hynek and of which few people in the world can fail to have heard. Hynek set up the Center for UFO Studies (CUFOS) in 1973 (renamed the J Allen Hynek Center for UFO Studies after his death in 1986). Within the "unexplained category", he proposed three different types of UFO based on the degree of "closeness" of the observer and what they reported. He is, therefore, best known as the creator of the three-level Close Encounters scale. Today, you will find websites which propose up to eight levels (some more justified than others),[53] but Hynek's categories remain powerful, and just about everyone has heard of *Close Encounters of the Third Kind*.

---

[53] The Wikipedia article on the subject provides more detail https://en.wikipedia.org/wiki/Close_encounter

Hynek's original scale encompassed Close Encounters of the First, Second, and Third Kinds (CE1, CE2, CE3) as follows:

CE1: Visual sightings of an unidentified flying object seemingly less than 500 feet away that show an appreciable angular extension[54] and considerable detail.

CE2: A UFO event in which a physical effect is alleged: for example, electronic interference; animals reacting; a physiological effect such as paralysis or heat and discomfort in the witness; or some physical trace like impressions in the ground, scorched or otherwise affected vegetation, or a chemical trace.

CE3: An encounter in which an animated creature is present. These include humanoids, robots, and humans who seem to be occupants or pilots of a UFO.

Dr Hynek was a thinking ufologist who viewed UFO sightings and events through a strictly scientific lens. An astronomer who had been recruited by the US Air Force to help them evaluate UFO sightings, he eventually became thoroughly dissatisfied with the way the events were being treated and set up his own UFO investigative body (CUFOS). His views and conclusions sometimes irritated other ufologists due to them being perceived as too conservative, but his thoughts were always carefully considered.

Towards the end of his career, he questioned the sheer variety in UFO sightings and experiences. He argued that there may be a different hypothesis to the standard ones – one which postulates an extremely old civilisation that has developed both mind and material capabilities (the M&M thesis). He was an adviser on Steven Spielberg's 1977 film *Close*

---

[54] A posh way of saying appreciable width or height from the observer's viewpoint.

Encounters of the Third Kind. In fact, he made a non-speaking, cameo appearance – along with his trademark pipe – in the final scenes.

Global Reach

There is another thing we need to get straight before delving into the bewildering mass of figures and stats about unidentified flying objects.

UFOs are a truly global phenomenon; they are not American or British or French, but worldwide. There are many, many countries for which it is difficult to get data, and there are incredible problems trying to combine data across different systems and different definitions of the phenomenon. Nevertheless, UFOs, in their hundreds and thousands, have been sighted right across the world, from Chile to China, from Austria to Australia, from the UK to Uruguay. Countries with very different cultures and histories, and with very different religions and political systems, have their own lists of sightings and their own ways of dealing with them.

For many people on the UK side of the pond, the UFO thing can often seem like an entirely American affair. Americans invented the terms flying saucer and UFO, launched the "aliens are among us" craze after Roswell, gave the world the first "I had sex with an alien" stories, and gave us piles of both A and B movies about aliens, visitations, invasions, cuddly extra-terrestrials, and so on – not to mention *The X-Files* (sorry, I didn't mean to mention them). In Britain, people probably know more about UFOs and events in the United States than they do about sightings in their own country. But however it sometimes appears, the phenomenon is truly global. I read recently that UFOs had been reported in 140 nations, but that is likely to be an underestimate.

Numbers

Getting at the actual numbers is surprisingly difficult in spite of all the publicity that UFOs receive. The most important reason for this is that only a very few nations maintain publicly-available databases of UFO sightings. Even fewer carry out formal investigations of the sightings, and only one European nation, France, has any form of nationally regulated system for accepting and investigating UFO reports.

This wasn't always the case. We've seen that the United States established a number of formal investigatory mechanisms between about 1947 and 1969. In the UK, the Ministry of Defence (MoD) tracked UFO reports to some extent between the early 1950s and 2009. Both governments conducted secret reviews and studies, and both decided, as we've seen, that UFOs do not constitute a threat in defence terms. Note that neither has explicitly said that unexplained UFOs do not exist, merely that they do not constitute a defence threat. How they came to this very specific, and very definite, conclusion is not revealed.

Today, therefore, in Britain and United States, the databasing and investigating of UFO reports is left to a number of independent, privately funded bodies. Each keeps its own data, and most of them keep those databases very close to their bosoms.

A further problem is that, even when UFO data were being gathered by organisations like Project Blue Book in the United States and by the UK MoD, it was widely understood that the numbers of formal reports represented the tip of the iceberg, that a high but unknown proportion of people either did not report what they saw or did not report it via official channels. Captain Edward Ruppelt once estimated that the number of unreported sightings was probably ten times that of the reported ones, and that proportion is supported to some extent by Nick Pope (ex-MoD) in the UK.

However, in the interests of trying to get the best possible view of the scale of the issue, I've gathered in Table 2 a few of the known and reasonably reliable figures. We have to be pretty careful with them; not so much because they are unreliable, as because they may well be just the tiniest tip of a gigantic iceberg. The figures for each nation are drawn from different sources and time frames so that you can see the basis on which the final calculations have been made.

Table 2: Estimated UFO Numbers

Country	Number of Recorded Sightings	Period	Average per Year	Percentage Remaining Unidentifiable	Number per Year Remaining Unidentifiable	Approx. No. per Ten Million Population
USA						
NUFORC(*)	96,607	1985–2015	3,220	1%	32	1.0
Blue Book(**)	12,618	1952–1969	742	5%	37	1.2
UK(***)	14,000	1950–2010	233	5%	12	2.0
France	2370	1951–2015	37	13%	5	1.0
	2310	1976–2015	59	13%	8	1.3
	1270	2007–2015	159	13%	20	3.3

(*) US figures from National UFO Reporting Center's detailed database. As the database includes cases from abroad and as the reporting system is an open one, I have arbitrarily reduced the "unexplained" percentage to a very conservative 1 percent.

(**) Project Blue Book. This project's "unexplained" percentages varied over the course of its existence from over 30 percent to 0.4 percent. There is some evidence to suggest that the gradual decline in the percentage of unexplained cases was a deliberate political decision. I have therefore opted to use the UK's 5 percent number as a proxy for the wide variation in Blue Book percentages. The French say the figure should be more than double, but I feel that the case is sufficiently well argued with the UK's middle-of-the-road figure.

(***) UK figures are combined MoD (via Nick Pope) and BUFORA averages.

Since the French launched GEIPAN in 1977, their total is some 2,310 sightings, or around 59 per year. In the eight years between 2007 and 2015, the French recorded 1,270 sightings – or some 159 per year on average.[55]

In the United States, after the three UFO formal studies (Projects Sign, Grudge, and Blue Book) were wound up in 1969, the tracking and investigation of UFOs has been left to private organisations:

> The National UFO Reporting Center (NUFORC), which keeps a very detailed database of all reported sightings and has extended it back historically to the year 1400 (!)[56]

---

[55] http://www.cnes-geipan.fr/index.php?id=198 . You should also remember that these figures for sightings reported through official channels may be far fewer than the "real" level of sightings.

[56] http://www.nuforc.org/

The Mutual UFO Network (MUFON), a membership organisation set up in 1969.[57] It keeps a database of sightings. MUFON has a science review board consisting of nine academics whose specialisms span most scientific disciplines, and it also fields investigators (who generally work for free) around the United States and in several other countries. Its database is searchable by many variables, and the website offers a live mapping of global UFO sightings on its "UFO Stalker" page.

The National Aviation Reporting Center on Anomalous Phenomena (NARCAP), established by Richard Haines to help pilots and aviation professionals report what they see.

Of the roughly fourteen thousand recorded UFO sightings in the UK over the past sixty years (most of which were recorded by the MoD's UFO desk), around 80 percent are listed as having been explained in conventional terms, some 15 percent suffer from a lack of evidence, and around 5 percent remain completely unexplained. This figure of 5 percent is quite important because it broadly mirrors what other nations have found. For example, it is roughly the official figure used by the Chilean government, among others. We should remember that this 5 percent statistic relates to those cases which remain unexplained. It does not necessarily mean that they are all alien spaceships, merely that there was no conventional explanation possible at the time of investigation, in spite of the fact that there was a good deal of evidence. Equally, it does not mean that every single one of the 80 percent that have been labelled "explained" is actually fully understood, merely that someone has decided, sometimes fairly arbitrarily, that it belongs in that category.

---

[57] http://www.mufon.com/

Statistical Research

A lot of nations can deliver basic statistics of UFO sightings, numbers per year, numbers unexplained, and so on, but one of the most interesting analyses in recent years was released in 2012 by NARCAP. Like many recent scientific approaches to the subject, they have avoided the use of the term UFO due to its emotive baggage. NARCAP was established in order to provide a formal, scientific conduit through which aviation people, particularly pilots, could confidentially report strange sightings without prejudicing their careers (a major danger in the US, unlike in the UK and France).

They asked Dominique Weinstein, of the French UFO research agency GEIPAN, to study six hundred pilot reports which had been collected over the previous sixty-four years (Weinstein, 2012). Of those reports, the bulk were American (275). French pilots turned in 33 reports, the British accounted for 18, and the Japanese 17, with many other nations accounting for smaller numbers.

Four out of ten reports over the period were from military pilots (41 percent), almost the same proportion from civil pilots (39 percent), and roughly a fifth from private pilots (18 percent). These proportions have changed in the last twenty years of the period (1990-2010). During those twenty years, commercial pilots were responsible for 70 percent of reports, with military pilots accounting for 17 percent, and private pilots 13 percent.

A little over half of all UFO sightings by pilots were made during darkness (54 percent) but almost half were seen in full daylight (46 percent). Keeping in mind that these were sightings by pilots, some quite interesting statistics emerged from Weinstein's study:

Some of M Weinstein's stats are fascinating. In no less than half of the cases he looked at, the object, whatever it was, had some sort of interaction with the aircraft. In no less than three quarters of cases the object was seen as an object and not merely as a light in the sky. In addition we should note that over a quarter of sightings were corroborated by radar (150 sightings) and almost the same proportion were seen by more than one aircraft at the same time. We should not be surprised at the proportion witnessed in the cruise phase of flight (that's when pilots have more time for scanning their surroundings) and the fact that only 16% were corroborated by witnesses on the ground is also unsurprising given the aforementioned fact that most were seen during the high-level cruise phase of flight.

It is probably not surprising that different countries arrive at different percentages of UFO sightings as "unexplained". The timespan over which UFOs have been recorded since World War II has enabled our understanding of such things as meteorological phenomena to improve, different nations investigate UFOs to different levels of rigour, different social attitudes influence the "acceptability" of seeing and reporting UFOs, and different levels of political and social pressure are brought to bear upon those who show an interest or, if they are pilots, who report sightings.

Stats and analysis on UFOs can, therefore, never be taken at face value in the same way one would usually accept government statistics on such things as road accidents. We can be fairly sure, however, that the stats we have are the minimum numbers. What the real totals might be is anyone's guess.

The Magic 5 Percent

We need, therefore, to have some way of narrowing the field to only those sightings of UFOs which are currently unexplained in conventional terms. I've called this "the 5 percent rule". Why 5 percent?

One has to be completely frank here. It's because, after quite a lot of research, it *feels* modestly right as a starting point. If you check Table 2, five percent would seem a reasonably conservative compromise between the ultra-narrow, less than 1 percent of the final Blue Book years (when it was alleged the USAF was being pressured to "explain" as many sightings as they could), to the 13 percent of the recent GEIPAN calculations in France. Indeed, it is entirely arguable that the GEIPAN statistic is a *more* reliable average indicator of the proportion of UFO sightings which cannot be explained. GEIPAN's sightings are much more up-to-date, and a fair number are investigated by police, scientists, and other experts.

In the 1950s, Project Blue Book's "unknowns" percentage was much higher than in its later years. Edward Ruppelt reported as follows:

> "Of the several thousand UFO reports that the Air Force has received since 1947, some 15 to 20 per cent fall into this category called unknown. This means that the observer was not affected by any determinable psychological quirks and that after exhaustive investigation the object that was reported could not be identified. To be classed as an unknown, a UFO report also had to be "good," meaning that it had to come from a competent observer and had to contain a reasonable amount of data."

Interestingly, the ex-Canadian defense minister, Paul Hellyer, was reported in a British newspaper in 2011 as saying that the "unknowns" percentage in Canada was also around the 20 percent mark.[58] And the experienced UFO researcher Richard Dolan proposes 10 percent as the most probable figure for the number of really inexplicable UFO sightings.[59]

If the resources of the Canadian government and the French GEIPAN conclude that 20 percent and 13 percent of sightings, respectively, are inexplicable, then I'd be very justified in using 10-15 percent as a base for all future calculations.

But I haven't.

The arguments become more powerful when we use a much lower figure – 5 percent – because, let's face it, if we can build a convincing argument on that basis, the real-life situation may be significantly more impressive. That's why I think my "5 percent rule" is about right.

So where does that get us?

It permits us to be confident of applying the figures in Table 2 to

---

[58] http://www.dailymail.co.uk/news/article-1360737/I-believe-UFOs--Ive-seen-says-ex-defence-minister-Paul-Hellyer.html
[59] Dolan, 2014.

make some fairly reliable estimates. That table shows that, together, the UK, the United States, and France rack up a recorded average of around four thousand sightings per year (and that is almost certainly a massive underestimate; Richard Dolan estimates around ten thousand per year in North America alone). In the UK, the "5 percent inexplicable" statistic results in around 700 "unexplained" UFOs over the past sixty years, or about eleven to twelve per year. That's roughly two unexplained UFOs per 10 million population per year, and that figure is almost the mid-point in the range of results for other nations: between 1 per 10 million per year and 3.3 per 10 million per year.

The four thousand sightings of UFOs per year for the UK, the United States, and France equate to a global total of around sixty-three thousand annual UFO sightings (assuming of course that all nations experience the phenomenon equally, which is not necessarily the case). If that sounds like a lot, we should bear in mind that around 95 percent are probably explicable, and that there are around 38 *million* commercial aircraft flights each year.

Using the 5 percent rule, the estimated global total of sixty-three thousand sightings translates into a world total of over three thousand *totally inexplicable* sightings *every year*. Whichever way you cut it, that's a lot of mysteries.

And there is one more wrinkle in all this. It would certainly seem sensible to assume that not every UFO sighting is reported. After all, a good many people may discount what they have witnessed or may fear ridicule if they say they have seen a UFO. Equally, many pilots, police officers, and other professionals are said not to report such things. They fear ridicule more than most. In the United States, pilots also fear for their careers if they start reporting strange things in the air.

If one takes a conservative figure of (say) 50 percent of sightings going unreported (one in two), the global sightings total would increase to over one hundred twenty thousand per year, and the numbers of inexplicable sightings to around six thousand per year worldwide (roughly 1 inexplicable sighting per million people). Even if many, or even most, of these cases are eventually explained beyond reasonable doubt, it would still leave quite a few extremely interesting cases for which conventional scientific explanations are not possible.

A possible global total of between 4,000 and 6,000 inexplicable UFO sightings every year.

Playing with figures is fun, and the assumptions and processes in any model can always be questioned, particularly when they are as rough and ready as those above. But outsiders should, nevertheless, give them some serious thought. Taking the *most* conservative figures in relation to population, the United States, UK, and Europe could, conservatively, be looking at around two hundred inexplicable UFO sightings *every year.* That's sixteen things in the sky *every month* which simply cannot be explained within our current understanding.

If 5 percent of the population – one in twenty people – were suffering from an unknown ailment, would we decide that it wasn't worth investigating? If a particular make of car had a fault in the braking system which occasionally caused the car to lose all its brakes, would we be satisfied if the makers said they'd solved the fault on 95 percent of cars? If a swarm of asteroids was going to collide with Earth and each one of them could wipe out all life if it impacted, would we let the authorities off once they'd dealt with 95 percent of them?

After a century or more of the modern era, we've recorded hundreds of thousands of UFO cases globally. Surely, it is well past time that we get to the absolute bottom of the phenomenon, no matter where that leads.

CHAPTER 7

Is Seeing Believing?

DID YOU KNOW THAT last year, a Royal Navy petty officer on his way to a new posting at the nuclear submarine base at Gareloch in Scotland spent several minutes filming a huge, long-necked creature as it swam down the loch? Furthermore, the whole episode was confirmed by sonar recordings from a submarine just leaving the base?

No? Well, that's not surprising because neither event happened. I made it all up. But if it *had* happened, what would you think? Probably something along the lines of "Wow! Weird, but it sounds pretty credible, and surely someone is doing some serious work searching the loch and its associated lochs".

Yet, incidents like this have happened where UFOs are concerned. Objects have been filmed by very professional people, and objects have been tracked by electronic means. But the result, as you'll see in this chapter, has not been a serious investigation by the authorities. No, siree!

Where evidence of UFOs is concerned, we, as human beings, adopt a strange and almost unique philosophical position. Across the globe, there exist literally tens of thousands of photographs of strange objects in the sky. Most now seem to be available on the Internet. Alongside this plethora of photographic visual evidence, stretching back at least until the early years of the twentieth century and arguably earlier, there are scores – possibly hundreds – of films and videos of alleged sightings.

We will explore just a fraction of this evidence, including four fascinating cases where film seems to support the existence of something in our skies.

An important point needs to be made right up front: We're dealing here with many, many thousands of photos (I kid you not) taken since the mid-nineteenth century and perhaps hundreds of movie-film and videos shot since the 1950s. The sheer depth of visual evidence is staggering, but, of course, not all of it is of anything but a misidentified natural phenomenon or a hoax.

The Internet, and its countless servers, forms an appropriately futuristic library for this store of digital data. It is a store, almost in its entirety, which is available for most of the world's citizens to study and consider. Admittedly, the repository of UFO evidence is pretty unusual, but its contents form the only publicly-available visual evidence that we have to work with.

But the weirdest thing is not the photos or the videos themselves. The most stunning fact about all this UFO visual evidence is that governments seem to take no notice of it whatsoever. In the United States, the Condon Committee, and in the UK the Condign group, looked at a few films and some photos and effectively said they were hoaxes or natural phenomena.

If there were tens of thousands of photos of the Loch Ness monster, would we take the same stance? Would we assume that *every* photograph, bar none, was a fake, or would we perhaps investigate, or at least ask ourselves what the laws of probability would have to say? On the surface, it appears that we are saying that 100 percent of UFO photo and videos are fake or of natural phenomena.

In spite of our natural disinclination to be taken in by silly pranks, are we really saying that not a *single* photo or video of a UFO is of a real and totally inexplicable object?

That's the question that you must ask yourself when smothering a titter as you examine a UFO photograph or video. Some are of lights and glowing spheres, some are of triangular objects with lights underneath, some are clearly of discs, some are cylinders or cigars, some look like upturned trashcan lids, and some look like something out of a 1920s space movie: cumbersome, unattractive, not at all aerodynamic.

Yet might it be that my 5 percent rule (see Chapter 10) applies as much to photographic and video evidence as it may do with eyewitness accounts? Conservatively, if we assume not 5 percent but 1 percent, that means that for every ten thousand photos, there will probably be a hundred genuine images of totally inexplicable objects.

Perhaps the best way for outsiders to get a brief, arm's-length view of the visual evidence, a way of dipping their toes in the water without anyone seeing, is to watch a couple of very good DVDs, both of them directed by James Fox, the US filmmaker. I considered a whole basket-load of DVD films of UFOs and of "experts" telling of their certainty of cover-ups and of the attitudes and activities of aliens, but only these two DVDs really hit the spot for the discerning outsider. They cover similar, but not identical, ground and from slightly different perspectives, and they offer an excellent way for the outsider to get a feel not only for the subject but for the credibility (or not) of some of the witnesses.

The two DVDs are:

1. *I Know What I Saw* (2009),[60] a History Channel compilation of clips and interviews covering ground from *Life* magazine's 1952 article to a conference in 2007 at the National Press Club in Washington DC . It includes some fascinating interviews, clips, and presentations from most of the attendees at the latter event (including the ex-White House Chief of Staff John Podesta and a number of generals and pilots, and some compelling quotes from the people involved in the Hudson Valley and Phoenix sightings, the Rendlesham Forest incident, and Captain Ray Bowyer's sighting above the English Channel (all discussed in chapters 11–17).

2. *Out of the Blue* (2012),[61] another compelling set of interviews and clips. It covers a bit of the same ground as the previous film but also includes the Disclosure Press Conference of 2010 and some different people, including a Russian general and a cosmonaut.

---

[60] History Channel DVD, released 2009. Director James Fox.

[61] *Out of the Blue: Definitive Investigation of the UFO Phenomenon.* Released 2012.

You might also take a look at the *Daily Telegraph's* collection of 140 years of the best UFO photos: eighty-four photos in three parts, containing some truly fascinating material, especially from the early years, when anything approaching a "UFO culture" was non-existent.[62] There are glowing lights and balls, saucer-ish shapes, a few triangular objects, and even a few which look like a 1950s schoolboy's idea of what a flying saucer might look like (ie, a disc with a dome or sawn-off trashcan on top).

The following photos are worth checking out:

- 1942 Los Angeles "UFO Raid": searchlight photo (retouched, so make your own mind up but it was a very strange event);
- 1950 McMinnville, Oregon: one of the three most famous UFO photos of all time. There are two photos by Paul Trent and his wife of objects seen from their backyard (see below);
- 1951 Lubbock, Texas: Carl Hart's famous Lubbock Lights photo. This was "solved" as being reflections, but those explanations have been challenged;
- 1952 Washington DC: the famous Capitol photo of glowing lights over and behind the US Capitol building;
- 1958 Trindade Island, Brazil: Brazilian navy photos of a UFO seen over a nearby mountainous island six hundred miles east of Rio;
- 1966 Zurich, Switzerland: glowing red spheres;
- 1966 Perna photo from Lake Tiorati, New York: bronze and silent;
- 1967 Joe Ferriere photo from Cumberland, Rhode Island: a large, cigar-shaped object, estimated at seven hundred feet long. You can see how such an object might be have been mistaken for a Zeppelin in the early 1900s

---

[62] Part I: http://www.telegraph.co.uk/news/picturegalleries/howaboutthat/3447508/UFO-sightings-140-years-of-UFO-pictures.html?image=28; Part II http://www.telegraph.co.uk/news/newstopics/howaboutthat/3452381/UFO-sightings-140-years-of-UFO-pictures.html?image=27; Part III http://www.telegraph.co.uk/news/picturegalleries/howaboutthat/3458222/UFO-sightings-140-years-of-UFO-picture-Part-III.html

Also on the Internet, you will find a few of the more intriguing short-clip films and videos. These four are a fair selection over a span of about fifty years:

- 1950 movie by Nick Marianna (August 15, 1950; Great Falls, Montana);
- 1952 movie by Delbert Newhouse, US Navy photographer (July 2, 1952; Tremonton, Utah);
- 1984 video by Bob Pozzuoli (June 10, 1984; Brewster, New York);
- 1997 Phoenix lights video (March 13, 1997; Phoenix, Arizona).

One could write books about the individual cases (and people have done so), but quick summaries of six strange and fascinating photo/video cases (two of them from the list above) will serve to illustrate the issues inherent in still and movie visuals.

Trent Photos, 1950

At about 7.30 p.m. on a spring evening in May 1950, Evelyn Trent was walking back to her farmhouse after feeding animals. As she gazed around, she saw a strange, metallic, disc-shaped object moving slowly in the sky nearby. It was moving towards the farm from the north-east. She called for her husband, Paul, who came out, watched the object for a short while, and then went to get his camera. When he came out again, he managed to get two photographs which appear to show an a clear disc-like object. He did this shortly before it sped away to the west.

Paul Trent did not immediately send the photos to the newspapers. At first, his banker, having heard about them, asked Mr Trent to let him display them in the bank's front window. Then a local reporter persuaded Trent to loan him the negatives. The reporter, Bill Powell, said he found no evidence of the photos being faked at that time. That was the start of the extensive press coverage of the photos, including a spread in *Life* magazine. Unfortunately, this is also where the all-too-familiar tale of lost photos and negatives rears its ugly head. *Life* magazine told Paul Trent that they had "misplaced" the negatives, so he did not get them back. But he and Evelyn were not paid for them and, as far as can be ascertained, never received a penny for the massive publicity they received.

One of the most famous UFO photos of all time. Taken by Paul Trent standing alongside his wife Evelyn at their farm in McMinnville, Oregon, in 1950. Sceptics claim it as a hoax, but it has been authenticated by an expert optical scientist. (Granger, NYC/Topfoto.co.uk)

Enlargement of a section of the Paul Trent photo taken at McMinnville, Oregon, in 1950. Almost certainly not suspended, and no sign of movement on what would have been a slow film and camera. (Granger, NYC/Topfoto.co.uk)

It was almost seventeen years before the lost negatives were found in the files of United Press International (UPI). Somehow, the Condon Committee got to hear about this, and the freshly rediscovered negatives were loaned to one of the committee's investigators, Dr William Hartman, an astronomer.

At that point, the Trents were not informed that their negatives had been found, but Hartman interviewed them and said he was struck by their honesty and sincerity. He confirmed that the Trents never received any payment at all for their photos. Hartman's analysis for the Condon Committee included the following paragraph:

"This is one of the few UFO reports in which all factors investigated, geometric, psychological, and physical, appear to be consistent with the assertion that an

extraordinary flying object, silvery, metallic, disk-shaped,
tens of meters in diameter, and evidently artificial, flew
within sight of two witnesses."

For some reason, UPI held onto the negatives for a long while. They seem to have been extremely sticky items because, after UPI had eventually returned them to the local paper, the *News Register*, that paper also held onto them without telling the Trents. It was only when the UFO investigator Dr Bruce Maccabee visited the newspaper to look at the negatives and, subsequently, carried out his own analysis of them that the Trents were finally reunited with them (and then only because Maccabee made sure that they were returned). That was in 1975, a quarter of a century after the couple had first snapped those two legendary shots of an object near their farm.

Naturally, Philip Klass, the sceptic, got involved along with another sceptic, Robert Sheaffer. In the early 1980s, they argued that the photos were a hoax because they felt the shadows on the barn proved that the photos had been taken in the morning and not the evening. They also felt that the object may well have been a vehicle's detached rear-view mirror which had been suspended from a power line. When this conclusion was sent to William Hartman, he withdrew his own conclusions. Subsequently, three other sceptics argued the same thing: that the object was a model hanging from a thread, which they claimed to have detected on the photos (although no one else can see that thread and there appears to be no change in the background emulsion at very high magnifications). Dr Bruce Maccabee, however, who was a US Navy optical scientist, refuted these analyses and said that he remains convinced that the photos are genuine.

Evelyn and Paul Trent died in 1997 and 1998, respectively. As far as can be ascertained they received not a penny for their photos or their story and never wrote a best-selling book about them. In reality they could have made a lot of money out of a well-crafted book, and then a bit more when they eventually revealed that the whole thing had been a hoax through an exclusive to a Sunday newspaper. But they didn't, they both stuck to their story that the photos were genuine, right to the end.

The Mariana Film, 1950

This old film and the story behind it are still extremely compelling.

On August 15, 1950, at 11.25 a.m., Nick Mariana was with his secretary in an office car park near Great Falls, Montana, when he filmed two white circular or disc-shaped objects as they moved across the sky. They were equally spaced and, according to Ruppelt and the Blue Book team, they were moving too fast to be birds and too slow to be meteors. Unlike the later Tremonton film in 1952, these objects were filmed passing a steel tower, which affords some perspective in the resulting images.

The objects, also seen by others in the town, were described as "spinning, metallic disks with a 'notch or band' along their outer edges". And, an important thing for the outsider to note, video and photo evidence of UFOs can often look pretty unconvincing – the film can be over-exposed, the distance too great for the lens, the action too difficult for the camera-operator to catch. Listen to the detail which the witnesses themselves observed, however, and the photo or the footage takes on a different level of credibility. We all know that feeling when we see something special happening but the photo or the film we take does it no justice. That situation is, I think, all too common for UFO witnesses.

Mariana accused the Air Force of "losing" the first frames of his film which, he claimed, showed the objects clearly as spinning discs. There were evidently two USAF F-94 Starfire fighters in the area on that day, but the witnesses[63] said that they saw the jets separately from the objects on the film. Ruppelt's Blue Book team examined the objects against the reported movements of the two F-94s, which had landed about two minutes after Mariana had filmed the objects, and they ruled them out as the objects which Nick Mariana and his secretary had seen. In view of the landing pattern, they could not have been the objects on the film. In spite

---

[63] Mariana was with his secretary, who also saw the objects.

of all this, the film was rejected by the Robertson Panel, which claimed that they were simply reflections from the F-94s.[64]

A rare still from the film shot by Nick Mariana in 1950. It is impossible for a still-frame to do justice to a movie, but you can just make out the two objects and the arrows which have been added to indicate their flight path. (Fortean/Topfoto.co.uk)

The Tremonton Film, 1952

In July of 1952, a US Navy chief photographer, Warrant Officer Delbert C Newhouse,[65] was in the middle of a transcontinental car journey with his wife and family. On the morning of July 2, when the family was a few miles north of the small town of Tremonton, Utah, Mrs Newhouse saw objects in the sky and pointed them out to her husband. At first, he was not interested, but she eventually persuaded him to stop the car. After a short delay, while he looked at the objects and then found, and extracted, his professional camera and film from the luggage, CWO Newhouse shot about seventy-five seconds of film of the objects.

The family all confirmed they heard no sound from the things in the sky, and at one point, before Newhouse could locate and arm his

---

[64] The Montana film – supposedly for the Robertson Panel https://www.youtube.com/watch?v=ogQUnT_ROBQ

[65] According to Ruppelt, Newhouse had twenty-one years of Navy service and some 2,000 hours' flying time as a photographer.

professional 16mm camera, they said that the objects were very close above them.

Newhouse's testimony was that the objects were like nothing he had ever seen before and that one of the objects detached from the others towards the end. He said that he filmed this "lone UFO" and deliberately allowed it to pass across the frame of his camera several times to give an impression of the high speed at which it was travelling.

Unfortunately, on this almost cloudless, 80°F day, there were no ground-based objects in the field of view which might have provided some perspective. So in the end, the sighting was judged to be birds, and that's the way it remains to this day. As with almost all of these early reports, some of the key evidence has disappeared over the years. Newhouse said he filmed the lone object as it departed in the opposite direction to the others, but that that portion of the film seems to have been lost. The lone object is mentioned specifically by Edward Ruppelt, who watched Newhouse's film and saw it depart many times when the footage was shown to his team. USAF photo analysts and (separately) US Navy photo analysts decided (in the latter case, after a very detailed analysis) that the objects were not birds.[66] One has to remember, too, that the witnesses said that the objects were much closer to them before the film was eventually shot. It's hard to believe that Mrs Newhouse, and then her husband, would have been fooled by birds at close range.

---

[66] The Tremonton film, with interview with Newhouse. The film is old and indistinct but the interview is interesting – even persuasive. https://www.youtube.com/watch?v=vbLvzgJMsIQ

A still from the film shot by US Navy Warrant Officer Delbert Newhouse near Tremonton, Utah, in 1952. The objects are clearly visible, but Newhouse claimed clearer and closer images were "lost" by the authorities. (Fortean/Topfoto.co.uk)

This case is important because it is based on the testimony and film evidence of a professional film cameraman and twenty-year military man who saw something strange and thought it important enough to interrupt his journey by filming it on 16mm stock. He testified that the objects were silvery and metallic, and like nothing he'd ever seen before. That is pretty strong from a photographer who'd spent twenty years in the Navy and had flown two thousand hours taking film.[67] Newhouse said he'd never

---

[67] Note that the Condon Report said the figures were nineteen years of service and "over 1,000 hours" of flight time. The Condon Report reviewed this case as No 49 and

seen a UFO before, and there is nothing recorded about him ever seeing one again.

It will probably always be an "unknown" because the bird theory is more than a little weak. The US Air Force, itself, initially said it wasn't birds. Kevin Randle's excellent summary will give you a real sense of how confused and contentious even the best of cases can become as time passes.[68]

Edwards AFB Photos, 1957

"Missing photos" is a very common theme in the UFO world. The widely read enthusiast encounters numerous stories of photos "borrowed" by the authorities and never returned, photos which mysteriously failed to come out when developed, films with missing segments, and variations on these mishaps. In most cases, these tales are simply more strange elements in even stranger stories. They get submerged in the sea of UFO detail.

Some of the stories endure, though, especially when they originate with USAF colonels who are also decorated astronauts. One such tale was told by Colonel L Gordon Cooper, the famous Mercury/Gemini astronaut who spent a total of nine days in space in the incredibly dangerous early years of orbital missions.

If ever there was a hard-nosed, unyielding, intelligent, stubborn, highly skilled, incredibly brave military officer, Cooper was it. He was so cool he actually fell asleep during the countdown for one of his Mercury missions and was the first of those gallant solo astronauts to sleep while in orbit. On his second mission, the automatic control systems went wrong, and he calmly took *manual* command, steered by the stars, and used his wristwatch to time the firing of his retrorockets (a bit like using an abacus to calculate the landing of a modern jetliner in dense fog). He also flew in the follow-up Gemini programme.

There is some evidence that he claimed to have seen a UFO while on

---

concluded that the film showed birds: http://files.ncas.org/condon/text/case49.htm
[68] See http://kevinrandle.blogspot.co.uk/2013/12/newhouses-tremonton-utah-movie-revisited.html

military service in Germany in 1951, but he does not appear to have made much of it. However, it was an event in 1957 which perplexed and frustrated him through the rest of his illustrious military career and numerous high-level civilian jobs. In fact, until the day he died.

Back in 1957, Cooper was an Air Force captain, assigned to Edwards Air Force Base in California. He was a test pilot working at that time on an experimental landing system. On the day in question (May 3), he had a team of two photographic specialists setting up high-tech cameras on the dry lake bed. The idea was to get a slow-motion movie of the aircraft as it landed using the new approach system. The two photographers, James Bittick and Jack Gettys, started setting things up at about 8 a.m.

Later that morning, a considerably agitated pair tracked down Captain Cooper. They told him they'd seen a "strange-looking, saucer-like" aircraft that did not make a sound either on landing or take-off. Needless to say, Cooper was astounded and perhaps a little suspicious that his leg was being pulled (as if anyone would ever dare pull Gordon Cooper's leg), but he recognised that these two men were experts, not only in camera work but also in the highly secret aircraft being tested at Edwards. They were clearly upset and flustered as they recounted what had happened. Evidently, a disc-like object had actually landed on the dry-lake bed just fifty yards away from where they were working. It landed on three legs and took off again as the two men started towards it for a closer look.

Cooper naturally asked them if they had taken any pictures, and they replied in the affirmative: They'd got 35mm and 4-by-5-inch stills, plus some movie film. With such good evidence, Cooper reported the sighting up the chain of command and was ordered to get all the films developed, but to make no prints of the stills. He was told that a courier would come, and he was to send everything, locked in a security pouch, with that courier.

The captain's only orders were to not make prints of the images. So he felt entitled to take a quick look at the negatives, which he did in the short space of time before the courier arrived (it took a good while for the material to be developed, of course). Cooper said, and stuck by this story for the rest of his life, that the images were of very good quality and that they showed the object clearly. The movie film had been developed, too, but Cooper did not have a chance to look at that before the courier arrived and everything got taken to headquarters.

The young captain expected that he and his men would be interviewed and assumed other investigations would be made. After all, something had actually *landed* without permission within a highly classified military zone. But he heard absolutely nothing, was never interviewed, and never saw the photographs or the film again.

One has to bear in mind that Cooper was a USAF officer and that he worked and socialised with other active military pilots. He heard stories, therefore, which were never made public; ones which were probably not even reported to senior officers.

It was this event, and the disappearance of those images, that caused Cooper to claim that the US government was engaged in a cover-up. He cited the "hundreds" of sightings by other pilots which, he said, had been suppressed by the government. Col Cooper, national hero, knew that those photos and the film from Edwards on that long-ago day in early May had been suppressed like all the others. The material is probably still lying in some deep US Air Force vault. The question we'd all like to ask – and Gordon Cooper, too – is why?

An excellent opportunity to get a feel for this decorated hero is provided by the video documentary *Out of the Blue* (Fox, 2012). In his distinctive Oklahoma drawl, Cooper takes no prisoners.

Balwyn, Victoria, 1966

On April 2, 1966, at about 2.21 p.m. local time, James Kibel saw an object from the garden of his home near Melbourne, Australia. He saw it for just six seconds but managed to get a Polaroid photo. He'd evidently taken his camera outside in order to get photos of his house and garden. He said he noticed the object because it reflected a patch of sunlight onto his garden, and he looked up.

It looked a bit like a child's old-fashioned spinning top tipped onto its side. Kibel said that it turned at one point with its flat face towards him and that he could see it spinning on its central axis. It was, at first, moving slowly, then stopped for a second, and then turned and sped off at a speed "faster than an aircraft".

The photo is quite spectacular. It can be seen along with other details and explanations on the Project 1947 website[69] and is reproduced below. The original colour photo shows the object as being having a bronze, metallic surface.

A fascinating shot of an object photographed over Balwyn, Australia, in 1966 by James Kibel. (Fortean/Topfoto.co.uk)

---

[69] http://www.project1947.com/kbcat/kbpdbalwyn1.htm

Hannah McRoberts, 1981

This young lady (she was aged twenty-five at the time) took possibly one of the most impressive UFO photos on record, except she did not know it at the time.

Between October 8 and 15, 1981, she, her husband, and their daughter were taking a short vacation. Driving through Victoria Island, Vancouver, the family had stopped at a rest area near Kelsey Bay (on the north-east side of the island). While sitting there, they noticed a cloud near the top of a nearby mountain and thought it looked like the smoke plume from a volcano. So, as a humorous addition to the family vacation album, Hannah McRobert took a snap.

When they got home, the family had their vacation photos developed and only then noticed something in the sky beside the mountain. It was a disc-shaped object which has baffled experts ever since.

Among other people, the negative was closely examined by Richard Haines, the distinguished UFO investigator, who could find no signs of tampering or negative damage.

It's an amazing photo and no one has been able to explain it convincingly.

The object photographed by the vacationing Hannah McRoberts near Kelsey Bay, Victoria Island, in 1981. (Hannah McRoberts/Fortean/Topfoto.co.uk)

CHAPTER 8

There Are No Such Things as UFOs

THERE WILL ALWAYS BE things in the sky that you don't immediately recognise and which might take some thought to understand. But the question is, are there things in our skies which are not explicable in any conventional terms as being either natural phenomena, human failings, or human-made objects? Note, this is not asking whether the UFOs are from outer space. There could be many other explanations. The question is simply whether there are things being seen, whatever they are and wherever they come from, that we don't yet understand.

The diehard sceptic answer would be that there are no such things.

What the Sceptics Say

We know that inexplicable UFOs exist. There are more than enough cases from extremely credible witnesses citing objects which can hover and then move with extreme speed, objects which are able to defy the laws of gravity and inertia and which can almost toy with conventional fighter aircraft. Credible witnesses have also described objects of very different shapes and colours. The sceptics, however, see this mass of data from a very specific perspective.

Philip J Klass was, for well over thirty years, an editor for the US aviation magazine *Aviation Week* (now *Aviation Week & Space Technology*). His contributions to US aviation journalism were legion. He was highly respected for his work and well known for his efforts to "debunk" UFO claims. Among many other things, he is reputed to have said that 97 to 98 percent of the people reporting UFOs are genuine people, honestly mistaken. The rest, he said, are frauds.

Along with many highly respected scientists and academics, Klass was a founder member, in 1976, of the Committee for the Scientific Investigation of Claims of the Paranormal (CSICOP). It changed its name to the Committee for Skeptical Inquiry (CSI) in 2006 and has remained a major force in sceptical research into the UFO phenomenon as well as other claimed paranormal events.

Klass had a wry sense of humour but also had a reputation for vindictiveness. We will see, when we come to look at the Washington National sightings, that he could also be positively insulting (see chapter 16). Back in 1966, he called what he regarded as the ufologists' bluff. He offered a cash prize to anyone who could meet a number of his requirements (the Klass Prize). He updated the offer in the mid-1970s, offering to pay $10,000 to

1. anyone who could convince the American National Academy of Sciences that a part of, or a whole, crashed spacecraft was of extraterrestrial origin, or
2. anyone who could get the academy to announce that other evidence proves that the Earth has been visited by extraterrestrial spacecraft during the twentieth century, or
3. a bona fide extraterrestrial visitor, born on a celestial body other than the Earth, who appeared live before the General Assembly of the United Nations or on a national television program.

As part of what was intended as a fully-legal contract, Klass also required the people who felt that they might meet his challenge to sign up to pay him $100 a year for ten years for every year that none of the above occurred. None of the most active supporters of UFOs accepted his offer. Only one person signed up but the agreement lapsed within a couple of years after a failed attempt to claim the prize. The challenge stood for the rest of Klass's life (through to 2005) without being successfully claimed.

In the 1960s, Klass came up with the theory that ball lightning and plasmas could explain many, if not all, UFO sightings. It is interesting that the plasma possibility was also a major element in the explanations offered by the UK's Condign report forty years later. But even today, plasmas and ball lightning are not fully understood and have not yet been proven to be capable of duplicating the characteristics of UFO sightings.

He also proposed a process of mass delusion, which worked in the following way:

The Klass Process of Mass Delusion

1. Newspapers announce a UFO sighting.
2. People are hopeful of seeing one and so go outside and identify all sorts of natural things as UFOs.
3. These reports add to the mass hysteria.
4. UFO organisations add to the mix by encouraging reports.
5. More observers go out and "see" UFOs.
6. This process becomes self-powered and self-fulfilling.
7. But eventually, newspapers get tired of the reports, and the sightings slowly die away.

There are more than a few problems with this superficially neat process. The first is how one explains the initial sightings: the ones which prompted the first newspaper articles. Are they *all* misinterpretations of natural phenomena?

A second problem lies with Klass's oft-stated theory that ufologists encourage people to report things (stage 4). In cases like the Hudson Valley wave (Chapter 16), for example, it is difficult to see how the presence on the ground of a handful of ufologists trying to contact witnesses and get detailed statements and evidence works to encourage hundreds of other people, in very different locations, to see things in the sky. UFO organisations are notoriously poorly resourced, and their (unpaid) investigators generally arrive days after an initial sighting. They manage to interview only a fraction of the witnesses (and even then only those who will come forward and brave potential ridicule). Meanwhile the press is gently deriding and mocking the sightings while making good money from increased sales driven by the exciting news. In the case of the Hudson Valley, the police were also pretty dismissive of claims which were phoned into them, and the press were cool on the subject, to say the least.

One could argue, contrary to Klass's theory, that rather than the process working on general excitement, driving more and more hysterical sightings, that UFO sightings would be more likely to have a built-in *dampener* which acts to prevent or discourage reporting. The dampening effect would be based on the following factors:

1. People's natural tendency to explain things for themselves. "It's a plane, isn't it? No, it's a cloud. No, it's just a bright light on that hillside. No, it must be one of those meteor things". Virtually all the halfway-credible sighting reports which have been submitted over the decades (and continue to this day) begin with the phrase "At first, I thought it was a plane/cloud/star/reflection from the factory nearby ...".
2. The fear of ridicule. "I'm not phoning *that* in. They'll think I'm crazy" or "For goodness sake, don't let the Smiths know what we think we saw. Our reputation in the neighbourhood will be shot to hell" or "I'm not giving my name to the newspaper. I'll never be able to hold my head up at the office again".
3. Natural laziness. "No point in phoning the police. They've got enough to do, and anyway, if it was something, then someone else will have seen it and will let them know".
4. The well-known "morning after" effect as memories fade. "We couldn't possibly have seen that. It must have been something else".
5. Press and police "explanations": "You saw what? (giggle, giggle); Yeah, sure, I'll write it down, but, take my word for it, it was those micro-lights from the airfield up the road".

Unfortunately, Klass's theory also does not explain why different witnesses in different locations, on the nights before media coverage, manage to see similar or identical objects.

The third problem is that newspapers *never* tire of a good story. Anything which sells the paper is grist to the mill. If sightings and incidents kept coming in, they'd keep reporting them. The difficulty with the Klass theory is to explain the process by which a newspaper "tires" of a story and whether it is an editor refusing to print any more stories about UFOs regardless of how many juicy reports are coming in (somewhat unlikely, one would imagine), or whether it is more to do with a fall-off in sightings, which causes the newspapers to have less to report.

In spite of some flawed logic, Klass could use humour and sarcasm against UFOs in a very effective way. His shrewd, acerbic humour is well illustrated by an insightful statement he made in a *Washington Post* article in 2002:

> "If there are UFOs and they want to make themselves known, land! And if they don't want to make their visits known, turn off the lights!"

It hits at the core of the UFO conundrum. Why, indeed, are there so many sightings? Why are they so visible? Why do they seem to actually enjoy cavorting around in full sight of scores of people?

At the time of writing, the billionaire Yuri Milner, with a large team of the most eminent scientists and engineers, is planning to send clouds of tiny chips, powered by space-sails and lasers, to do a fly-by of the nearest star, Alpha Centauri. The plans are astounding, but the technology is pretty much achievable within our current knowledge and skill set[70] within the next couple of decades. The point is that, if our current civilisation can send $5mm^2$ chips to Alpha Centauri to conduct surveillance in a nearby star system (the chips would have multiple cameras, sensors, and radios within their tiny frames), why would a civilisation capable of sending flying saucers to Earth need such relatively large, clumsy, and eminently visible technology? If the object is surveillance, why not simply send tiny chips or whatever the advanced technology equivalent would be?

---

[70] See *Scientific American*, March 2017.

CSICOP (the initials are still in constant use, in spite of the change of name more than a decade ago) carries on the good work. Its website and magazine publish solutions to UFO sightings researched by its officials and associates. The biggest headlines are, of course, reserved for when CSICOP feels it has solved one of the most stubbornly elusive cases on the records (for example, see the Exeter explanation in chapter 11).

On the British side of the pond, the battle lines are drawn in exactly the same way as in the States (something that would probably be true of any nation you care to mention). One of the interesting things about sceptics is that, in an almost equal and opposite way to those who are convinced that UFOs are alien spacecraft, they tend to use a single fundamental argument which can be shown to be fairly applicable to one or two instances, and then imply that that logical conclusion applies to all cases.

The extreme ufologists tend to point to one or two very interesting cases for which explanations have proved elusive and then treat the whole subject as though those inexplicable cases apply to everything. If one case with some coloured lights can be shown to be devilishly difficult to explain, they will conclude that all sightings with coloured lights must be equally inexplicable.

The extreme sceptics take exactly the opposite stance. Ian Ridpath is a British sceptic who has put forward many very interesting explanations for a range of sightings. He believes that all UFO sightings would be explicable in everyday terms on the single proviso that we had sufficient evidence.

He also argues that what are usually seen as "credible" UFO sightings often depend on so-called "credible" witnesses: military and civil pilots, police officers, air traffic controllers, and so on. His argument is that even such people can make mistakes.

We look at a good number of credible sightings in this book, and most of them do, indeed, depend on credible observers. So yes, anyone can make a mistake. But, just because it is possible that an expert witness can be mistaken cannot mean that *all* expert witnesses are mistaken on every occasion. The same rebuttal must apply where his corollary is concerned: that non-expert witnesses cannot be considered credible. The crucial problem with many of the sceptics' arguments is that they often fall prey to generalisation and smear tactics. Does the fact that a witness is a twenty-year-old waitress with bad skin necessarily make her any less credible than a good-looking, forty-year-old airline pilot? Does the fact that one police officer is proven to have been mistaken necessarily imply that all police officer testimony must be discarded?

On his website, Ridpath says that by studying UFOs, we are really learning about human nature and not about extraterrestrials. He argues that if we cannot find alien life through studying UFOs or intergalactic radio signals, we will come to what he considers an "even more exciting conclusion": that humanity is the only high-tech civilisation in the galaxy at present and that the stars belong to us and to us only.[71]

It's a strangely arrogant proposition, but whether you are excited by this possibility or not (assuming you ignore the very slight difference between "galaxy" and "universe"), Ridpath's points are straightforward:

- Even the most professional of observers can make mistakes. Allan Hendry, he says, investigated over thirteen hundred cases reported to the Center for UFO Studies (CUFOS) in the United States during the course of a year and explained 75 percent of pilot sightings and 94 percent of police officer sightings (Hendry, 1979).[72]
- No physical evidence has come to light, and all of the unexplained sightings will be explained in due course once we have sufficient evidence.[73]

Unfortunately, his explanations allow much room for questioning. His research leaves no less than 25 percent of pilot sightings and 6 percent of police officer sightings unexplained (and that is discounting whether

---

[71] http://www.ianridpath.com/ufo/ufoindex.htm

[72] Whether the explanations are actually correct or not is something the reader will have to investigate.

[73] And this one could well be absolutely wrong. The French "Trans-en-Provence" case came up with a decent amount of physical evidence, for example, there were probably some very convincing photos and movie film from Edwards AFB during the time of Col Cooper, and the extended research by the Norwegians in Hessdalen might also provide some.

one accepts his explanations for the rest of them). It is highly debatable whether physical evidence is in our hands or not. The ufologists would point to suspected evidence in government hands, to a high number of inexplicable photos and videos, and to the scientific evidence (albeit scant) from a couple of French "landings".

The extreme sceptics point to the (roughly) 95 percent of explicable sightings and say that the same underlying reasons apply to *all* sightings; it's just that there's not enough evidence in 5 percent of cases. This approach conveniently forgets that some researchers (the MoD's UFO desk and GEIPAN in France) have found that there is a reasonably large "uncertain" group in the middle and that some calculations put the "inexplicable" proportion as high as 28 percent.[74] Even the US Condon report found that an amazing 30 percent of their study's cases were impossible to explain.

Some, like Dr David Clarke of Sheffield Hallam University, a lifelong UFO researcher, argue that the whole thing is simply a cultural "myth," like the old stories about witches, ghosts, mysterious creatures in the woods, and things that go bump in the night. He points to the "fact" that UFOs only began to be seen and reported in the latter two-thirds of the twentieth century, conveniently alongside such books as *War of the Worlds* and the introduction of children's comics such as the Marvel series.

But we have no proof that UFOs only began to be seen from the late 1930s, and in fact, as we saw in Chapter 1, there is some evidence (although obviously not provable) that such strange objects have been sighted over many more years. As with many sceptical arguments, Dr Clarke takes up an apparently unassailable position. He cannot prove that witches do not exist, but he can argue that they are a myth. He cannot prove that ghosts do not exist, so it's a safe proposition that they might be a myth too. Ditto with UFOs. To be blunt, it is a logically weak position for an academic. Dr Clarke's specialism is journalism but that does not release him from the academic duty of replicable proof. There are massive problems with

---

[74] The old MoD UFO desk and the current French researchers (GEIPAN) specifically distinguish between three categories of sighting – those which are explainable after investigations, those for which there is insufficient evidence either way, and those which are definitely inexplicable in known or conventional terms.

labelling the UFO phenomenon a modern myth. We haven't space to debate this issue in full here but we can certainly skim over a few points.

Myths almost always differ subtly across cultures. There may be the same sort of myth in numerous countries (a monster in the lake, a terrifyingly large carnivorous animal, giant humanoid beings such as Big Foot and trolls), but there are always differences in the localised version of the myth and, strangely, the myth does not necessarily become global simply through global publicity. People in Scotland, for example, are well aware of the Big Foot myth, of the stories of the Abominable Snowman, and of the tales of evil Trolls in the Norwegian mountains but none of them has ever been reported in the snowy forests of the Scottish Highlands.

UFOs do not really demonstrate the differences in similar myths; almost all sightings all over the world, whether explicable or inexplicable, are of the same types of objects (discs, cigars, triangular, wedge, rectangular), and they demonstrate the same characteristics of rapid changes of speed, hovering, different coloured lights, and silence. Clarke would probably argue that this is due to modern communications, but such an explanation would still not answer the question as to why the myth has followed an entirely different line to popular culture.

There are a number of rational, balanced sceptical approaches, exemplified by Dr Bernard Haisch's ufoskeptics.org website, but most of the sceptical organisations take a stance which begins with "UFOs are all in the imagination" and which works from there. This may indeed prove to be absolutely true, but many serious people still want to know more. Simply because a sighting *could* have been swamp gas, or a meteorite, or a balloon, or a plasma does not mean that it was or that *every* similar sighting *must* be one of those things.

Bernard Haisch uses a quote which he attributes to Winston Churchill:

"Men occasionally stumble over the truth, but most pick themselves up and hurry off as if nothing had happened".[75]

[75] This appears to be a slightly modified version of Churchill's comment about Stanley Baldwin: "Occasionally he stumbled over the truth but hastily picked himself up and hurried on as if nothing had happened."

The words could apply as much to the more ardent flying saucer fans as to the diehard sceptics. Both sides ignore key elements of the logic chain or important pieces of evidence when it suits them. But in the centre ground and on the moderate fringes of both camps, there are a great many people willing to think logically and extensively about the evidence. Some sceptics, such as J Allen Hynek, become gradually convinced by the evidence and move much closer to the ufologist camp. And occasionally, a ufologist, such as David Clarke, drifts closer to the sceptical encampment. Others seem to make abrupt switches. Among these would be Edward Ruppelt.

In 1960, at the close of the second edition of his *Report on Unidentified Flying Objects*, Ruppelt declared very definitely that UFOs were *not* extraterrestrial. He pointed to the lack of material evidence and called UFOs "a space age myth".[76] His change of heart came very late in the second edition, having said pretty much all the same things he'd said in the first. The change was abrupt and, for such a massive shift of belief by one of the most important writers on the subject, it lacked detailed and convincing argument and explanation. The second edition of Ruppelt's book consists mainly of his earlier explanations and thoughts, tending towards the possibility that the objects might be of exotic origin, followed by a short section which essentially reverses the argument. His change of stance left a number of scholars of the subject wondering although without hope of a solution.

We could do a lot worse than to leave the sceptics' case with one of the most eminent scientists and intelligence officers of World War II: Dr R V Jones. He was one of Britain's most influential scientists during the war and, afterwards, wrote an essay entitled *The Natural Philosophy of Flying Saucers*.[77] It sums up the sceptics' case against UFOs being anything extraterrestrial. His final words in that essay neatly summarise the wish of many people even today:

---

[76] This was a strange 180° change of mind in a man who had carefully assessed many cases and the rationale he provided was pretty weak.

[77] R V Jones. "The Natural Philosophy of Flying Saucers." *Physics Bulletin, 19*, 7, 1968: http://www.project1947.com/shg/condon/appndx-v.html

"And while I commend any genuine search for new phenomena, little short of a tangible relic would dispel my skepticism of flying saucers".

Perhaps the real issue here is not that between believers and non-believers but between the factions of the "still curious" and the "convinced one way or the other". Whether one believes or disbelieves is fundamentally irrelevant because we still have no proof either way. What might, however, be important is whether one simply writes off the whole phenomenon as myth or misperception, or whether one decides that we still don't know for sure, and until we do have conclusive proof one way or the other, we should keep researching and keep our minds open.

Twenty Explanations for UFOs

There is no one (I sincerely hope) who would argue against the fact that the majority of UFO sightings are explicable in terms of normal phenomena. This means that a high proportion of UFO sightings might be explicable in terms of what I call the "Twenty Explanations for UFOs":

1. Meteorological events: certain cloud formations, temperature inversions,[78] so-called ball lightning, and so on. Lenticular clouds, for example, can look remarkably like a hovering flying saucer. They are flat, lens-shaped clouds which can appear disc-like. Seen in particular light by someone not familiar with the type, and against ordinary cumulous clouds, misinterpretation is possible. Under this heading must also be listed the various putative electromagnetic causes such as plasmas and sprites.

---

[78] There are many types of temperature inversion – including radiation, subsidence, frontal, marine, and so on and there are photographic examples of almost all types on the internet but it has to be said that I have not seen a single photo – even ones showing bulbous inversion cloud formations which could seriously be taken for a UFO. And inversion phenomena tend not to dart around the sky.

A lenticular cloud formation. One can see how, if illuminated from below by town or city lights, such a formation might possibly be interpreted as a UFO. (Sheryl Williams/Shutterstock.com).

2. Meteors: "rocks from space"; meteors are chunks of rock which enter the Earth's atmosphere and, as meteorites, burn up with the friction. They are called shooting stars in many countries. Large meteorites have possibly caused immense damage on Earth in the past.

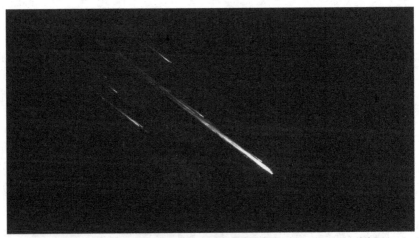

A meteorite. The fundamental differences between such objects and those reported as UFOs is that UFOs can travel slowly and hover, they lack a tail, and they make sharp changes of direction. (Vadim Sadovski/Shutterstock.com)

3. Fireballs: large meteorites, called bolides, which burn until they achieve a highly gaseous state and reach fairly low levels. They often explode and can be spectacular. It was one of these which is suspected of causing huge damage at Tunguska in Russia in 1903. Whatever it was probably exploded at a height of between ten thousand and fifteen thousand feet, destroying almost eight hundred square miles of forest. If a bolide was responsible we were very lucky it did not explode over London, Paris or New York.

4. Planets: Some planets can look bright and large in certain weather conditions and in certain positions in relation to the viewer and the time of year. The planet Venus is the most common heavenly body mistaken for a UFO. It is very bright in certain circumstances and can appear like a green light floating near the horizon when magnified by the lower atmosphere.

5. Stars: Similarly, groups of stars can seem to be flashing lights in the sky or can even be misinterpreted as squadrons of UFOs. The constellation forming the Pleiades – called the Seven Sisters – is very prone to such misidentifications when the stars are particularly bright.

6. Earthbound lights: lighthouses and warning lights on tall chimneys, radio masts, and buildings. Even when people are extremely familiar with the lights in their area, they can sometimes be fooled by seeing them from unusual angles or by their appearance through unusual weather conditions. Fog or mist, for example, can completely change the colour of distant lights and can make them appear to move and float.

7. Aircraft: Researchers know that aircraft lights can be misinterpreted but also that certain advanced aircraft might be mistaken for UFOs. An aircraft can be high in the sky and virtually invisible to the naked eye, yet the sun glancing off its metallic body will flash a very bright light. Sceptics have argued that certain delta-shaped aircraft might be responsible for the triangular UFOs.

8. Satellites: Low-orbit satellites can reflect sunlight or moonlight and move fast in the sky. At dusk and dawn especially, they can seem like red lights moving through the sky.

9. Satellite re-entry: Old satellites burn up on re-entry and can break into pieces, creating a small set of lights and trails in the sky which might look like a group of UFOs streaking into the atmosphere.

10. Weather balloons: The larger, advanced ones with metallic skins can look remarkably like strange air vehicles hovering in the sky. In high-altitude winds, they can also move quite quickly.

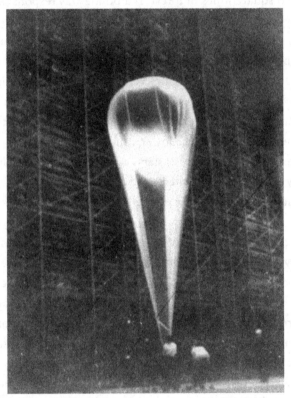

A weather balloon. At altitude, these can appear to be silver globes and, if high-altitude winds are speedy, can appear to travel quite fast. (Fortean/Topfoto.co.uk)

11. Light aberrations: Certain weather conditions and times of the year can create stunningly different variations in light, even on a localised basis. Sun-dogs, for example, are particularly spectacular. They usually consist of a pair of mini-suns to the left and right of the sun and some distance from it. Caused by ice crystals in

the atmosphere, they can be very misleading when the sun itself is partially obscured by cloud.

12. Earth-bound surface phenomena: Volcanic eruptions on a localised basis, swamp/marsh gas, dust devils, and earthquakes all have been linked to sightings at one time or another.

13. Satellite fuel burn: The final insertion of a satellite into orbit may create a bright light in the sky. Satellites also often dump and ignite unused fuel, causing a cloud of flame in a small shape high in the sky.

14. Rocket launches and stages: More and more rockets are being launched by numerous nations, and each rocket covers a huge distance before it reaches orbit. As it goes, not only is there a bright light streaking across the sky, but the separation of each stage also creates a burst of bright flame in a localised area. As the spent stages fall back to Earth, they are almost always red-hot for a time.

The separation of a rocket stage seen from the ground. Bright lights in the sky can be caused by such events as well as satellite fuel-burn and vehicle re-entry. (vicspacewalker/Shutterstock.com)

15. "New" atmospheric phenomena: A number of scientists have mooted new, and not yet fully understood, atmospheric phenomena as causing sightings, including plasmas, so-called blue sprites, charged fields, buoyant masses of plasma, and such like.

And finally, of course, there are:

16. Deliberate hoaxes: and there have been a huge number.
17. Mass suggestion: the tendency of a crowd to believe and follow a strongly stated view of a single person or a sub-group. The power of suggestion is extremely potent. At the simplest level, one can persuade people to "see" the man-in-the-moon or view a cloud as an automobile. At more serious levels, people can be misled by other witnesses into "remembering" a totally different set of events which might have led to, for example, a shunt between two cars or a fight in a bar.
18. Mass hallucination: not so common and very difficult to prove, but a possibility in some cases.
19. Socio-psychological factors: for example, the power of myth to cause people to interpret ordinary things in ways which support and substantiate the myth.

In addition to all of the above:

20. Einstein: There are some who argue that, while UFOs may exist, they cannot be from other planets. The argument generally relies on the assertion that Einstein's theory of relativity determines that nothing can ever exceed the speed of light.[79] As most star systems which might contain life-bearing planets could be hundreds or even thousands of light-years away from our own star system, the argument concludes that no civilisation would be able to reach

---

[79] His beautifully elegant equation – $e = mc^2$ – means that anything reaching the speed of light (c) must have infinite mass. In simple terms, it means that it would "weigh" more than the whole universe.

us, and even if they had the capability of building near-light-speed craft, why bother with such lengthy journeys?

Some eminent physicists have developed a pretty strong set of formulae and theories supporting the possibility of wormholes and other folds in space-time which might, if they can be proven, allow a vehicle to travel vast intergalactic distances in the blink of an eye. *Star Trek's* warp-drive may be a science-fiction dream, but so was landing on the moon to the Edwardians. The fact is, we just do not know for sure. The bottom line on faster-than-light travel is that we simply have no real idea whether there are ways to get around Einstein's light-speed brick wall. Human history shows that we have often believed that certain things were not possible on the basis of existing scientific understanding. Rocks falling from the sky were impossible until science found out that, actually, they were possible. Travelling faster than the speed of sound was also once thought to be impossible. The wonderful thing about humans, at least to date, is that, collectively, we eventually find ways around virtually everything.

CHAPTER 9

Strange Characteristics

ONE OF THE THINGS which fascinated me when researching this book was the weird and wonderful characteristics which UFOs exhibit. They are said to do some strange – sometimes ludicrous – things. These features matter because, illusory or real, they are what people see and are therefore vital to a solution, whichever side of the debate you may find yourself on.

Incredibly, UFOs have exhibited remarkably similar – although diverse – characteristics throughout the post-war period. As far as can be ascertained, many of those characteristics also apply to sightings from before 1939 and possibly before 1900. Some of them are well known, and others not so well-recognised.

Here is a baker's dozen to think about:

1. High Speed

Ever since Kenneth Arnold and Fred Johnson saw nine objects in the summer of 1947, high speed has been a common denominator in UFO sightings. Not just high speed but speeds which were much higher than aircraft of the time could manage. It's also noteworthy that speeds of well over 1,000 mph appear to be achieved by these objects without any form of sonic boom. Sceptics argue that this proves that the objects do not exist, but we now know that there are aerodynamic ways of reducing or eliminating sonic booms. NASA has conducted shaped-fuselage and flexible wing tests in recent years, and Spike Aerospace's S-512 project is said to be capable of building and flying a supersonic transport aircraft whose sonic boom will be low to negligible. If *we* can get to the point where a sonic boom could sound no louder than a "muffled handclap", who is to say that someone else might not have taken the matter a little further?

2. Hovering

Very low speeds and hovering are also commonly reported. From Fort Hood in 1948 through the Hudson Valley wave in 1982, to Belgium in 1989 and England between 2007 and 2017, UFOs are said to move very slowly or to actually stand still in mid-air.

The Portuguese air force pilot Julio Guerra and a couple of his fellow officers saw a UFO whiz around in a wide circle around Guerra's aircraft and suddenly stop dead above it, before shooting off.

3. Incredible Manoeuvrability

In addition to hovering and travelling at high speed, large numbers of witnesses say that the objects are incredibly manoeuvrable. There are many reports of them literally zigzagging as they travel. At Lakenheath in 1956, one was watched on radar as it travelled short distances at high speed and then changed course radically and instantly. A meteorologist at RAF Cosford also initially testified that the object which he saw zigzagged. Even the NORAD reports from 1975 confirm this characteristic.

4. High Acceleration/Deceleration

This characteristic is one of the ones which impresses most pilots, along with the manoeuvrability. Everyone who has ever taken a jet-passenger flight will understand the acceleration which pushes one back into the seat when the pilot first opens the throttles for take-off. That additional G-force is minimal: around half a G at most, and usually much lower.

Fighter pilots, physically extremely fit, can pull 10G and more in their turns.[80]

However, pilots who say they have watched UFOs accelerate and decelerate, and who have witnessed the rapid climbs and descents (such as that at Chicago O'Hare), have been awed by the potential G forces involved. In one case, the object went upwards from zero to 300 mph in an instant. That speed, over that distance, if it could have been duplicated by a man-made aircraft, would have squashed its human occupants.

5. Silence

This is a very strange characteristic and one which tends to go almost unnoticed in reports. Yet there are only a few which say that the object made any noise. It's one of those things which makes the outsider ponder. If UFOs are a myth, where did the silence thing come from? Given the way humans think, would a myth not be a lot more enticing and exciting if the objects roared through the air or emitted a deep and threatening growl? And yet silence is the rule, even when apparently moving very fast.

6. Lights

Much to Philip Klass's amusement, almost every UFO that is spotted at night (and some during the day) sports an array of lights which would shame a young SUV driver. If there is any consistency, however, it has yet to be deduced. In both arrangements and colours, the objects' lights exhibit significant variety, even where the shape is the same.

Many people report the lights as flashing and some as flashing in sequence, like that scene in *Close Encounters* but without the melody. The witnesses during the Exeter incident reported just such sequential lights. The other, slightly weird, feature of reported UFOs is the large degree of variation in flashing frequency. The presence of lights is almost universal,

---

[80] Half a G means that for a few moments, you weigh 50 percent more. If you are a 100-pound person, you feel as though you weigh 150 pounds. A 10G turn makes a fighter pilot feel as though he or she weighs ten times their actual weight.

but not only do the colours vary but so too do the number of lights and the way in which they flash.

Klass did not ask enough questions: he should not merely have asked "why the lights?" but why the colours, why do the colours vary so much, why flashing or changing, and why the frequency can be so different? Over the years, most witnesses have reported lights, but if this were a myth, why haven't they all reported the same sort of thing, particularly within a given "wave" of sightings?

There are many reports of equally spaced lights in symmetrical formations: three on each side, one in the middle, or lights equally spaced around the circumference of an object. But there are also reports of odd numbers of lights, of non-symmetrical placing of lights, and even of lights coming together to give the appearance of a single object but then whizzing off in different directions.

Sometimes, one reads an account of lights flashing in a simple sequence, but mostly it *seems* the flashing is random. Unfortunately for the outsider, however, there are no readily available analyses of the phenomenon of lights on such objects either by colour, number, brightness, frequency of flashing, or any other variable.

If witnesses are seeing lights because they are following fashion, then perhaps we need to know what social or psychological forces are causing them to do this. Not what forces do a few psychologists think *might* have led to this result, but what has actually, in proven and replicable experiments, caused such perceptions to prevail.

Some people report quite strange characteristics for UFO lights, such as that they are very bright but do not hurt the eyes, that they are pastel shades, that they'd never seen colours like that before, and that they are very "pure" colours. These are extremely specific observations and are compelling because the witnesses really did not have any need to invent yet more strange things about a sighting.

Finally, there's the issue of objects whose lights are "switched off" when fighter aircraft get too close, only to be switched on again once the fighters have returned to base. As far apart in time as Washington DC in 1952, the Loring AFB incidents in 1975, and the Belgian objects in 1990, there are official reports of UFO lights apparently being turned off when the fighters got too close and then being cheekily relit once the aircraft had left the area.

7. Electromagnetic Interference

Interference with car radios, vehicle engines, aircraft communications, electronics, and even aircraft systems have been reported on occasion as far back as the 1940s and 1950s. And then there's the small matter of the number of times that air force pilots have reported weapon lock-ons being broken. Fighters throughout the decades, from the early F-94s and British Vampires to the F-4s over Tehran in 1976[81] and the F-16s used in various North American sightings and in Belgium, have suffered the frustration of achieving lock-on but then having it broken very quickly. This could be because the objects, whatever they are, are too agile and manage to speed upwards, downwards, or to one side quickly enough to fool the radar, or that the objects are gaseous or plasmas and do not reflect the radar for long enough, or perhaps even that the objects somehow manage to interfere with the aircraft's electronic systems.

There are reports by pilots that their weapons systems were temporarily disabled, only to come back on line the moment the UFO had gone. Civilian pilots have said sometimes that their radios and navigation equipment became unserviceable.

8. Shapes

UFOs are reported in a number of shapes and sizes, from gigantic to pretty small. Sometimes, single objects are seen to break up into several

---

[81] Ground sightings of a bright light plus official corroboration sent two Imperial Iranian Air Force F-4s into the sky north of and over Tehran in September 1976. The F-4s were alleged to have suffered communications and radar problems when approaching the objects, which corrected themselves when the aircraft turned away. It's a fascinating event which the sceptics explain with planets and aircraft maintenance issues, but the whole event, with multiple visual and radar sightings, remains extremely interesting.

smaller ones, and on other occasions, there have been reports of the UFOs seeming to change shape. Yet again these features would seem counter-productive from a witness point of view. If you want someone to believe that you have seen a space-ship why invent things which make it seem impossible and unrealistic?

The reported shapes break down into a number of fairly common descriptions:

- triangle/wedge
- disc
- cigar/cylinder
- globes
- bell

The myth explanation could be applicable to the shapes people report, but the only problem with that, apart from the fact that it requires thousands of people in scores of countries to believe so much in the myth that they all report similar things, is that there are arguably much more powerful stories which could, perhaps even, *should*, determine what they see.

A "spaceship" has always had a pretty standard cultural norm in each generation, and if the UFOs were a myth acting on human psyches, one would expect the myth to be an imprint of existing cultural beliefs. So 1950s witnesses should have seen needle-nosed space fighters à la Dan Dare or Flash Gordon, and the phenomenon of the 1990s should really have morphed into huge, complicated alien spacecraft with seven different lobes and huge claw-like appendages.

I hope you can see what I am getting at. Since 1945, UFOs have not morphed into vast rumbling galactic freighters with pods and multiple levels. They have not changed into globe-like Death Stars, and they have never been described by witnesses as needle-nosed space fighters in the *Star Wars* or even the old Dan Dare or Flash Gordon moulds.

All myths tend to reflect the prevailing cultural beliefs and fears. Lake monsters tend to be shaped like huge prehistoric dinosaurs; forest humanoids are like gigantic apes with dripping fangs. Yet UFOs in the second decade of the twenty-first century remain pretty much what they were just after World War II. Consistently, over seventy years of sightings, UFOs are reported as exhibiting weird flight characteristics: abrupt changes of course, incredibly rapid acceleration and deceleration, and impossibly fast ascents and descents.

The consistency of description against a backdrop of highly imaginative fictional space sagas is fascinating (and slightly disturbing) for the outsider.

Sceptics suggest that the UFO craze is just that: a fictitious story based on mass hallucinations and suggestibility in which almost the whole of humankind is enmeshed. Yet witness after witness reports ultra-fast, darting movement, impossibly abrupt changes of course, and a good many have described strange fluttering motion. Someone should tell all those witnesses that they'd have a much easier time if they stuck to the film myth.

Ask any youngster today what an intergalactic spaceship looks like, and they will almost certainly come up with something from the examples below.

Fictional Spaceships through the Ages

1950s: Through the late 1940s and the decade of the 1950s, fictional spaceships tended to be of two varieties: either slender objects with a pointed nose and tail fins – like a V2 rocket – or space fighters, which looked pretty much like a modern F-16 fighter aircraft. The stubby wings, sharply pointed nose, and all-over glass cockpit were the trademark of Dan Dare.

1960s and 1970s: Fictional spacecraft began to become larger and more imaginative. *Star Trek* introduced a number of huge ships with separate power pods and huge circular crew structures. "Alien" spacecraft were deliberately fashioned to look evil and menacing, with multiple sharply pointed or even serrated, claw-like protrusions.

1980s onwards: The idea of huge, intergalactic freighters and warships took root, and we got the whole mass
of *Star Wars* craft: space fighters similar to those of the
early post-war years, rumbling freighters with scores of
decks and cavernous, factory-like holds, and vast, menacing battleships studded with gun turrets and airlocks.
Today, the variety has been multiplied many times over
by the advent of computer and video games. We now have
everything from cumbersome, girder-enclosed cargo vessels to alien fighters which look like birds or insects.[82]

What the largest proportion of those youngsters will *not* come up with
are discs which look like a 1950s trashcan on a plate, silly discs which look
like two soup-plates stuck rim to rim, equilateral triangles with a light at
each corner, or coloured cigars. All far too boring.

9. Light Beams

Beams of light shooting down to the ground or into bodies of water are
pretty common in UFO reports. USAF reports state that objects shot
beams down into weapons storage areas. Lt Col Halt says that the objects
which he watched at Rendlesham in 1980 shot a beam to the ground not
far from where he and his men were standing. The meteorologist in the
RAF Shawbury affair said that the object he saw was illuminating the
ground as though searching for something. Even the witnesses to the airship over the eastern counties of England in 1909 told the press that it was
illuminating the ground with searchlights. Mr White in 1914 said that his
light sometimes sent lights to the ground and back up again.

To paraphrase Philip Klass – why the light beams? That's a question
no one can answer but, again, leaves one wondering about how that could
tie into copycat reports due to mass hysteria or into the "myth" theory.

---

[82] Take a very brief look at https://www.quora.com/What-are-some-of-the-best-
looking-fictional-spaceships-ever-designed

Other people have said they've seen balls of light, smaller than the main object, exiting it and then darting around, sometimes while the object is emitting beams of light. Stephen Spielberg took up both features – the light beams and the tiny, independent red balls of light – the his film *Close Encounters of the Third Kind*.

10. Water

The association of UFOs with water is something that we have not really addressed in this book. It is a subject about which several books have been written and one which is every bit as fascinating as the general subject of UFOs.

UFOs have apparently been witnessed emerging from the sea and from inland water and showing great interest in lakes and rivers. For example, two separate witnesses, Jim Cooke and Linda Nicoletti, watched different objects shooting a red beam down into water during the Hudson Valley wave in 1983. There are a number of unsubstantiated accounts of USN vessels reporting underwater UFOs – known as USOs (unidentified submersible objects) and fishing boats of various nations have also said they've seen such things (including a couple off the coast of Yorkshire).

The issue from the outsider's standpoint is that very few of these water-UFO events were corroborated by other witnesses and particularly not by officials or pilots.

11. Interacting with Aircraft

Events where UFOs appeared to interact with aircraft – circling them, tracking or following them, even playing with them – are much easier to find. More importantly, several have been investigated by the military, by aviation authorities, or by organisations such as GEIPAN in France.

Several civilian pilots have mentioned that the UFOs they saw seemed to track their aircraft. Captain Phil Schulz in 1981 and Captain Terauchi over Alaska in 1986 are excellent examples.

12. Wobbling

This is arguably the most uncanny physical characteristic of all. What myth-maker would have invented this one?

Many accounts, widely separated in both in time and location, tell of UFOs having a "rocking motion" or descending like a "falling leaf" or "swaying back and forth" or actually wobbling. One witness mentioned a high-speed change of altitude by one object which ended in an abrupt hover, in which the object wobbled and appeared to be correcting itself until it reached a state of equilibrium, after which it hovered in perfect stillness.

Dr Bruce Maccabee recounts the case of the prospector, Frederick Johnson, who in July 1947 probably saw the same objects as seen by Kenneth Arnold from his aircraft. Johnson said the objects "tilted back and forth as they flew" (Maccabee, 2014), and this, of course, corroborates Arnold's own statement that the objects seemed to skip as they flew along.

Accounts containing these sorts of words have been recorded since 1945, and if you think about it a bit, the words and the phenomenon they describe are incredibly strange on many levels. Why would anyone make up a wobble on a UFO? It makes the objects sound comical and unbelievable, as though the operators of the objects are not quite fully competent. And yet witness after witness, decade after decade remarks on the fact that the things often exhibit short periods of unstable flight and then steady themselves.

Other accounts say that objects would stand on their ends and tilt. Like wobbling, it seems counter-intuitive to imagine that any sort of craft would be able to function when standing on its edge or hovering at an angle. For a human-made aircraft, standing on end or skipping through the air is not only dangerous but, for its occupants, just a little uncomfortable.

Among the witnesses who allege that the objects can be prone to wobbling or unstable flight are Stan Hubbard, the test pilot in England in 1950, the witnesses at RAF Topcliffe in 1952, the police officers at Exeter, New Hampshire in 1965, and a chap named Herbert Proudfoot, at Danbury, Connecticut in 1983.

Surely, if a witness was making up a sensational story of a spaceship from another galaxy, come to Earth for all sorts of nefarious reasons, the last thing they would want is for their flying saucer to appear comical or even physically impossible. If you want a newspaper to laugh at your story, tell them the thing wobbled or, like the Trents, send them a photo of the thing tilted at a weird angle.

Little green men can scoot across millions of light-years in arrogant confidence, their cold, dark eyes glinting with the prospect of conquest. But when they reach the final destination and flash menacingly into Earth's lower atmosphere, in full view of human witnesses, they cannot seem to get the brakes to work properly, and they are forced to wobble a bit before getting the thing under control.

Anything wrong with this picture?

13. Mental Connections

Hold on to your hat.

Read through a good few reports of UFO sightings, and you will inevitably come across people who are baffled by an apparent link between them and the object. The sceptics would say that this is not surprising, as the objects are figments of their imagination. But the open-minded outsider would probably question this in many cases, based firstly on the apparent sincerity and honesty of the witnesses, but also on the fact that their accounts are corroborated by others close by or resonate closely with other people's sightings years previously and thousands of miles away.

The accounts in question generally mention, in the midst of a traumatic sighting, that there was a feeling that the object did what the observer was thinking, perhaps even what they wanted. A frightened observer might say that they became scared, and suddenly the UFO sped away or disappeared. Intrigued observers have on several occasions mentioned that they sort of wished the UFO would come closer, and it did. Pick the bones out of that if you can.

The UFO phenomenon involves a variety of common characteristics which seem to prevail and persist in spite of powerful social myths and stories embedded in films and science fiction books. One very interesting exercise is to compare what I've listed above as the common characteristics with what senior USAF officers identified as the characteristics of flying saucers almost exactly seventy years ago.

First, then, the things I believe, from decades of sightings, are pretty common to the 5 percent "unexplained" element of the UFO cases:

1. Extremely high speeds
2. Extremely low speeds
3. Ability to hover indefinitely
4. Transitions from high to low speed (and vice versa), which would imply very high G-forces
5. Rates of climb and descent which, equally, imply high G-forces
6. Abrupt changes of direction which would be impossible for human craft
7. Silence (or virtual silence)
8. Bright lights
9. Flashing lights
10. Coloured lights
11. Occasional periods of unstable flight (tilting and wobbling)
12. No apparent hostility towards aircraft trying to chase them (even when the aircraft have locked weapons onto them or even fired upon them)
13. An almost playful attitude when being chased – stopping to let the aircraft catch up and then dashing off again

Compare this list with the one contained in a memo from Lieutenant Colonel George Garrett, US Air Force Intelligence, in 1947 (see Maccabee, 2014):

a. relatively flat bottom with extreme light reflecting ability
b. absence of sound except for an occasional roar when operating under super-performance conditions

c.   extreme manoeuvrability and apparent ability to al-most hover

d.   a plan form approximating that of an oval or disc with a dome shape on the top surface

e.   the absence of an exhaust trail except in a few instances

f.   the ability to quickly disappear by high speed or by complete disintegration

g.   the ability to suddenly appear without warning as if from an extremely high altitude

h.   the size most reported approximated that of a C-54 or Constellation type aircraft

i.   the ability to group together very quickly in a tight formation when more than one aircraft [i.e. object] are together

j.   evasive action ability indicates possibility of being manually operated, or possibly by electronic or re-mote control devices

k.   under certain conditions the craft seems to have the ability to cut a clear path through clouds--width of path estimated to be approximately one half mile. Only one incident indicated this phenomenon.

The last item makes one recall the Chicago O'Hare case of 2006 (chapter 12).

Sceptics would probably say that these characteristics have been passed down through generations of people by word-of-mouth, by the media, and, especially, by sensationalist films. This may turn out to be what has happened, but can we be certain that those social and communication mechanisms (if they exist) are the driving forces behind every sighting and event?

Notwithstanding all this, what gets at me, personally, are a small number of perplexing features which I have real problems trying to fit into a standardised myth model. Why would witnesses need to invent

- abrupt changes of course and zig-zags,
- "pure" colours,
- bright colours which do not hurt the eyes,
- apparently random (rather than standardised) flashing of lights,
- apparently unstable flight, and
- mental connections?

Most of the above are almost guaranteed to make others disbelieve the story when, according to the sceptics, what people are seeking is attention, belief, and publicity.

CHAPTER 10

Strangers in the Night

AS OUTSIDERS, WE HAVE to conclude that there is almost certainly a small proportion of UFO sightings which would be difficult for even the "as yet unknown natural phenomena" explanation to solve. Good photographic evidence, together with compelling witness testimony, throws a good deal of weight behind those who believe there is a phenomenon at work here which is not natural or a result of human frailty.

Before we start looking at the "what are they" question, we need to ask "why so many" and "why so obvious?"

If, as I have shown, there are literally thousands of inexplicable sightings *every year* across the globe, that's a lot of visitors. The sheer number would probably lend weight to the "as yet unknown natural phenomena" argument.

And there's also the Philip Klass question. If these objects wish to be unseen and secret, why all the lights and the slow cruising just above people's heads? If, on the other hand, they actually want to be seen, why not simply land on the lawns of Buckingham Palace, the White House, and the Palace of Versailles and get it over with? Instead, the objects fly conveniently alongside aircraft, to be seen by experienced pilots and their bewildered passengers; they appear to taunt fighter aircraft; and they wander slowly up and down densely populated areas so that people can witness them at extremely close quarters (e.g. Belgium, Washington, English Midlands, Hudson Valley). If these are not natural phenomena, Philip Klass's question needs to be answered.

Incredible as it might seem, if the UAPs/UFOs are not of this world, one of the strongest explanations which fits all the variables (number of sightings, lots of different types of objects, deliberately allowing themselves to be seen, and incorrigibly showing off) is "tourism with a smattering of scientific and military investigation". Is a galactic civilisation running tours to Earth? Are our future selves running sight-seeing tours to the past?

Modern theories about UFOs have evolved somewhat since the 1940s in both prosaic and profound ways. They tend to fall into four categories:

1. Intergalactic craft (sometimes with bases within the solar system);
2. Made on Earth;
3. Time or dimensional travellers; and,
4. Even stranger theories such as mental images or even living creatures

1. Intergalactic Craft?

If there are UFOs which cannot be explained by our science, even by hard work to expand the boundaries of atmospheric, electromagnetic, nuclear, geological, and other sciences, what are the best theories of where they come from?

The most popular theory as to what they are is that they are spaceships from another solar system (within or without our galaxy).

We have no way of deducing the origins of these objects without much more information and, crucially, without finding enough information to be able to reject all other theories. We need verified and scientifically calibrated photos and video, we need radiation measurements, we need magnetic and gravitational measurements, we need to understand why they "appear" and "disappear", probably by tracking them more effectively, and we need advanced instrumentation established according to scientific principles to get the data required on the various manifestations of UAPs.

If they are from someplace other than Earth, it's possible that, even if they originate in a galaxy far-far-away, they may have bases in the solar system. People have wondered whether there are alien bases on the dark side of the moon, or on any of a score of different planets and moons. So-called "fast walkers", anomalies which seem to speed across the face of the moon and planets, have been recorded for decades. If the objects which have been witnessed on Earth for the past seventy years are ultimately from outside our solar system, then having bases within it would make sense.

We still do not know enough about the planets in the solar system to be certain that they do not contain life. But the possibility of space-faring creatures having *originated* on Saturn or Jupiter or even Mars is a genuine stretch of logic.

If the UAPs/UFOs are coming from another star system, however, the time taken to reach the Earth is an issue, one that has often been raised as a killer punch by sceptics. We have no way of knowing how fast the craft can travel, but even at a high percentage of light speed, it could take decades, centuries, or even millennia to reach the Earth from their galactic homes. But "they" could, of course, have found ways to circumvent light-speed limitations in the form of wormholes and so on.

Sceptics often use Einstein's light-speed barrier (i.e. that nothing can ever exceed the speed of light) as a final nail in the UFO coffin. Why, they ask, would any alien species bother to travel for such long periods of time just to buzz the Hudson Valley for a while, frighten commercial airline pilots with near-misses, and bedazzle thousands of humans with their light shows?

It's a good question which becomes even more powerful if one turns the argument around. Say the "aliens" have discovered a way to travel faster than light and can reach the Earth a lot quicker. Even if it takes them seconds to travel to our planet, why are they bothering to use their sophisticated spacecraft to hover over Washington, Yorkshire, France, and Belgium in full view of the inhabitants?

2. Earth Origins?

Remember here that we are speaking of the tiny proportion of sightings which remain "unknowns" even after a fair degree of investigation. So

Earth origins are only likely if we pin down a nation as being capable of developing truly exotic vehicles and keeping the fact totally secret for decades. There are a fair few people who argue that some UAPs/UFOs are actually manufactured on this planet and are secretly deployed by certain governments for, presumably, disreputable reasons.

Let's examine that as a possibility. Having reached this point in the book, the outsider will know that UFOs are seen doing some amazing things: abrupt changes of direction; super-fast speeds with an absence of sonic booms; rapid ascents and descents; even transiting from air to water and back again. If we discount 95 percent of sightings as either mistaken or natural, we are still left with many hundreds of inexplicable sightings per year across the world.

The implications of these UFO characteristics boil down to one thing: incredible technology supported by lots of money, lots of human resources, and some extremely advanced science. Any human-made UAPs with these sorts of characteristics would need manufacturing facilities, supply chains, bases, and hundreds, if not thousands, of support personnel plus the necessary logistical networks. Who would have the financial resources to research, develop, manufacture, staff, and supply such craft on such a scale and then fly them on a global basis over seventy years?[83] Who, also, would have the capacity to keep such an enterprise totally secret? One might essay that there are only four nations or blocs which could achieve this (and two of those really only in the past thirty years). Russia, the United States, China, and the European Union could theoretically marshal the resources, but China has probably only had the ability within the last thirty years, and the EU, in all fairness, could never keep such a secret across its twenty-seven nations. So, given the length of time over which sightings have been made, the only realistic options are: number one, the USA, and number two, the Soviet Union/Russia.

Can the outsider really swallow the idea that one or both of these nations has been able to keep entirely secret, technologies which would

---

[83] A look at the global supply chain for components for modern aircraft goes a long way to rendering such theories highly unlikely. To build a sophisticated space craft takes new materials, advanced manufacturing techniques, and scores of different suppliers.

shift virtually every paradigm we know? If either had developed such technology, where are the supply chains, the bases, the thousands of ex-employees, the spy exposés, the whistle-blowers, the leaks of emails and documents, and so on?

But assuming for an instant that the United States had developed such craft and found a way to keep their base in Antarctica, or under the ocean, completely secret for seventy years, why would the machines be swanning about, festooned in fairy-lights, in plain sight like particularly garish models on a catwalk?

Possession of such technology, if it exists at all, would imply that the owner could also dominate the near-Earth environment, launch any number of satellites without the risk and expense of crude rockets, save billions by not having to develop, test, and build newer forms of rockets (as each of the four nations/blocs have and are doing), and could almost certainly translate some of the whizzo ideas into ordinary life. If gravity and inertia could be ignored, for example, what would that mean for trains and cars?

If the United States or Russia had known for decades how to avoid such a relatively simply phenomenon as a sonic boom, why are both nations spending huge amounts of cash trying to achieve that feat right now (as well as China and the EU)?

A number of ufologists argue that the US government would have kept such things covered up because the technology would destroy businesses worth billions of dollars (e.g. oil, aviation, rail manufacturing, and automobiles to name but four). But seventy years is sufficient time for those industries to have adapted to new technologies, and if the conspiracy theorists are right, those same businesses would, by now, have long since abandoned their oil, gas, and aircraft and would have transitioned to producing billions of dollars' worth of gravity-defying ground vehicles, space vehicles which could mine minerals on Jupiter's moons, and trains which could float above their tracks and stop instantly. Which would Exxon, Shell, and BP really want: profits from an expensive, dirty, and rapidly diminishing resource in the form of liquid hydrocarbons, or a virtually free, quiet, and infinitely more powerful form of energy derived from secret, crashed UFOs?

Even the Earth-bound strategic implications of such technology would be epoch-changing. If either the United States or the USSR had possessed a technology capable of floating silently in the night sky and travelling effortlessly into space, could they have resisted using it to revolutionise earthly manufacturing and products over the past seventy years? Given such silent, radar-invisible craft, could the Americans have resisted the chance to sneak in and stop North Korean rocket trials?

Any critical outsider must conclude that, whatever they are, UFOs are almost certainly not man-made.

3. Time or Dimensional Travellers

But there are other theories, of which two of the most interesting are that the inexplicable proportion of UFOs consists of time travellers from our future, or that they might be from this Earth but from different dimensions. I can hear you laughing from here but neither possibility is theoretically impossible.

Time travel is a science fiction stalwart, forming the basis of a steady stream of books and movies ever since the early years of the twentieth century. It's an exciting, thoroughly absorbing, and intellectually challenging concept which millions of us love.

While, as a subject, it remains on the fringes of conventional studies, scientists admit that it is *theoretically* possible under very, very special circumstances. On the most fundamental level, we know that time slows down the faster you travel. Find yourself a spaceship which has the oomph to get up to a high fraction of light speed, and you could return to Earth scores, hundreds, or even thousands of years into the future having barely aged. We have also begun to suspect that time, as with most things, operates at the quantum level in a different way to time in normal space.

Could a suitably advanced civilisation, knowledgeable enough to have conquered gravity and inertia, have also worked out how to travel in time?

The idea that UFOs may be from another dimension is a bit like time travel but even more towards the very fringes of theoretical scientific possibility. Nevertheless, multi-dimensions have been seriously posited by certain eminent scientists who work in the quantum world and string theory. It is at least theoretically possible that there may be other versions of the Earth on which the inhabitants have found ways to bridge the dimensional gap to come and visit their close but primitive cousins.

4. Even Weirder Theories

J Allen Hynek came up with the theory that UFOs may actually be manifestations or mental illusions created by beings who have mastered both mind and matter. He called it his "M&M" (Mind and Matter) theory. Hynek wondered whether UFOs might actually be pure mental images created by those advanced beings. Subsequent thought leads to the possibility that these manifestations may be created by "ourselves from the future" or other civilisations from another dimension.

Hynek also warned that we might be mistaken if we believe that UFOs are the result of a *single* cause. He proposed that, whatever the objects might be, they might stem from more than one origin or cause.

It simply adds to the fascination, but there are some who believe that the unexplained UFOs are actually living creatures. Followers of Charles Fort and Ivan T Sanderson set a certain amount of store by Sanderson's theory, expounded in his book *Uninvited Visitors*.[84] Sanderson was a brilliant Scottish-American biologist (Eton and Cambridge) who invented the term "cryptozoology". He propounded a theory that our "visitors" may be entire living organisms.

You pay your money, and you take your pick.

And just like rocks from space, UFO sightings keep coming, no matter how impossible scientists and governments claim they are.

---

[84] Sanderson, Ivan T. *Uninvited Visitors: A Biologist Looks at UFOs*. Cowles Education Corporation, 1967.

PART 2

Introduction

We know that people see things in the sky, and we know that we can be pretty sure that around 5 percent is a good working number for those which are inexplicable, according to our current understanding of science and psychology.

What we need to do now is to take a peek at some of the most credible events. And when I say "some", I mean it. I've selected a couple of dozen, but it could easily have been treble that number and still only scratch the surface of fascinating and pretty credible cases.

By "credible", I mean that the sheer weight of the professionalism of the witness, the numbers of unconnected witnesses, the degree of corroboration by radar, and the fact that the sightings have never been convincingly explained all make one confident that something happened that cannot yet be explained.

Almost all authors of books about UFOs experience grave difficulties in the task of dividing sightings up in order to help the reader cope. The easiest way is to divide them up chronologically or geographically. In this book, for example, I could have segmented the sightings by decade or perhaps by place: the United States, the UK, and Europe. Such segmentation helps to show that sightings have occurred over the last seventy years or across two continents plus an offshore island nation, but those approaches ignore the central premise of the book, which is that these objects get seen in roughly the same way whenever and wherever they are seen. So dividing them according to time or place is pretty senseless. Possibly even misleading.

The problem is that there are many other ways of doing the job. One could look at who saw them, what time of day, where the witnesses were at the time, what the objects did, what they looked like, how they behaved, and on and on. I just hope you appreciate the anguish I've been through.

In the end, I opted to arrange the sightings under headings related to who saw them and where, but the bottom line is that every single case could be categorised in a different way and still be every bit as fascinating. Most could appear under more than one heading, and quite a few under all.

Still, there it is.

I also make no apology for including cases from as far back as the 1950s. The types of object, features, actions, and characteristics of UFO sightings over time are pretty similar across several generations of people who cannot have known each other. They are also uncannily similar across cultures and nations.

What follows are a few chapters containing the plums, the most mysterious and intriguing of the hitherto unexplained cases.

CHAPTER 11

UFOs and the Police

SCEPTICS USUALLY DISCOUNT THE police as witnesses for the same sorts of reasons that they ignore trained professional pilots: because "they can make mistakes no matter how professional they are". So what's new? Doctors make mistakes too but we still go to consult them and still trust them with our lives.

I've included these three cases because police officers were important witnesses, and I am afraid that I am one of those people who believes that, whatever the situation, it is simply more probable that a police officer will be a reliable witness. The police are certainly as fallible as the rest of us. Nevertheless, while a single officer can sometimes get it wrong, it is much less likely that several officers will do so on the same occasion.

Police sightings in Britain go back to the Peterborough sighting in 1909 and the Devon Cross incident of the 1960s. In the US they include the Lonnie Zamora case and several other cases cited in this book, such as the Hudson Valley and some of the airbase events. The best European example in this book is that of the bewildered policemen who chased a UFO during the Belgian flap of 1989-91.

When a policeman says he's seen something strange, one has to sit up and listen. When no one else can convincingly explain what he's seen, then that constitutes real grist to the outsider's mill. And when two or more police officers see the same thing on the same occasion, the mill really begins to hum.

Exeter, 1965

Date: September 1965
Location: Route 150 near Exeter, New Hampshire
Type of Sighting: Visual
Type of Prime Witness: Young male civilian and several police officers
Other Witnesses: Female car driver

A good example of the way in which sceptical organisations and individuals deal with UFO issues is that of the famous Exeter incident in 1965. It's now a fifty-year-old sighting, but it remains extremely difficult to explain away. CSICOP's researchers claimed in 2011 that they had finally nailed it down; they announced "CSICOP Solves the Exeter Mystery".[85] The case, the CSICOP solution, and some thoughts on that solution are set out below.

The state of New Hampshire is usually associated with mountains and verdant valleys in the summer and snow and ski slopes in winter. Even those who know New England quite well sometimes forget that the state also possesses a seashore. For about eighteen miles, this sliver of shoreline extends south of the port of Portsmouth, and it is in this rough area that these events took place back in 1965.

Three locations are important in this incident: the town of Exeter, New Hampshire, Pease US Air Force Base, which lay near Portsmouth, and the Kensington area. They form an elongated, narrow triangle, with Pease at the northern end, Exeter about six or seven miles south-west, and then Kensington about five miles further south from Exeter.

At the time of the incident, Pease AFB was one of the largest bases in the US Strategic Air Command. It has since been transformed into a joint civilian airport and Air National Guard base. In late August and

---

[85] See James McGaha and Joe Nickell. "'Exeter Incident' Solved! A Classic UFO Case, Forty-Five Years 'Cold'. *Skeptical Inquirer* 35, 6, Nov./Dec. 2011: http://www.csicop. org/si/show/exeter_incident_solved_a_classic_ufo_case_forty-five_years_cold

early September 1965, Pease, with its strategic jet bombers (B-47s) and their refuelling aircraft (Boeing KC-97s and KC-135s), was involved in a Strategic Air Command/NORAD exercise called Big Blast.

A Boeing KC–97 tanker aircraft of the type involved in Exercise Big Blast in August 1965. (Raimundo79/Shutterstock.com)

But the story begins miles from the noise and bustle of an airbase coming to the end of a major military exercise. It begins, like all great thriller stories, on a quiet and nearly deserted main road, very early in the morning of September 3, 1965.

At around 2 a.m., an eighteen-year-old lad named Norman Muscarello was hitch-hiking north on Route 150. He was walking to his home in Exeter from his girlfriend's house in Amesbury, Massachusetts, a distance of about ten miles (young love, huh?). Traffic was sparse at that time in the morning; it was not exactly prime hitch-hiking time, so he'd had trouble getting a lift.

The young man had reached about the two-thirds mark in his journey home. As he was passing some houses and a farm, he noticed, off to his right, flashing red lights which appeared to be in some woods. The red lights were very bright, and there were five of them describing an angle of approximately 60 degrees. They lit up the woods and a nearby farm-house. He later mentioned that the animals in the barn were making a lot of noise, and this was corroborated by one of the police officers who later witnessed the lights.

Just after he first saw them, the lights evidently came towards Muscarello at a good speed from the north. They scared him, and he fled across the road, only to trip into the ditch at the side, from which somewhat ignominious position he could see the red lights bathing the side of the house next to the road. Now completely spooked, he heaved himself to his feet, ran to the front door of the house, and hammered hard. It turned out that the owners (the Russells) were in bed. They heard him hammering but, understandably at that time in the morning, decided not to answer the door. At that moment, Muscarello heard a car and ran back into the centre of the road to flag it down. There was no way, he said later, that he was going to allow it to get past him.

The couple in the car took him to Exeter Police Station, where the desk officer (named Toland) said he wasn't surprised at Muscarello's story because he'd heard two similar reports that very night. One of the reports was from Officer Eugene Bertrand, Jr. It described a lady who'd told Bertrand that her car had been chased down the road by red lights. Toland now asked Bertrand to look into Muscarello's story.

Almost certainly with a shrug and the thought that it was to be one of those nights, Bertrand ushered the youngster out of the station. Together they got into his police cruiser and the officer drove them back to the place where the lights had been seen. Amazingly, when they arrived, the lights were still there. Almost immediately, Bertrand and Muscarello saw an "object" rise up from the woods. Bertrand described it as "this huge, dark object as big as a barn ... with red flashing lights on it".

The object moved slowly towards them, swaying back and forth. Bertrand was so concerned that he actually drew his firearm before he and the lad scooted back to the patrol car.[86] They watched the object hover "100 feet away and at 100 feet altitude", rocking back and forth. The red lights evidently flashed in a regular sequence, right to left, then left to right. At that point, a second police officer, named Hunt, arrived from Hampton

---

[86] Both Muscarello's and Bertrand's full statements can be found in Hynek, 1977.

and also saw the object until it flew away over the woods and disappeared towards the east (that is, towards Hampton and the sea). Hunt also saw a B-47 bomber fly over just after the incident and stressed to an interviewer (John Fuller) that he could tell the difference between the bomber and the object. There was no comparison, he said. There were other similar sightings around Exeter over the following weeks.

The accounts of this incident have been pretty consistent over the years, apart from the occasional small error. For example, some accounts have the young man hammering on the door of the nearby farm (the Dining farm), from which the owners were absent that night. Readers who want to scan what must be a fairly trustworthy version, from the horse's mouth, should read the accounts placed on a local website which is run by the author J Dennis Robinson. In 1980, fifteen years after the event, Muscarello gave a unique interview to the students of Exeter High School. The transcript and accounts of the event, and his interview with the students, are available on the SeacoastNH.com website.[87]

Theories

There have been lots of theories as to what Muscarello and the two policemen saw that September morning. They began with the USAF suggestion that they had mistaken stars and planets twinkling in the clear air. The Air Force then came up with weather inversions[88] and planes from the SAC/NORAD Big Blast exercise. But the witnesses stuck to their stories, even though the two policemen said they were being ridiculed at work. The two officers who, it must be repeated, were from different counties, said that at

---

[87] http://www.seacoastnh.com/Famous-People/Link-Free-or-Die/norman-muscarello-recalls-his-ufo-incident-at-exeter/?showall=1 plus further details and photos of Muscarello: http://www.seacoastnh.com/History/As-I-Please/The-Incident-at-Exeter-High/

[88] It's not at all clear why weather inversions were mooted as a cause by the Air Force. An abrupt change of temperature at a given altitude can create what is effectively a barrier to radar waves and produce false reflections. But inversions do not produce red lights or objects in the visual spectrum.

the time of the sighting, they had checked and rechecked with each other that what they were seeing was not one or more aircraft. They confirmed that whatever the object was, it was absolutely silent, and they also said it lit up the entire field and nearby houses and barns.

When Norman Muscarello died at the very early age of fifty-five in April 2003, he still insisted that what he had witnessed was real and not an ordinary object.

There have been many attempts by sceptics to explain the sightings, including "fire balloons" (hot air balloons) and "flare balloons". Given that some of these carry red lights, the theory goes that they might have misled the young Muscarello and the two police officers. But quite apart from the facts that there's absolutely no corroboration of balloons being in the area that night at that time, and that it staggers the imagination to believe that people were out at well after 2 a.m. setting off flare balloons or doing a little hot-air ballooning, Muscarello clearly said the object *approached* him from the north or a little east of north. A balloon, no matter how many red lights it was showing and flashing, would have drifted with the prevailing wind, which Pease AFB said was westerly that night (that is *from* the west). It could not have drifted against the wind in a south or south-westerly direction, an objection supported by the way the object is said to have behaved when Officer Bertrand was on the scene.

There's also the small matter of fire (hot-air) balloons being bathed in their own light once they are aloft. Even on the darkest of nights, the light from the burners cannot help but illuminate the balloon itself. It is fairly certain that two policemen and an eighteen-year-old would, between them, recognise one or more balloons.

In spite of all the theories, the incident has never been explained.

Until, that is, CSICOP's *Skeptical Enquirer* published a proposed solution in December 2011.[89] Researchers James McGaha and Joe Nickell had looked again into the case and had decided that the answer was that the witnesses had simply seen the lights of an aerial refuelling event.

---

[89] James McGaha and Joe Nickell. "'Exeter Incident' Solved! A Classic UFO Case, Forty-Five Years 'Cold'". *Skeptical Inquirer* 35, 6, November/December 2011: http://www.csicop.org/si/archive/category/volume_35.6

McGaha is a retired air force pilot and says he recognised the sequence of red lights described by the witnesses as being the same as those flashed from the underside of a KC-97 air refuelling aircraft to guide other aircraft seeking to dock with the refuelling boom. The boom deployed, he said, at an angle of 64 degrees (this was roughly the same angle as Muscarello said the red lights were being displayed when he first saw them). The CSICOP solution, therefore, was that the flashing red lights from the tankers were what the witnesses saw, sometimes reflected from the refuelling boom at the 60 degree angle.

The lady who said she was "chased down the road" by flashing red lights was, in their opinion, also seeing the lights from a refuelling boom.

It's absolutely true that KC-97 radial-engined refuelers were operating out of Pease AFB at that time. The KC-97 was obsolete and was retired completely in December 1965. Nevertheless, it may have been used during the September Big Blast exercise to refuel the B-47 jet bombers. It's also very possible that the exercise had aircraft in the air well after its official 2 a.m. completion time on September 3 (Officer Hunt said he saw one).

A more modern Boeing KC-135 air-refuelling tanker showing the type of boom which would have also been deployed by a KC-97. (InsectWorld/Shutterstock.com)

The problems with the CSICOP solution would seem, however, to be as follows:

1. Air refuelling generally takes place at safe altitudes (too much danger of mid-air collisions and other accidents) and, wherever possible, over the sea or uninhabited land. In the event of an accident, the authorities tend to frown upon tons of burning fuel falling over an inhabited area. The way it worked (and still does) is that the refuelling aircraft are given a set "circuit" to fly and an exact geographical location for the circuit; a little like airliner "holding patterns" which most major airports today are forced to use at busy times. The big refuelling planes establish themselves at the assigned altitude, in the right location, and then wait for the planes in need of fuel to come to them. The roughly oval refuelling circuits might be fifty or more miles or more in length and twenty miles or so in width. They are strictly adhered to so that other aircraft keep clear, and the planes in need of fuel know where to find them.

    The main refuelling areas for Big Blast were well out to sea. But in the unlikely event that part of a refuelling pattern on that day was over land, any tanker aircraft would only have been above a given spot for a few seconds – even at the KC-97's slow cruising speed of 260 mph.[90] The normal altitude for refuelling was about fifteen to twenty thousand feet, and at that altitude, some three or four miles up, those red flashing lights on the underside of the KC-97 would have been mere specs among the stars. And that's if they were directly overhead. There is almost no chance at all that they would bathe an entire wood, and then a neighbouring house, in red light for minutes at a time, or appear as an "object" which moved towards the observers.

---

[90] The speed had to be at least 260 mph but not much more (too much fuel would be burned) because the jets that the aircraft was refuelling would struggle to maintain such a slow speed unless they were quite close to their stall speeds at that altitude. Sometimes, the KC-97s would have to go into a shallow dive when refueling certain jets simply because those aircraft would have come close to stalling at a mere 260 mph.

2. The lights were seen brightly by Muscarello, Bertrand, and Hunt, low in the sky, in the trees, and down behind a house. If the two men were seeing a KC-97 through or just above trees, the aircraft must have been a long way away for it to also be at refuelling altitude (and that's the only time the red lights would have been flashing). There is no chance that the red lights from a refuelling boom way out to sea would have illuminated the trees or the farm. Muscarello said he watched the lights in roughly the same place for fifteen minutes: enough time for the KC-97 to have covered around sixty miles.

3. The lady whom Officer Bertrand helped, before he returned to the station and met Muscarello, told him that the flashing red lights had followed her car on Route 101 for twelve miles and had stopped over her car before flying away. The CSICOP report does not explicitly deal with this episode (one wonders why), but for this to be a KC-97, it would have been breaking all sorts of major air force flying rules as well as a few laws of physics and self-preservation. Beating up civilian cars on highways at night is not in the rule book. A stunt like that would also have been suicidally stupid. For the lady driver to have been so scared by the red lights, the plane would have had to be very low indeed with its boom extended. At night, no sane pilot would have risked such a prank, and most especially not in a large and unwieldy, four-engined aircraft with fuel tanks full of fuel or fumes. The thunder of those four radial engines might also have given the game away. There's also the slight problem of the words "followed" and "stopped". The lady said the lights followed her and stopped overhead. A plane travelling at 100 mph or 150 mph would very soon overtake a car doing 40 mph – that's not what a driver would call following or stopping overhead!

4. Both Muscarello and Bertrand stated very clearly that the object, whatever it was, came towards them and got quite close. In fact, it got so close to Muscarello that he ran and fell into a ditch and, later, so close to Officer Bertrand that he drew his gun. It

was pretty late, so one could forgive a lone hitch-hiker having an optical illusion and getting scared. But for two men to have the self-same illusion half an hour or so later and for an experienced policeman to get so worried that he drew his gun would be stretching things a bit far. All three of the witnesses spoke about an "object", not simply lights.

5. The two CSICOP researchers suggested that the red flashing lights were visible to the witness at an angle of about 60 degrees because they were being reflected off the refueler's boom. Setting aside the fact that refuelling lights would only have been used at well above fifteen thousand feet and that they would almost certainly have been miles away, there is also the problem that the boom on those aircraft was either a dulled aluminium or painted white. At that distance, the red lights, even if they actually could have been reflected off the boom, would have been faint to invisible. Indeed, if a refuelling boom could throw bright red lights many miles into the night, it would be an absolutely gift to an enemy fighter plane, and if that's the case, the USAF probably needs to rethink that particular gadget.

6. Quite apart from the surface material of the refuelling boom (either dull aluminium or white paint), the booms were tubular. Therefore, any reflection from the red guide lights would be dispersed and substantially dimmed across a 90 or 180 degree area by the shape of the boom.

7. Intelligence officers from Pease were at the scene very quickly to interview the witnesses, but CSICOP argues that they missed the significance of the red lights amid a "welter of paperwork". That is stretching the outsider's credulity to breaking point. These were intelligence officers; their whole *raison d'etre* was detail and putting together vital facts. They asked many questions, and one has to sincerely doubt that they would miss something as significant as red lights flashing in sequence. No one during those investigations by air force professionals came up with the "refuelling boom" theory, and there's probably a good reason for that. If it

were even remotely plausible, USAF intelligence officers from a base from which tanker aircraft flew on a regular basis would have had their suspicions and just might have questioned the refueler's pilots quite closely.

Whatever scared Norman Muscarello and Officers Bertrand and Hunt half to death on that September morning near Exeter, New Hampshire, is still unexplained.

Michigan, 1966

Date: March 1966
Locations: Several mainly rural locations
Type of Sighting: Visual and radar (alleged)
Type of Prime Witness: Police officers, sheriff's deputies
Other Witnesses: Many civilians

This was the famous "swamp gas" affair which bedevilled Dr J Allen Hynek for almost the rest of his life. In fact, he once called it "the low point in my life".

It all began on March 14, 1966, at about 3.50 a.m., when seven police officers and sheriff's deputies saw lighted objects near Dexter, Michigan (which lies to the north-west of Ann Arbor). There were also around a hundred other witnesses to the collective sightings. The law officers recounted that they watched objects travelling at fantastic speeds, rising and diving, hovering, and making sharp turns.

During the night, objects were seen by different county sheriff's officers, and at one point, the police evidently logged that Selfridge AFB (north of Ann Arbor) had tracked unidentified objects over Lake Erie.

Students, from a Michigan University campus to the north of Dexter, watched a football-shaped object swanning around for no less than four hours. The police and other witnesses later put together a composite sketch of the object which stressed its shape and that it had a surface which seemed "quilted", plus lights to each side and in the middle. The "quilted surface" aspect was reported on at least two occasions by different witnesses.

Three days later, on March 17, two local sheriff's deputies watched red, white, and green circular objects oscillating and glowing near Milan (about eight miles south of Ann Arbor) at about 4 a.m.

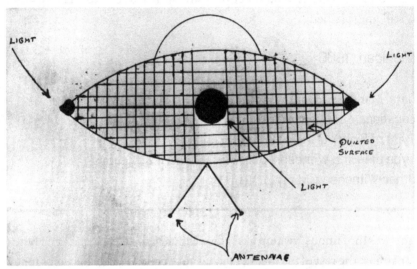

A drawing of the "quilted" object seen by many witnesses during the Michigan sightings in 1966. (Granger, NYC/Topfoto.co.uk)

On March 20, a patrolman from Dexter (Robert Huniwell) reported seeing an object in the sky between 9.30 p.m. and 9.45 p.m. He described it as having red and green flashing lights and said it came close to the ground, hovered, and was then accompanied by a second object when it ascended. That sighting was convincing enough for the Washtenaw County sheriff, Douglas Harvey, to divert all his available deputies to the scene. That meant six patrol cars and a dozen officers, plus three detectives. Later that evening, some of them chased a flying object northwest along Island Lake Road without catching up to it. A chap called Frank Mannor, together with his family, also saw the lights from their farm, which lay near McGuiness Road (a little to the east and north of Island Lake Road).

Mannor explained that the object came within five hundred yards. He described it as pyramid-shaped with lights and what seemed to be a porthole. He said it made noises like a siren at times, and then like a bullet ricochet, and it changed colours several times. A local police chief and patrolman who attended the scene also heard the noises. They later said it sounded like an ambulance. Sheriff's officers chased it, or another similar object, for five miles at up to 70 mph (they said the object was doing around 100 mph at the time) but claimed that it disappeared in an instant. Mannor and his family were clearly upset by the events. His wife evidently wanted to leave the area. On March 22, several dozen residents of Dexter, and nearby Hillsdale, reported more flying objects with lights which, they said, emitted strange sounds.

At that point, Project Blue Book's then chief, Major Hector Quintanilla, sent in astronomer Allen Hynek, who, at a local press conference, dismissed the sightings as "swamp gas". Hynek famously explained that the lights of swamp gas "resemble tiny flames, sometimes seen right on the ground, sometimes merely floating above it. The flames go out in one place and suddenly appear in another, giving the illusion of motion. The colours are sometimes yellow, sometimes red and blue-green". He went on to say that the gas was odourless but could give off slight popping noises.

Needless to say, Hynek's explanations caused a major fracas. Local people were almost incandescent with rage at his words. A man named Van Horn, a resident of the Hillsdale area, who grew up on the edge of a swamp, was particularly upset by Hynek's explanation. He said he knew more about swamp gas than Hynek did and that the astronomer had ignored the fact that the lights were higher, moved more, and that there was a convex surface between them. He claimed that the US Air Force (i.e. Project Blue Book) was ridiculing a lot of good people. There were more sightings in late March and beyond, some clearly hoaxes, but at least one credible sighting was by a sheriff's deputy and a police chief.

The Michigan sightings of 1966 have received their fair share of attention from sceptics; there have been many proposed explanations, but the quality and numbers of the original witnesses and the sheer number of additional sightings (including one of an alleged landing) are fascinating. Clearly, Hynek's swamp gas theory does not explain sightings in non-swampy areas or those reported by police officers as being high in the sky, moving erratically, and at very high speed. From the outsider's viewpoint, there is also the very strange way in which the objects were reported as sometimes appearing to be "in trouble" – coming very low, then rising, and then descending again, making loud noises (the unstable flight characteristic is fairly common but the loud noises are not).

J Allen Hynek addressing the press and others during the famous "swamp gas" explanation. (Fortean/Topfoto.co.uk)

Cosford, 1993

Date: March 30 and 31, 1993
Locations: Devon/Somerset/Staffordshire; RAF Cosford(*); RAF Shawbury(**); UK
Type of Sighting: Visual
Type of Prime Witness: RAF police and RAF officer
Other Witnesses: Civilian police officer and members of the public

Notes

(*) Cosford has almost always been a major RAF training site. In 1993, it focused on technical training, and today it offers a wide range of associated training services.
(**) In 1993, Shawbury had a few Air Training Corps Chipmunks as its only fixed-wing aircraft. Its main role by then was as a helicopter training school, operating mainly Gazelles.

Although these UK sightings in 1993 are generally known by the name RAF Cosford (situated to the north-west of Wolverhampton), the sightings were actually spread over a much wider area, including another RAF base at Shawbury. Members of the public, civilian police, and RAF police all witnessed one or more triangular craft or sets of lights travelling at high speeds. In the case of the Cosford sighting, military police testified that a craft shot over the base at a height of around a thousand feet.

Nick Pope, who was then on the MoD UFO desk, wrote to his boss on April 16, 1993:

> "It seems that an unidentified object of unknown origin was operating in the UK Air Defence Region without being detected on radar; this would appear to be of considerable defence significance, and I recommend

that we investigate further, within MoD or with the US authorities."[91]

His boss agreed and wrote to the assistant chief of the Air Staff on April 22, 1993:

"In summary, there would seem to be some evidence on this occasion that an unidentified object (or objects) of unknown origin was operating over the UK."

The sightings which comprise the Cosford incident are extremely interesting for the outsider. The story involves almost every aspect of the UFO issue, from sightings of objects by trained people to some ingenious potential explanations by sceptics. I have appended some comments on those explanations.

Today, it is one of the most bitterly contested incidents between sceptics and ufologists. But we'll come to that later. First, let's look at the main account of the sightings.

According to West Country UFO investigators, it began with a series of UFOs being reported in the south-west of England from early evening on March 30 to early morning on March 31.

At about 8.30 p.m. on the evening of March 30, 1993, a civilian reported a UFO in Somerset. About half an hour or so later, in the Quantock Hills (which stretch to the Bristol Channel in North Somerset), an off-duty police officer and a group of scouts saw a wedge-shaped "something" that the policeman famously described as looking like two Concordes stuck together. A later witness, further north, in Staffordshire, repeated that approximate description and said that whatever it was, it was about two hundred metres across.

Just a little further to the north of that sighting lies the city of Wolverhampton and, near it, to the north-west, the RAF training base of Cosford, where a two-man RAF police patrol saw an object travel over the

---

[91] Nick Pope, 1996.

base at very high speed at an estimated one thousand feet. They said it was silent, and they saw two white lights and a red glow at the rear.

Early the next morning, at about 2.40 a.m., an RAF meteorological officer saw a slow-moving object in the distance. Based at RAF Shawbury (which is to the north-west of Cosford), the officer was on his way to release a weather balloon when he saw an object moving slowly over the countryside at about 30 mph or 40 mph. He saw its lights first, about eight to ten miles away. As the object neared the base, it shot a beam of white light down onto the ground and swept it backwards and forwards, as though searching for something just beyond the base boundary fence. The officer said that he could hear and feel a low humming sound coming from the object. It was large. He estimated its size as somewhere between a C-130 Hercules and a Boeing 747. He watched as the object then passed over his head and sped away to the horizon at an incredible speed.

That is the account as it would be recognised by the UFO investigators and, indeed, in the records which were created by the police and MoD. The sceptics have been examining this case for many years, but recently, they announced that they had solved it, and the explanations were perfectly rational and commonplace.

Their solution falls into three parts:

1. Mistaken stars/planets/objects sighted by civilians in the West Country, which were then talked up by the local UFO investigator;
2. A Russian rocket stage burn-up, which fooled the RAF Security police at Cosford; and,
3. A police helicopter seen across an airfield at night, which was mistaken for a totally unknown object by the RAF meteorologist.

Some sceptics have raised the additional possibility of "secret" aircraft flights being responsible, but no one has really accepted that explanation as being plausible.

The first part of the suggested solutions has been to ignore the sightings in the West Country on the basis that they were by civilians and were reported to the MoD by a UFO investigator who, the implication is, "encouraged" the witnesses or, in some accounts, actually twisted the facts to suit the hypothesis that it or they were inexplicable objects. The sceptics have, however, failed to explain why the scoutmaster described "stars and planets" as two Concordes stuck together and why a separate witness in Staffordshire agreed with him.

The second part was to explain the RAF Cosford sighting by the two-man RAF police patrol. The sceptics say that the military policemen actually saw the burn-up of the final stage of a Russian rocket. That evening, the Russians had launched a Tsyklon rocket to place the Cosmos 2238 satellite into orbit.

NASA believes that the debris from this final booster would have re-entered the Earth's atmosphere at between 1 a.m. and 1.15 a.m. on the morning of March 31, leaving burning debris falling through the upper air in a direction from north-west to south-east over Ireland and the south and Midlands of Great Britain.

The NASA plot concluded that almost anyone in the UK and Ireland, as well as the inhabitants of northern France and Spain, could have seen the debris burn up. David Clarke wrote up the sceptics' answers in an article in 2005 which is now on his website.[92] The article effectively argues that the whole thing was misinterpreted and exaggerated by Nick Pope, who was then responsible for receiving and analysing UFO reports for the MoD. At one point in the article, Clarke says

"... the correct time for the decay [according to the NASA simulation] was in fact 1.15am local time, leaving no doubt this indeed was the source of the UFO flap."

It's quite amazing when reading the debates between ufologists and sceptics how frequently one side or the other can state something as a definite "fact" or in very exact terms when, in reality, the event is much less certain. In this case, there are two sources of doubt: whether the two policemen really misinterpreted a rocket burn-up for "two white lights"

[92] David Clarke. "The Cosford Incident." *Fortean Times, 199;* 2005.

and a red glow behind which were just a thousand feet above them, and secondly, whether NASA's timeslot was as firm as it sounds.

NASA ran a simulation based on its best guesses as to the re-entry time. It got an answer of 1 a.m. to 1.15 a.m., but as the United Nations was informed by Dr William Ailor, the exact time of *any* re-entry can be out by as much as 10 to 25 percent.[93] And this is when the precise speeds and data from the launch are known. Space debris does not run to a time-table. Its decay can be influenced by a million variables. In the case of the Russian launch, NASA would have had a pretty accurate launch time but no telemetry from the rocket. The exact time and speed at which it reached orbital height and at which the final stage of the rocket separated from the payload could only be estimated. The time at which the final stage itself started to burn up would depend on factors such as the angle at which it first encountered serious resistance from the air, its precise speed at that point, and the extremely variable density of the upper atmosphere at that specific point above the planet.

The time frame therefore was exactly what NASA said it was: based on best-guesses. The error could have been anything from thirty minutes to an hour either way. There are also the characteristics of a rocket-stage burn-up to take into account.

A rocket stage is, unlike a decaying satellite, very prone to break up quickly and to decay quite fast. It burns up faster because the individual pieces are lighter. This is because it is fundamentally a tube with one or more empty fuel tanks which have high aerodynamic drag. As the tube and its contents encounter the upper atmosphere, the air rips the casing apart and can then proceed to rip out the contents. Each will burn up separately. It takes about sixty seconds for the trail of the debris, breaking up as it goes, to travel right across the sky. That sort of display would leave no doubt in the RAF policemen's minds that what they were seeing was either a meteorite or some space junk.

There are scores of videos online showing space debris breaking up, including some good ones of the final stages of the huge Chinese Long

---

[93] http://www.unoosa.org/pdf/pres/stsc2012/tech-39E.pdf

March rockets. One was filmed in 2016 by numerous witnesses in the western United States.[94] Almost all debris provides a spectacular show, quite like a meteorite at first but then more like a good firework display. You will have to make up your own mind as to whether these events look like what the police witnesses were describing in England back in 1993.[95] Would *you* have mistaken any of them for a strange object at a thousand feet?

Then there is the sighting of something by an RAF meteorologist. David Clarke says that the officer actually saw a police helicopter searching for something, perhaps cars, on the nearby main road.

In his original handwritten note, the meteorologist said he'd seen an object with three red lights, which was, in size, somewhere between a C-130 Hercules and a Boeing 747. He said it shot a laser-like beam of white light down onto the ground as though searching for something. The police report says he told them that he'd first seen the object about eight to twelve miles away and that it came towards him "travelling at hundreds of miles per hour". It was, he'd said, unlike anything he'd seen before.

His original, very brief, handwritten report said that he'd seen the object at 2.40 a.m. local time. It had been stationary but then began to move – first upwards and then in a zigzag motion. He'd noted two red lights and the narrow, laser-like beam. At its lowest, it reached about four to five hundred feet about half to one mile from the airfield. The officer's report then stated quite clearly that the object departed "directly overhead, at approximately 4,000 feet, heading almost due south". At this point, he saw three red lights (two side by side and one larger flashing red light behind the others). It was in this handwritten report that the meteorologist estimated the object's size at between that of a C-130 (Hercules) and a Boeing 747.

Nick Pope claimed that the witness told him that the object made no

---

[94] Burn-up of the final stage of a Long March rocket, July 2016: http://spaceflight101. com/long-march-7-maiden-launch/fireball-over-western-u-s-chinese-rocket-debris/

[95] The Long March re-entry object weighed about six tons. In its shallow trajectory and at relatively slow speed, it took about one minute to cross the sky. The Russian Tsyklon stage weighed less than four tons and would have burned up a little faster.

sound except a low humming. David Clarke interviewed the officer more recently and quotes part of the interview as follows:

> "At the time it did not strike me as being something familiar," he [the meteorologist] told me. "However, it's clear in hindsight that what I saw was not the same object seen at Cosford as it was much later. I never made anything of it, I just reported what I had seen. Nick Pope was very excited about it and made a great deal of the fact that I was an official observer which was true. He assured me that he had checked with all the military sources for aircraft and ruled them out ... I believed what I was told at the time, but now I'm convinced that what I saw has been explained. I have to accept that the noise like a humming and the beam of light are very similar to what you would expect of a police helicopter".[96]

But there's something in his choice of words which might make one think that, being now very senior, and in the national and international spotlight, he might well want to put that strange sighting well behind him. His statement seems carefully worded: "are very similar to what you would expect of a police helicopter". This is not the same as saying "I made a mistake; what I saw was a police helicopter". His original statement also says that the object approached the base at "hundreds of miles an hour". This is too fast for any police helicopter. Neither does his retraction address the size as being between a C-130 Hercules and a 747. That's a very large police helicopter. There is also the fact that he said the object passed right over his head.

Again, the outsider has to decide whether, working on a base from which helicopters were operating day-in and day-out, he mistook a police helicopter as it passed right over his head for something much less familiar. I live beneath a regular tourist and military helicopter run and,

---

[96] David Clarke. *The Cosford Incident*. 2011.

even though they pass over at about 2,000 feet or more, they make a tremendous racket. I would never fail to identify them as helicopters (day or night) or report their infernal noise as "humming".

For some reason, and one has to assume it is to throw yet more doubt on the capacity of the meteorologist to observe accurately, David Clarke also points out that the man did not report an aircraft which, by Clarke's estimation, was directly overhead at 2.46 a.m. The MoD radar report could not find anything unusual, but for that night, it had one entry which Clarke thinks is important:

310140z Clee-Hill Squawk 2304/200 descending on A25. At 0146z overhead Shawbury squawk 5231/203 southbound.[97]

This is aviation-speak for "aircraft interrogated at 0140 Zulu (0240 British Summer Time) is at 20,000 feet and descending on Airway Alpha 25" (which runs south roughly from the Scottish borders south of Glasgow, along the Welsh borders and then across Cardiff, the Bristol Channel and Devon, and out into the English Channel from about Exeter). There's no indication of whether the aircraft whose identifying squawk was 2304 was travelling north or south. Neither are we told whether it was the same aircraft, travelling south at twenty thousand three hundred feet (squawk 5231) six minutes later (if it was, then it was not descending in accordance with normal aviation practice. For a decent-sized aircraft usually between about fifteen hundred and eighteen hundred feet per minute). So if it was the same aircraft, it should have been reporting an altitude of about eleven thousand feet.

However, the key for Dr Clarke is that the aircraft reported itself as "overhead Shawbury" and should, he believes, have been noted by the meteorologist. But why? Dr Clarke's implied conclusion is that, because the officer did not see the aircraft, this places doubt on whether he also saw the object. Firstly, high flying aircraft are a fact of our modern lives,

---

[97] AIS Memo of April 19, 1993.

night or day. How many of us even notice them anymore? If one can assume for a moment that the RAF officer *did* see something very strange on the boundary fence and travelling very fast across Shawbury airfield, is it any wonder that he did not notice the pinpoint navigation lights of an airliner at twenty thousand feet in an entirely different direction to the one in which he was looking? The aircraft, also, may not have been exactly "overhead" anyway.

Clee Hill Radar Station was, that night, not able to use its primary radar and was using only what is called secondary surveillance radar (SSR). This does not sound like much to be concerned about, but actually it makes a big difference.

SSR is not radar at all; it is a sophisticated communications system which uses a directional antenna to "interrogate" a gadget called a transponder on the aircraft. SSR is very definitely not a positional radar (that's what primary radar is for: giving operators a location and height for the blips it paints on the screen). With SSR, the aircraft is asked a question and in return sends back an automatic message giving the aircraft height. The operators at Clee Hill got a time, a height, and the direction of their antenna would give a *rough* bearing to the aircraft. When the aircraft was interrogated again a few minutes later, a second bearing would indicate direction of travel. The pilot would have to tell the controller roughly where the aircraft was.

So, "overhead Shawbury", given the pilots' view from three and half miles in the sky, would be anything from absolutely dead over the runway centre-line to possibly ten or fifteen miles either side.

It has to be said that Clarke is pushing it to try to imply that the meteorologist's testimony is suspect simply because he did not mention that particular aircraft.[98] But Clarke is sure that the man was watching a police helicopter searching for something with its powerful searchlight. That might well be the case, but any RAF meteorologist at Shawbury could not be a novice around helicopters. It is pretty difficult to imagine any of us mistaking a police helicopter a few hundred yards away for something

---

[98] See also http://www.uk-ufo.org/cosford/index.html

the size of a 747. When a helicopter is in the air, it banks and turns; one would never describe its flight as a zigzag (as the RAF officer described that of the object). The lights (see below) are also a problem; the noise from those beasts is ear-shattering at low altitudes, and the meteorologist said it departed right over his head. It beggars belief to imagine that he would not have recognised the object as a helicopter in those circumstances.

However, Clarke and several others use the following quote, supposedly from an airman at Shawbury to explain what really happened:

> "The UFO supposedly seen at RAF Shawbury was later identified as a Dyfed-Powys police helicopter following a stolen car down the A5 between the A49 junction [sic] ... The observer was using his NiteSun to illuminate proceedings."

It's a strange quote because it is difficult to understand what "down the A5 between the A49 junction" means. Assuming the police helicopter was searching the junction area (where the A5 and A49 meet) or perhaps the A5 itself, it would be to the south-west of the base. One wonders therefore why the object that the meteorologist saw would be searching to the north of the base – well away from those main roads – to be seen approaching by the meteorologist, and then fly south across the base at four thousand feet and not be recognised as a helicopter by someone who worked around them every day.

Hands up those of you who would not recognise a helicopter's flight pattern, lights, and noise at that height.

One really wants to ask the ex-RAF meteorologist where, exactly, he first saw the object, what course and height it followed, how the lights might have differed from normal aircraft navigation lights, and so on. But we are a quarter of a century too late because he has now changed the testimony he gave in all seriousness to the police on that night. Not for the first time one is left envying the French attention to detailed records and immediate investigations of such events.

CHAPTER 12

UFOs and Airbases

THERE ARE SCORES OF good quality reports of UFOs being seen around military airbases, missile sites, sensitive research establishments, and civilian airports. Nobody has yet published an analysis of decent-sized databases, which would be necessary to understand whether these types of areas attract proportionately more sightings or whether they simply occur in places where the guards and employees are a great deal more vigilant and observant than the average civilian.

Lakenheath, 1956

Date: August 13 and 14, 1956
Locations: RAF Lakenheath; RAF Bentwaters; UK
Type of Sighting: Multiple radar and visual
Type of Prime Witness: USAF radar operators in two separate bases
Other Witnesses: Control tower staff and RAF pilots

Although relatively unknown, this event is probably among the top ten UFO incidents of all time. The reason is that unknown objects were tracked by radar on this night, during an event for which even the Condon report failed to find answers. An object or objects were recorded on at least two separate ground radars, seen by a transport pilot and a ground observer, located on a fighter's night radar, seen briefly by that pilot, and then watched on radar as it moved rapidly around the sky. The event lasted not seconds or minutes but hours.

At about eleven o'clock on the evening of August 13, the radar at RAF Bentwaters[99] recorded an object passing across the base against the prevailing wind, moving from east to west. The apparent speed of the object was between 2,000 mph and 4,000 mph. A light was seen by control tower staff at the same time at an estimated height of about four thousand feet. A transport pilot flying over the base at four thousand feet at the time reported a similar object passing below his aircraft.

Because the object was travelling west (inland), Bentwaters called up their colleagues at RAF Lakenheath (another USAF base), whose radar operators spotted a stationary object about forty miles south-west of the base. The radar operators then watched as the object suddenly went from a standstill to between 400 mph and 700 mph, changing direction frequently and going between eight and twenty miles before stopping abruptly for a few minutes and then starting off again.

Lakenheath was obliged, at the time, to send a telexed report to the US Project Blue Book. In that report, they said that the instances of radar confirmation of rapid acceleration and abrupt halts, allied with visual observations from the ground, gave the sightings "definite credibility".

The RAF despatched a Venom twin-seat night-fighter, which the American controllers vectored onto the object which was, by now, about six miles east of Lakenheath base. The crew of the Venom got the object on their radar, and the pilot saw it ahead but then lost it. The object had now moved very quickly twelve miles east of the airfield, and the Venom was, once more, vectored onto it by the ground controllers. Once more, the pilot achieved visual and radar contact and locked his gun radar onto the target. Again the object evaded the night-fighter. One can only imagine the crew's feelings when they were told by radar controllers that the object was now behind them. For the next ten minutes, the pilot tried everything

---

[99] In reality, it was a USAF base, having been leased to the United States as part of its NATO commitment.

he knew to shake the object from his tail, but ground radar could see that it was keeping a constant distance and was not to be shaken.

The Venom was low on fuel by this time, so the pilot returned to base, first asking the radar operator to tell him if the object followed him. Evidently it did, but it eventually stopped and, after making several short moves, went off in a northerly direction at about 600 mph. It disappeared from the radar screens at 3.30 a.m. after leading American and British forces a merry dance for over four hours.

No one has satisfactorily explained this detailed and coherent set of separate visual and radar sightings. Apart from other sources, the event is recorded in detail in the 1999 COMETA Report.

Malmstrom AFB, 1967

Date: March 1967
Locations: Missile sites
Type of Sighting: Visual and electronic effects (alleged)
Type of Prime Witness: USAF missile officers
Other Witnesses: US security personnel

Back in the mid-1960s, not only was the Vietnam War well into its nastiest stages, but the Cold War was simmering quite nicely. The Cuba missile crisis of '62 had brought it to boiling point, after which the temperature of the stand-off between the Warsaw Pact and the US and its NATO allies never dropped far. In those days, the bulk of the West's deterrent (apart from British and French nuclear bombers) was based on America's main intercontinental ballistic missile (ICBM) system, which was firmly rooted in the vast open spaces of the US mid- and far West. The philosophy was MAD: mutually assured destruction. In theory, neither the United States nor the Soviet Union would be crazy enough to launch a pre-emptive nuclear strike against the other if they could be sure that a devastating return strike would be despatched as soon as the pre-emptive one was detected.

Long-range radar stations, in a string from Alaska to Yorkshire, gave a few vital minutes' warning of a Soviet missile attack, and those minutes allowed a crushing, probably final, blow to be struck by hundreds of US ICBMs. To all intents and purposes, the nation which tried to launch a pre-emptive strike would be bringing the curtain down on human civilisation and, in all probability, the entire species. So no stress there, then.

The MAD strategy was crazy, but that Mexican stand-off kept the world safe from nuclear Armageddon for half a century. And it still does. Today, the situation is more complex and much more multilayered, but back then, it all depended on hundreds of deeply buried missile silos set up in small groups (called "Flights") in widely separated areas. Each Flight, with around ten missiles each, was situated many miles from other silos and was connected by secure telephone and data cables to other groups and to their headquarters, from which any order to fire would come after being approved by the president.

The missile bases are some of the most secure military installations in the world. Let's face it: They could not be otherwise. The missiles are a necessary evil, and the Mexican stand-off which they represent is as close to ideal as this imperfect world is ever going to see. The greatest fear on both sides is that somehow, someone might neutralise their missiles, thereby ending the stand-off and allowing the other side to launch a war-ending first strike without fear of retaliation. The debates continue as to whether such a strike is sane, given the irradiated clouds of dust which would cover most of the globe within weeks. One side would "win" the war, but whether it would have much of a future to gloat about is a moot question.

But MAD was what we got. Not to put too fine a point on it, the United States armed forces were a bit sensitive about nuclear missile silos, so they took pretty good care of them. That's the background to what happened in the state of Montana in March of 1967.

The details of what happened at Malmstrom Air Force Base, Montana, were kept top secret for many years. At the centre of the affair were two Air Force officers: Captain Eric Carlson and First Lieutenant Walt Figel, who, on the morning of Thursday, March 16, 1967, comprised the Echo Flight Missile Combat Crew. Each flight of ten missiles was given a letter designation, and each was assigned teams of officers in command plus technicians and security guards sufficient for twenty-four hour cover. The place where the missile combat crew were based was not where the missiles were located. Each of the ten missiles in their flight were miles away from the control centre and miles away from each other (to try to avoid a single nuclear attack from wiping out an entire missile flight).

A group of flights came under the overall command of a specific Air Force base (in this case, Malmstrom). Generally, two officers at a time were stationed in the underground capsule (control room) twenty-four hours a day in shifts. The above-ground entrance to that capsule was a small military enclosure, guarded by teams of soldiers day and night.

At the cutting edge of the system were the two very carefully vetted and psychologically cleared officers in the capsule. It was their job to push the fire buttons when the order came. Why two people? Because no one wanted to take the chance that a single person might go rogue and try to launch some missiles as an April Fool's prank. This was actually theoretically impossible, as the men in the capsule only had one set of codes; the other was with the president. But there was no point in taking chances. Another reason was to guard against the possibility that a lone missile commander in the capsule might refuse to launch when ordered. There's no point in spending all that money and setting up the MAD strategy if individual commanders were going to be given the option of firing or not as the mood took them.

Carlson and Figel were on duty in the control centre's capsule when, at 8.30 a.m., one of their missiles suddenly went off-line. That is, the alarm sounded to tell the capsule crew that that particular ICBM was no longer operational. Puzzled, they phoned the security guards at the silo containing the now-defunct missile. The guards told them that a UFO had been spotted that morning, and that no maintenance had been started on the missile that day. So, still puzzled, and not a little startled by the news from the security team, the two officers put the phone down and thought it was all over, bar the repairs to the missile in question. A maintenance crew would be called and the missile brought back to its duty very soon. But then alarms began to sound, one by one, as every one of the other nine missiles in the flight also went off-line. Checks showed that the guidance and control systems of each of the ten missiles had failed at roughly the same time.

One of the deputy commanders at Oscar Flight, located about twenty miles south-east of Echo Flight, was Lieutenant Robert Salas (who has since become a staunch and fervent supporter of the extraterrestrial hypothesis). He has written that several of his security guards at the control centre reported watching lights zigzagging across the sky in the early hours of March 16: shooting one way and then stopping and changing direction. Salas said that at the time, he did not take this report seriously, and he had no way of knowing what had apparently been seen above ground at Echo Flight.

However, he then received another call from the guards in the compound far above his head. They informed him that a UFO was hovering just outside the main gate. Red, glowing, and saucer shaped, it simply hovered there silently. Salas decided it was time to take the reports seriously. He woke his commander, Lieutenant Fred Meiwald, and they were talking things over when klaxons sounded, and one by one, six of the missiles in Oscar Flight also went off-line.

Below ground, Salas and Meiwald followed their Air Force routines and checked and phoned and investigated. Above ground, there is some testimony that the security team fired on the object without effect. In fact, they are said to have fired until they literally had no ammunition left.

Boeing, the company which made the missiles, looked into the matter and wrote a report entitled "Report of Engineering Investigation of Echo Flight Incident, Malmstrom, Mont - 16 Mar 1967". Salas says that this very detailed Boeing investigation could not come up with an answer as to why *all* the missiles had failed at virtually the same time and with the same fault. One of the Boeing engineers found that he could simulate the fault 80 percent of the time by injecting a 10 volt pulse into the circuit at a specific point. If this was the cause of the failures, the only viable explanation was a powerful electromagnetic pulse which, in those days, could not be generated externally in sufficient power to penetrate the silo's shielding.[100]

The sighting of a glowing object hovering outside the main gate of a missile site in 1967 has been officially ignored. The sceptics have explained it as either being made up by the people telling the story, or as the planet Mars being

---

[100] For a detailed account from the horse's mouth, see www.cufon.org: Robert Salas and Jim Klotz. "The Malmstrom AFB UFO/Missile Incident," originally dated November 27, 1996, updated May 15, 2000.

seen at the brightest point in its two-year cycle (ignoring for the moment that it seems the planet was actually in almost the exact opposite position in the sky to the direction which observers were seeing the object). There is a similar set of proposed explanations for what happened at the missile silos themselves, even though most of the witnesses, who include a couple of full colonels and an Air Force captain, have stuck to their stories for over forty years.

The sceptics have presented an interesting technical case which argues that such shut-downs were not unknown and that the most likely reason for the Malmstrom missile failures was the use of diesel generators producing a noise-pulse which disabled the missiles. Later sceptics have proposed a variety of alternative possibilities (again including the planet Mars). Richard Haines of NARCAP has discussed one of the latest explanations on his blog,[101] and for those who are interested, there's an interview with Robert Salas on YouTube.[102]

Whatever you might think about the 1967 events at Malmstrom AFB – mass illusions or unexplained UFOs – it was not the end of the matter, for whatever they were, they came back again eight years later, in 1975, and Malmstrom was again on the list of locations.

Loring AFB, 1975

Date: October/November 1975
Locations: Loring AFB, Maine; Wurtsmith AFB, Michigan; Malmstrom AFB, Montana.
Type of Sighting: Visual and electronic effects/possible landing
Type of Prime Witness: USAF missile officers
Other Witnesses: US security personnel; civilians in Caribou, Maine

The incidents which occurred in late October and early November 1975 are, for the outsider, extremely fascinating. As usual, they are not an

---

[101] http://www.theufochronicles.com/2014/02/skeptic-robert-sheaffer-solves-famous.html
[102] https://www.youtube.com/watch?v=zjbhq4P_sZI

isolated set of events but feature within a much larger collection of sightings at about the same time. Witnesses include USAF officers and enlisted men, and the sightings have been scrutinised and criticised by a number of sceptical investigators.

If that was where it ended, it would be very similar to all the other sightings by credible witnesses in this book. But the log entries from the NORAD[103] files add unique corroboration and even some thought-provoking extra detail.

The Loring incidents began, as far as the records show, on October 27, 1975, at 7.45 p.m. in the evening, when a staff sergeant of the 42nd Security Police was on duty guarding the top-secret nuclear weapons "igloos" at Loring Air Force Base in Maine. The igloos are domed bunkers of considerable strength within which armaments, including nuclear weapons, are stored.

Loring AFB is almost the furthest north you can drive in Maine before crossing into Canada. It was built because it was the closest the United States could get to Europe. Its positioning was also ideal for releasing bombers and interceptors over the southern Arctic Ocean.

Nuclear weapons storage areas are among the most heavily guarded installations on any base, patrolled by heavily armed security police and dogs (K-9 patrols) twenty-four hours a day. At 7.45 p.m., Staff Sergeant Lewis saw what he thought was an aircraft fly low along the base perimeter and then cross into the base at a height of about three hundred feet. Lewis noted what he thought were a red navigation light and white strobe light. Another non-commissioned officer saw the same object on radar from the base control tower. Staff Sergeant James Sampley had spotted the object on his set about ten miles north-north-east of Loring. He tried every communication band but could get no answer from the "aircraft", which

---

[103] Established in 1958, the North American Aerospace Defense Command (NORAD) is responsible for aerospace warning, aerospace control, and maritime warning in the defence of Canada and the United States. It coordinates US and Canadian armed forces from its central command centre located at the Cheyenne Mountain complex in Colorado. http://www.norad.mil/About-NORAD/

began to circle, getting to within nine hundred feet of the nuclear storage area at an altitude of around a hundred and fifty feet.

Lewis warned the 42nd Bomb Wing of the intruder, and the base went immediately to a major alert status. In the control tower, Sgt Grover Eggleston took the alert call at 8.45 p.m. and began watching the unknown object on his screen. He saw it circle, about ten miles east-north-east of the base, for three-quarters of an hour before disappearing. He thought that the object must either have got below the radar coverage or may have landed.

Back at the weapons storage area (WSA), the commander requested fighter coverage from the 21st NORAD Region (Hancock Field, New York) and the 22nd Region based at North Bay, Ontario, but apparently his request was denied by both regions. The commander then requested help from the Maine State Police. Everyone assumed the object was a helicopter. He had the security police check all the areas over which the object had flown, with no results. There were no further sightings that night, but the base remained on high alert.

At 7.45 p.m. the following evening (October 28), three security policemen at Loring (Sgt Blakeslee, Staff Sgt Long, and Sgt Lewis) saw what they thought were the running lights of an aircraft, about three miles north at about three thousand feet. It or a similar object was reported at irregular intervals for the next few hours. Lewis said it had a white flashing light and an amber or orange one too. Again the base commander sped to the weapons storage area and watched the object himself. Its speed and motions suggested to the observers that it was a helicopter, but the object seemed to be able to appear and disappear at will. It appeared over one end of the runway at an apparent hundred and fifty feet, shut off its lights, and was then seen over the weapons storage area, again at about a hundred and fifty feet.

While all this was being monitored by the commander and various tower staff, a maintenance crew was working on a B-52 bomber on the flight lines. The crew chief, Sgt Eichner, together with Sgt Jones and others in the maintenance crew saw a red and orange object, looking like a stretched-out American football. They watched as it hovered. It then put out all its lights before reappearing over the north end of the runway. Eichner and his men were curious (and presumably excited by the distraction). They clambered into their maintenance truck and drove towards the object down a base road called Oklahoma Avenue.

They made a turn towards the weapons storage area and immediately came upon the object right in front of them, about a hundred yards away and about five or six feet off the ground. They said it was the length of about four cars, quite still and silent, and that it looked to be a reddish-orange in colour. Eichner said the colours seemed to blend into each other. At that point, evidently, security vehicles started to approach at high speed with their sirens going and lights flashing. Because the maintenance crew was now in a restricted area without permission, Sgt Jones recommended that the crew get out of there, and they did. They did not immediately report what they had seen, because they thought they might have got into trouble for being in a restricted area.

Again, though, the object seemed to switch off its lights, and it disappeared, and, again, a thorough security sweep was carried out, without any result.

Also on October 28, local civilians and police in the nearby town of Caribou reported lights in the area which changed colours. Quite reasonably, the 42nd Bomb Wing commander (Col Richard Chapman) requested the use of a National Guard helicopter, which was then at Loring. The general feeling on the base, in the absence of the information which Eichner's crew could have supplied, was that the object was a helicopter making highly illegal incursions into a US Air Force base.

Chapman's request was approved, but for some unknown reason, he was ordered not to try to apprehend the object, not to overfly the nearby Canadian border, and to have only "official" personnel on board (presumably meaning no journalists). Chapman protested at the border restriction, and this prohibition was subsequently lifted. But the other restrictions sound strange, particularly the first. If a helicopter had been overflying the highly restricted airspace over a weapons storage area on a front-line USAF airbase, why would the authorities not wish to apprehend it? If the helicopter was suspected of drug-running or other crimes and it was part of a lengthy FBI operation, why not tell Chapman to back off and forget the matter? And if the colonel was barred from apprehending the object, what on earth did the authorities think was going to be Chapman's objective while he was stooging around in the National Guard helicopter?

The helicopter pilots were Chief Warrant Officer Bernard Poulin and Chief Warrant Officer Eugene Herrin. Early the following morning, the National Guard helicopter took off carrying a motley set of passengers, including a Royal Canadian Mounted Police officer, an officer from the Maine State Police, and a few security police from the base.

That night, and for a couple of further nights, the National Guard helicopter dashed around the countryside surrounding the base, chasing various "sightings". But radar never picked them up, and the helicopter never made visual contact, either.

Understandably, the senior officers on the base were very concerned that something had breached the base perimeter and overflown the WSA. Security was stepped up and a mobile patrol established for the WSA during the hours of darkness. All of the US northern tier bases – those along the US-Canadian border – were put on alert, too, against the possibility of potential helicopter incursions.[104]

More objects were seen and plotted on radar at Loring on October 30, but almost nothing about these events entered the public arena until, a decade after the main events, UFO investigators set in motion Freedom of Information Act requests which led to the gradual release of some extremely interesting NORAD logs. The letter releasing the log entries, signed by Colonel Terrence C James, director of administration, USAF, says in its opening paragraph, "The following log entries have been extracted for release", leaving you wondering whether any entries were *not* selected for extraction.

The NORAD log for Loring states:

---

[104] These comprised Pease AFB, New Hampshire, Plattsburgh AFB, New York, Wurtsmith AFB, Michigan, Kinchloe AFB, Michigan, Sawyer AFB, Michigan, Grand Forks AFB, North Dakota, Minot AFB, North Dakota, Malmstrom AFB, Montana, Fairchild AFB, Washington, and Barksdale AFB, Iowa.

"29 Oct/0630Z[105]: Command Director called by Air Force Operations Center concerning an unknown helicopter landing in the munitions storage area at Loring AFB, Maine. Apparently this was second night in a row this occurrence [sic]. There was also an indication, but not confirmed, that Canadian bases had been overflown by a helicopter."

The log entries which were allowed for release are quite stunning.[106] They show that NORAD controllers were not only taking unidentified objects very seriously but that USAF fighter aircraft were still being scrambled to chase them, twenty-three years after an earlier generation of fighter pilots were trying to find them in the skies over Washington DC. The logs also show that NORAD cannot have seriously believed the intruders to be helicopters. On one occasion, they were logged at thirteen thousand feet, and on another in groups at altitude.

What the outsider might also note is that the 1975 UFOs mirrored their 1952 comrades in using the disappearing trick. As soon as fighter aircraft got close, the objects' lights would go out, and they would effectively disappear. Then, when the fighters left, the lights would reappear.

At this point in the story, attention switched to other bases on the northern tier of US airbases. Specifically, to a base called Wurtsmith in Michigan, almost on the shores of Lake Huron. On October 31 at 0445 Zulu, Wurtsmith reported that a "helicopter" had hovered over the SAC weapons storage area before flying away. The entry mentioned that a tanker aircraft had been flying over the area at about twenty-seven hundred feet. The crew saw the object, painted it their radar and followed it by

---

[105] All times followed by the letter "Z" refer to Zulu time – that is, Greenwich Mean Time. In order to translate these times to local time, one has to subtract the difference between the location's time zone and GMT. Most of these sightings were between six and eight hours behind GMT. It sounds clumsy, but airbases and military locations all over the world can all operate on a standard time frame – Zulu time.
[106] NORAD Log – entries extracted for release – available on the NICAP website at http://www.nicap.org/norad3b1.htm

radar out over Lake Huron for about thirty-five miles before contact was lost. This was yet another incursion into a high-security area in the middle of a USAF base by a suspected "helicopter". This time, it was apparently plotted on the radar of an Air Force air-refuelling tanker and disappeared, flying south-east over the lake roughly in the direction of the Canadian town of London, Ontario.

And then, in early November of 1975, the US ICBM sites received more visits, starting with Malmstrom. The log entries begin with Sabotage Alert Teams (SATs) reporting a visual contact at approximately three hundred feet and possibly four miles. Jet fighters were deployed but without results.

US Time Zones (in the Month of November; GMT = UTC = Zulu)
Eastern Standard Time = GMT -5 hours
Central Standard Time = GMT -6
Mountain Standard Time = GMT -7
Pacific Standard Time = GMT -8

At Malmstrom, the military SAT teams at two missile sites – Kilo 3 and Lima 4 – reported visual sightings of objects at 0836 Zulu, at about three hundred feet altitude and five miles away. F-106 fighters had been scrambled, but they did not make contact. Similar incidents occurred repeatedly in Great Falls, at Stanford, and at numerous missile sites through November 1975. In some cases, security teams watched objects through binoculars.

The officers at NORAD took the reports seriously enough to log them and, sometimes, to scramble USAF fighters to try to intercept them. In one case, a radar station picked up an object at between ten thousand and thirteen thousand feet high, which it labelled "track J330". Even from the terse military-speak, one picks up the puzzlement of the staff, and even perhaps a little frustration. The log says that J330 was doing just 18 knots at ninety-five hundred feet and that up to seven objects were being tracked at the same time. A few minutes later, J330 was reported as stationary or moving at 7 knots at twelve thousand feet.

J330 was a strange track indeed. It varied in height between ninety-five hundred feet and thirteen thousand feet, and its speed varied in that hour between 18 knots (about 21 miles per hour) and stationary. Balloons could travel fast in a wind-stream at altitude, but they almost never become totally stationary and are never seen in groups of seven.

F-106 fighters had been unable to find the objects, and the ground lost contact with another track (J331). The NORAD log states that the objects were seen from four different points, and yet again, the lights went out when the fighters arrived and came back on when they departed.

The sightings across the northern tier USAF bases in October and November 1975 were spectacular and pretty compelling for the outsider. Some sceptics claimed that it was simply a case of mass suggestion. If the commanders asked, "Can you see a UFO?" it might just be that people would see UFOs. Others said these troops and airmen were simply seeing bright planets or stars.

The problem with either substantiating or rejecting such theories is that we do not have enough comparative evidence. What would a normal night in the NORAD logs look like? How come so many competent and experienced troops saw things in independent groups over several nights? Why were there multiple radar tracks, as well?

Chicago O'Hare, 2006

Date: November 7, 2006
Locations: Chicago, Michigan
Type of Sighting: Visual and radar
Type of Prime Witness: Airport workers, pilots
Other Witnesses: People outside the airport

Although not a military base, Chicago O'Hare International Airport was like all other such locations: it was filled with people who worked around aircraft all their lives, people who were as thoroughly familiar with things that flew as they could possibly be. But in November 2006, those people saw something they'd never encountered before, ever.

The events remained relatively unknown to the outside world for two months before the *Chicago Tribune* gave it a public airing. Once a single newspaper had revealed the sighting, the global media were not far behind, and the Chicago O'Hare UFO is now extremely well-known, although still not understood.

The story began at about 4 p.m. (local) on November 7, 2006. On that cloudy afternoon, a group of twelve United Airlines employees were working on the ramp at the airport when they noticed an object hovering over Gate C17. A ramp operative, who was helping to oversee the push-back of United Flight 446 to Charlotte, North Carolina, saw it first and called it to the attention of others.

It was a metallic disc which the group of witnesses variously estimated at between about twenty-two feet and eighty-eight feet in diameter (seven to twenty-eight metres). As the cloud base was at nineteen hundred feet, the object was definitely lower than that height. For somewhere between five and fifteen minutes, the object hovered over the airport building, in which position it was seen not only by the twelve ramp employees but by pilots in aircraft taxiing and waiting to take off, and by other airport staff. One of the United dispatchers phoned the control tower, but the staff there treated her enquiries with disdain.

After a while, with the observers' gaze still riveted on the strange thing in the sky, the object suddenly shot upwards at high speed, penetrating the cloud layer above the airport and leaving a hole through which they said they could see blue sky for a while until the winds gradually closed the hole again.

John Hilkevitch of the *Chicago Tribune* did most of the background research, including filing Freedom of Information requests, which prompted the key authorities into at least trying to explain things.

This is perhaps the most interesting thing about this incident: In the days following the sighting, both United Airlines and the FAA denied point-blank that anything at all had happened at O'Hare. For the FAA, in particular, this is very strange because absolutely any incursion into protected airspace over an airport is an incredibly serious matter. The danger to passenger flights is one that all aviation regulatory bodies take very seriously. So for the FAA simply to deny that anything had happened was weird, to say the least. Almost equally strange is the fact that not a single witness was prepared to go on record to say what they saw.

Most of them, of course, were United employees.

It took Hilkevitch weeks of research and FOIPA requests, but eventually both United and the FAA provided explanations for the event. The FOIPA process also uncovered tapes of the control tower communications at the time. These confirmed the calls from the United supervisor to the control tower. The FAA conducted an internal enquiry and announced, at first, that the object was an illusion caused by airport lights reflecting down from the cloud layer. The response from the UFO community was that it was still daylight and that the airport lights had not yet been switched on. Subsequently, the FAA announced that what the witnesses saw was a weather phenomenon known as a "hole punch" cloud and that there was therefore nothing for it to investigate. But hole-punch clouds are only created when freezing conditions above the clouds cause ice particles to fall through and create a hole. Evidently conditions above the clouds on that day were not below freezing.[107] And there is the additional issue of the object which was seen *before* the cloud was punched. If the ground crew had simply seen a "hole-punch cloud", why did they not report a cloud with a hole in it rather than a metallic disc?

The National Aviation Reporting Center on Anomalous Phenomena (NARCAP) assembled a scientific team led by its head scientist, Dr Richard Haines. Its 150-page report was published in March 2007 as "Case 18". It concluded that there definitely was something there to be reported, but that whatever it was could only be called "unknown". It went on, quite reasonably, to say:

> "Anytime an airborne object can hover for several minutes over a busy airport but not be registered on radar or seen visually from the control tower, (it) constitutes a potential threat to flight safety."

---

[107] A nine-minute segment of "off the air" videotape from an interview with Jon Hilkevitch has been posted on YouTube at https://www.youtube.com/watch?v=AlhiAFHHTM4

CHAPTER 13

UFOs and Civil Airliners

THE IMPACT OF RIDICULE is, of course, to lessen the number of reports, and this has been a particularly serious problem with respect to pilot sightings in the United States and probably in other countries too. In 2000, Dr Richard Haines launched NARCAP, the National Aviation Reporting Center on Anomalous Phenomena, to make it easier and safer for pilots and other aviation professionals to report aerial phenomena. Haines had become very concerned about what he calls "the law of diminishing reporting". As fewer pilots feel confident enough to report sightings, fewer and fewer sightings come in, and the authorities then have the opportunity to say, "There's nothing there because no one is reporting anything". He believes that, in the United States, only between 5 and 10 percent of aviation-related sightings are ever reported.

NARCAP's website invites pilots, air traffic officials, radar operators, and aviation professionals to report both current and historical observations of unidentified aerial phenomena. It also assures visitors that all reports will be held in strict confidence.

NARCAP approaches aviation-related sightings in a strictly scientific manner. An example would be the case of a glider in New York State in August 2015.[108] The pilot and passenger of the glider reported an encounter with an unidentified object which, among other things, sped up to it and then circled their glider on the outside of a turn (implying very high

---

[108] See http://www.narcap.org/files/aircat_UP_8-9-15_NY_final.pdf

speed for the object). It seemed to have red and green and white lights, and several other similar objects were seen. The NARCAP report addresses information from the FAA and the possibility of the objects being un-manned aerial vehicles (UAVs) but still concluded

"This case must remain open until additional data is [sic] available. The object(s) remain unidentified at this time."

NARCAP's researchers and contributors carry out detailed scientific investigations of many other aerial phenomena. For example, Richard Spaulding developed an interesting and somewhat high-level set of possibilities for what he termed "spherical luminous objects". They address the idea that some or even all of the various sightings of self-luminous circles and balls could be caused by new forms of electromagnetic phenomena related to ball lightning and "air threads". The argument, which repeats some of the arguments in the British Condign report, is highly technical, and Spaulding concedes that certain hypotheses are, as yet, unproven or that evidence is incomplete, but the paper appears to constitute a valid line of enquiry for fireballs and glowing globes.[109]

What follows are four of the most famous civil pilot sightings of un-identified aerial phenomena, two from the United States, one from the UK, and one from France. It is fascinating how the British and French aviation authorities treat such sightings much more openly and do not deride or ridicule pilots for reporting such things.

---

[109] Richard E Spaulding. *An Atmospheric Electrical Hypothesis for Spherical Luminosities Occurring at Aircraft Altitudes,* Jan. 2010 in Richard Haines, et al., *Spherical UAP and Aviation Safety – A Critical Review.* April 2010. NARCAP.

TWA 842, 1981

Date: July 4, 1981
Location: Over Lake Michigan
Type of Sighting: Visual
Type of Prime Witness: Airline captain
Other Witnesses: Co-pilot

Notwithstanding ridicule, reports of strange sightings by airline pilots are extremely common (and might well be more so if the US authorities were less aggressive in their mockery and derision). Well-recorded sightings include the Chiles-Whitted sighting of 1948, the 1952 Washington National airliners, almost innumerable equivalent sightings in modern times (refer back to chapter 2 for a few examples), and, of course, the examples in this current chapter.

Regardless of sceptical ridicule, such reports simply must carry a significant degree of weight in evidential terms. Airline pilots can make mistakes just like everyone else, but when it comes to being very familiar with the sky at all times of the day, how things look during the hours of darkness, keeping an eye out for dangers to their aircraft, and having the optical acuity to be able to see and describe what they experience, one cannot escape the fact that they are witnesses of the highest credibility.

As a young man, Phil Schultz was a Navy fighter pilot during the Korean War. By the age of fifty-four, he was captaining TWA heavy airliners on long-haul flights.

It was Independence Day 1981, and presumably having drawn the short straw and missed his celebratory barbeque, Captain Schultz was in charge of TWA Flight 842, a Lockheed 1011 Tristar, on a scheduled flight from San Francisco to JFK, New York. The flight had been uneventful until about the halfway mark; when the airliner was cruising above Lake Michigan and Schultz's life changed forever. From his command seat, he watched as an unidentified object sank into view and manoeuvred. At one point, he believed there would be a collision.

Even where pilot sightings are concerned, this sighting was unusual;

not only because a very experienced airline captain saw something extremely strange, but because, whatever he saw, it came very close to the TWA aircraft. He described its size at one point as being that of a grapefruit held at arm's length. Afterwards, he oversaw the drawing of some pretty detailed diagrams of his sighting.

Schultz described the object as a large, round, silver, metal object with six jet-black "portholes" equally spaced around the circumference. It descended from above into the left front quadrant of the pilots' view, and Schulz believed for a moment there would be a collision. But the object manoeuvred and then swept off to the left and out of sight.

The event also provides the outsider with a very clear indication of the atmosphere in the United States surrounding UFOs. Captain Schultz decided, in consultation with his co-pilot, not to file a report with the airline or the FAA. Instead, he went to an organisation called the Coalition for Freedom of Information (CFI). One of its most experienced and skilled investigators was a man called Richard Haines.[110] Dr Haines drew a diagram under Captain Schultz's directions and interviewed the TWA pilot at length (the co-pilot was deliberately left in considerate anonymity as indeed most young First Officers have been).

It was daylight, about quarter to five in the afternoon. The aircraft was cruising at thirty-seven thousand feet at an airspeed of 280 knots (about 320 mph). The sky was generally clear, but there were some lower clouds at about ten thousand feet. At that time on a summer's afternoon, the sun was still high and behind the airliner. Schultz saw the object descend until it was approximately three thousand feet above his altitude and to his left. During the course of just five to six seconds, it moved smoothly, slightly towards him, and then, in an arc, away from the aircraft at around 1,000 mph.

The full details can be read in the CFI report quoted on an independent website,[111] but evidently Schultz (who should be a fairly reliable judge

[110] Richard Haines is the chief scientist for the National Aviation Reporting Center on Anomalous Phenomena, an organisation he co-founded. Previously, he was a NASA and Raytheon scientist. He is a human factors and air safety specialist and considers UFOs a serious potential danger to air safety.

[111] http://www.ufoevidence.org/cases/case656.htm

of such things) estimated the G-forces experienced by the UFO in that rapid turn as being around 20G. A very fit and trained human pilot can withstand G forces of up to this amount and even beyond,[112] but it is still an exceptional turn (and one which could not be made by a weather balloon).

Phil Schultz had been a lifelong non-believer in UFOs, but that experience certainly made him think. He told Richard Haines that

"We have nothing that can do what that object did".

JAL, Alaska, 1986

Date: November 17, 1986
Location: Alaska
Type of Sighting: Visual and radar
Type of Prime Witness: Airline pilot
Other Witnesses: Radar operator

This is one of those sightings which has caused trouble for the person who reported it, and the whole affair was kept pretty much under the carpet for many years, with the inevitable result that a number of facts have been slightly blurred. One of those facts is the actual date of the sighting. It is given as anywhere between November 7 and 17, 1986. Either could, of course, be a simple typo, but for the purposes of this book, I have elected to go for the 17th, as that is the date most commonly used.

The incident caused serious trouble for the pilot, who was disciplined for reporting the incident and talking about it to the press. It also caused long-term hassle for a senior FAA official who disagreed with the official FAA conclusions and kept the details, including voice tapes and radar tapes, secret and in his own possession for fifteen years before startling the world with his evidence.

So what caused all this upset?

---

[112] A fairground roller coaster can subject passengers to about 5 or 6 G.

It was just after five in the afternoon on November 17, 1986. A Boeing 747 freighter was well into a westbound flight from Paris to Tokyo with a cargo of wine. Japan Airlines Flight 1628, with three crew, was cruising over Alaska at thirty-five thousand feet a little to the north of the town of Anchorage. In the left-hand seat, the captain was Kenju Terauchi, an ex-fighter pilot with around ten thousand hours' experience in the air. His co-pilot was Takanori Tamefuji, and the flight engineer, sitting behind the two pilots, was Yoshio Tsukuda.

The three crew became aware of two bright objects that they first thought were fighter aircraft. The objects were pacing the 747, about two thousand feet below them to their left. A few minutes later, both objects flashed to a position between five hundred and a thousand feet ahead of the freighter, one above the other. The objects, as described by the crew, were keeping exact pace with the 747 and were like two rectangles standing on their short ends. Each had a black band down the centre, lengthwise, with two bands of bright lights on either side of the band.

The first officer radioed Anchorage ATC at just after 5.19 p.m., and we can hear the tentativeness in his voice:

> "Anchorage Center, Japan Air 1628, ah, do you have any traffic, ah, eleven o'clock above?"

Over the next few seconds, the ATC controller, Carl Henley, did not actually answer the question but instead asked whether the crew could identify the aircraft above and in front of them. The crew said no but confirmed that the two objects were still there. ATC simply asked them to maintain visual contact.

Terauchi described the two objects as glowing brightly, enough to light up the 747's cockpit. He said that he and his crew could feel heat on their faces as the objects "sat" in front of the speeding air-freighter.

The objects then moved closer, to sit side by side, in front of the aircraft. They remained there for some ten minutes, just undulating slightly, with their glow sometimes bright and sometimes less so. For the crew, it must have been incredibly frightening. If the objects had failed for a moment to keep pace with the aircraft, there would have inevitably been a very nasty mid-air collision.

About a minute into the conversation, ATC asked another strange question: whether the JAL aircraft was requesting a higher or lower altitude, to which Flight 1628 responded in the negative. The ATC question was strange because if the air traffic controllers could see that there was an aircraft close to, and directly ahead of, the 747, they should have immediately instituted a height and distance separation move. If they could not see any aircraft (as indeed they first claimed), then why ask the question?

A minute later, ATC said

> "JAL1628 heavy, see if you are able to identify the type of aircraft, ah, and see if you can tell whether it's military or civilian".

The crew responded that they could not, but that they could see what they called navigation lights and strobe lights. After ATC asked for the colour of the lights and 1628 replied, "White and yellow," the controller simply repeated the colours (which were a pretty unusual, not to say illegal, combination for an aircraft) and thanked the crew. Incredibly, Carl Hendry did not query the colours or express any surprise that the supposed aircraft would flash white and yellow lights at another aircraft. Neither had he responded as to whether his radar had picked up the objects, and his actual responses could be taken to mean that he had, indeed, seen them but wanted the crew of JAL 1628 to try to identify them.

In the log, at this point, the watch supervisor at Anchorage notes that no known traffic was identified and that both the FAA Regional Operations Centre and Elmendorf USAF base at Anchorage had been notified. It also notes that Terauchi unsuccessfully tried to photograph the objects. Flight 1628 also asked for a change of frequencies due to heavy interference on their communications.

About four minutes into the event, the crew tell ATC that the objects have "extinguished". They also found that VHF transmissions had returned to normal. The ATC controller then explicitly confirms that he is no longer receiving any radar replies.

This response, some four minutes into the affair, raises the question as to why he did not tell JAL 1628 that he had contacts on radar up to that point. Presumably the crew thought the incident was over, but then the captain noticed a pale band at about 10 o'clock. His on-board radar confirmed an object about 7.5 nautical miles ahead, and Elmendorf AFB radar also got a "primary" return from that location.

In the reflected lights from the town of Fairbanks, Terauchi perceived the new object as huge – statements vary from twice to three times the size of an aircraft carrier (which would make it roughly six hundred to nine hundred yards). At that point, the captain requested a change of course in order to avoid what he saw as a major threat to the aircraft. He was given a 45 degree change, and the object simply mirrored it. He was permitted a descent to thirty-one thousand feet and allowed to make a full 360 degree turn, but still the object stayed in the same position relative to the freighter. Radar logs released much later confirmed that the radars had also followed these manoeuvres.

Terauchi later said that the object was like two deep soup bowls placed rim to rim and that it was about three times the size of their aircraft, with coloured lights flashing in a band around the circumference.

The flight crew sat and watched the object as it flew in level flight with the aircraft, until eventually, Terauchi decided to try a turn. Anchorage radar also plotted the object as it jinked backwards and forwards around the freighter. The radar's sweeps took ten seconds, and in one sweep, the object went from eight miles directly in front of the aircraft to six miles behind. To do this, its speed must have been around 5,000 mph. Terauchi described the apparent technology as "unthinkable". It appeared to have control over both inertia and gravity.

Anchorage then offered military intervention, but Terauchi rejected it as being unnecessary. The aircraft landed in Anchorage without further incident at 6.20 p.m.

The JAL captain called the object a UFO in his official FAA report of the incident, and the division chief for the Accidents and Investigations Branch for the FAA, John Callahan, arranged for all the data – radar, voice communications, and written reports – to be gathered together for detailed analysis. As part of this, he constructed a plan view display (PVD) of the incident, with correctly timed voice recordings coordinated with the radar returns. Essentially, this was a joined-up video of the radar plots and voice transmissions, showing how everything panned out over the course of the incident.

Callahan briefed his boss, and together, they then briefed Vice-Admiral Donald Engen and then, separately, a group of officials including representatives from the CIA, the FBI, and President Reagan's Scientific Study Team. After the meeting concluded, those attending were told by the CIA representatives that the meeting "never took place". Callahan says that the meeting agreed that the incident was the first ever to be corroborated by two sets of reliable radar evidence. All of the evidence presented at the meeting was taken away and never seen again.

In 99 percent of cases, that would have been the end of the story. We'd have been left with testimony from the crew, and FOIPA requests might have extracted some of the radar evidence, but then we'd be left to make of it all what we could.

However, uniquely, John Callahan had retained original copies of the radar video, the tapes of the voice exchanges, and the written reports. Mainly due to his seniority and the implications of the evidence, he kept it all to himself until 2001, thirteen years after his retirement. He later said that he'd been dismayed and disappointed by the FAA report's findings.

In 2007, he spoke at the now-famous press conference at the National Press Club, organised by James Fox and Leslie Kean, at which a number of senior, informed people from all over the world spoke about their UFO experiences.

There were two further possible sightings in the Alaska area, in January 1987. One was a radar contact by a civilian airliner, and the other a sighting of a large disc-like object by the crew of an Air Force KC-135 tanker.

In March of 1987, the FAA revealed the results of its three-month-long investigation into the JAL 1628 sighting. The apparent radar plots of an unidentified object were actually, they said, a "split radar image" of the 747. This doesn't even satisfactorily explain the fact that two separate radar units (at Anchorage and at Elmendorf) recorded the aircraft and the objects, never mind the fact that the 747's own radar had painted the large object at 7.5 miles.

Completely unlike the ultra-detailed and highly assiduous FAA reports that we are used to from aviation incidents, this report somehow completely ignored the visual reports from the 747's crew.[113] The report simply says that the FAA could not confirm what the crew said had been seen.

Captain Terauchi gave a couple of interviews about the incident to the Japanese press, and he was transferred to a desk job for many years. There are allegations that he claimed to have seen a UFO prior to this event, but simply because someone has seen a UFO on a previous occasion does not necessarily mean that they cannot see another. There appears to be no rule that says it has to be one-sighting per lifetime.

Radar Displays

Without going into too much technical detail, there are many different types of radar systems, and they have become more sophisticated as the years have gone by. Today, most operators watch aircraft blips on what is called a raster scan monitor. In essence, this is a very high-resolution version of your computer desktop or laptop monitor, on which the electronics draw a screen line by line, with the refresh rate of the screen being scores of times per second.

---

[113] This is a fascinating contrast. For civil aviation accidents, the FAA and the British CAA tend to start, first, with what the witnesses perceived, add to that testimony the technical data, and only then arrive at a conclusion. For a recent airshow crash in southern England, the CAA took the testimony of scores of witnesses in order to confirm the attitude, manoeuvres, and altitude of the aircraft. Where it was corroborated, the testimony of individuals was believed.

These modern displays give a much more stable and informative set of data for the operator than the old cathode ray tube (CRT) screens, which plotted the blips as the radar antenna swept around in a circle. Most people will be familiar with the pictures of blips gradually fading as the line sweeps further around the screen to highlight other contacts.

What John Callahan reconstructed on the PVD was a series of raster screens of data direct from the radar electronics saved during the JAL incident, plus the results of an older sweep display.

There is an excellent account of the incident on Wikipedia from which the communications transmissions quoted above have been taken. There is much more detail in the Wikipedia article.[114] John Callahan's brief but powerful account of the incident can be seen online as part of the 2007 al Press Club presentations, which were moderated by Fife Symington, former governor of Arizona.

The sceptics were pretty quick to try to debunk the JAL 1628 sighting. Some repeated the "split image" solution adopted by the FAA. Others, like Philip Klass, proposed a couple of answers. At first, he proposed that the pilots had been looking at the planets Jupiter and Mars, which were bright that evening. As a second line of attack, Klass also suggested that they had seen moonlight reflecting on the cloud layer below them. All of the critics have adopted the FAA explanation as far as the radar images are concerned and have stressed the fact that two other aircraft in the vicinity confirmed seeing JAL 1628's navigation lights but could not see anything else.

Klass proposed that the moonlight reflecting off what he termed "turbulent ice crystals" gave the appearance of coloured lights.

However, the man who held onto the hard evidence, the radar plots, voice communications, and written reports, has never strayed by so much

---

[114] See https://en.wikipedia.org/wiki/Japan_Air_Lines_flight_1628_incident

as an iota from his conviction that something very strange was near the 747 that evening and that the FAA did not provide a sufficiently accurate final analysis. At the National Press Club conference in 2007, John Callahan showed a few of the radar pictures on the presentation screen and explained what he'd been told during his own investigation in the months that followed the sighting. Towards the end of his presentation, he pointed at a radar plot and said he'd first been told by the radar hardware technicians at the FAA that the returns were a software problem. The radar software experts confidently informed him that the issue was a hardware one.

Callahan has told his story many times since 2001, and there are a few YouTube videos of his presentations which you might find interesting.[115] His closing line is a crowd-pleaser, but however slick it is, the outsider is given the very clear message that he honestly thinks so:

"Who are you going to believe," he asks, "your lying eyes ... or the government?"

Air France Flight 3532, 1994

Date: January 28, 1994
Location: Over Coulommiers, France
Type of Sighting: Visual and radar
Type of Prime Witness: Pilot/co-pilot
Other Witnesses: Chief steward

An Air France Airbus A320 was on a routine flight from Nice to London and was, at the time of the sighting, at thirty-nine thousand feet (ten thousand, five hundred metres) over Coulommiers, France (due east of Paris). The captain was Jean-Charles Duboc, and the first officer was Valerie

---

[115] The section where Callahan describes the incident is at about 1:06.19; that is just over an hour into the video of the National Press Club conference of 2010 https://www.youtube.com/watch?v=uDRkJn2NkE4 An earlier presentation is here https://www.youtube.com/watch?v=VgNvVqMEFdI

Chauffour. Conditions were clear, and at the time, the chief steward was standing behind the captain in the cockpit.

At 1.14 p.m., the steward pointed out of the cockpit window at an object which the co-pilot and pilot instantly saw and took to be a weather balloon. Then the captain said it was probably an aircraft banking and reflecting the sun off its wings. Soon, however, they all agreed that it was like nothing they had ever seen before. It was slightly below them, at about thirty-four thousand feet, and Duboc estimated that it was about thirty miles away over northern Paris. The men also agreed that, whatever it was, it must be large.

It appeared to change shape, from a brown bell to what they described as a chestnut-brown lens shape before disappearing off to the aircraft's left, almost instantaneously.

Local air traffic control at Reims had no contacts, but they reported the sighting to the military (CODA, *Centre d'Opérations de la Défense Aérienne*) and asked the pilot to follow the "air-miss" procedures on landing. French military radar recorded a blip crossing the track of the Air France aircraft at that time and location for about fifty seconds. It disappeared from their radar at the same time that Duboc reported the object disappearing from view. But, and this is one of the strangest things about this case, the radar track and the visual location for the sighting are not in the same place.

Neither Duboc nor his co-pilot reported the sighting after landing in London that day. The captain later said that it was because he feared ridicule. It wasn't until three years later that he heard a radio report of a "UFO" being seen over Paris on that day back in 1994, and he recognised that he and his crew had seen the same thing. He then made a formal report to the gendarmerie, and they passed it on to SEPRA (the successor organisation to GEPAN and the forerunner of GEIPAN).

SEPRA's investigations ruled out weather balloons. The radar records showed that the object was about two hundred fifty metres in length – about two-thirds the length of the *Queen Mary 2* ocean liner.

Captain Duboc and his co-pilot are still convinced of what they saw over Paris that day, but a great deal of confusion has been caused by the French military radar track which appears to show, for around a minute, a trace travelling across the nose of the aircraft (but at an undetermined height). Clearly, the two sightings cannot have been the same object (unless Captain Duboc's theory is correct – see below). The aircrew saw an extremely large object to their left, hovering over the city of Paris, and that object was reported independently by a witness on the ground. But military radar tracked an object travelling from the aircraft's right to its left. The trace and the visual object appear to have disappeared at the same time.

Captain Duboc, like everyone else, cannot explain the contradiction, but he has correctly noted that modern military aircraft are able to throw a false radar image of themselves onto enemy radar screens. This is technically possible, but it does not explain why an object – a UFO – over Paris would wish to construct a radar image of itself very close to a commercial airliner but only for a minute.

If you are interested in the radar issue, there is an excellent examination, together with a selection of good and bad map representations, on the website of the French ufologist, Patrick Gross.[116]

Aurigny Sighting, 2007

Date: April 23, 2007
Location: Aurigny airliner north of Alderney, Channel Islands
Type of Sighting: Visual and radar (faint, possibly anomalous)
Type of Prime Witness: Civil pilots (two separate ones in two separate aircraft)
Other Witnesses: Aircraft passengers; two pedestrians on the island of Sark

---

The Aurigny sighting is one of the weirdest in this book. If we were tempted to accept the argument that UFOs were things of the past, mass hysteria from the 1950s and 1960s, and figments of overactive imaginations, this event would most certainly make us think again. In one very ordinary,

---

[116] http://ufologie.patrickgross.org/ufology/af3532rt.htm

everyday story, it juxtaposes two experienced airline pilots on the one side, with two bright yellow, cigar-shaped objects on the other. The archetypal sublime and ridiculous, but it happened.

On a relatively clear and bright spring afternoon in 2007, Aurigny Airlines' Flight 544, a Trislander,[117] was about ten or twelve miles south-west of the Isle of Wight, at its cruising altitude of four thousand feet. It had taken off from Southampton a few minutes earlier at its scheduled time of 2 p.m. en-route for Alderney, one of the smaller Channel Islands. At that point, the pilot, who had been flying this route for the previous eight years, noticed a bright yellow light in the direction of the island of Guernsey, another member of the Channel Islands and some eighty miles distant (a little further than Alderney). This was a short trip, and on such a clear day, once at cruising height, the pilot and passengers could easily see ahead to their destination.

Captain Ray Bowyer gazed at the light, thinking it might be a reflection onto the clouds from the ground on Guernsey, an island famed for its acres of horticultural greenhouses. He kept an eye on the bright yellow light as the plane flew on, but it did not change, either in position or in its intensity. Another factor which puzzled him was that there was a low, hazy bank of cloud below the light which should have reduced its brightness if it had been a reflection from the ground.

Within a few minutes, Bowyer realised that the light was not changing much as his angle to it changed and could not, therefore, be a reflection. So, the plane being on autopilot, he reached for his binoculars. Through them, he could see that the brilliant yellow light had a shape. From his vantage point, it looked like an elongated cigar with length-to-width ratio of about 15:1. The object had what appeared to be a dark widthwise band.

The Trislander droned onwards, and soon two passengers, a couple who were sitting behind Bowyer (those aircraft had no separation between the pilots and the passengers), spotted the yellow object and pointed out that there was another one just behind the first. The pilot now described

---

[117] The Trislander was an eighteen-seater commercial aircraft with three propeller engines.

the objects as discs with a dark area to the right. He told an audience at the National Press Club that he estimated their size at up to a mile across.

Ray Bowyer now wondered whether there was any air traffic coming towards him, and he contacted Jersey Air Traffic Control, telling them what he was watching. They replied in the negative as to air traffic heading towards him and added that they could just make out a faint primary radar return in the rough position indicated by Bowyer.

A second aircraft, which was then some twenty miles south of Bowyer, also told Jersey they had seen the object. Captain Patrick Patterson, the pilot of a Blue Islands' Jetstream aircraft, inbound to Jersey from the Isle of Man, reported from above the tiny island of Sark: a different angle of view from that of Bowyer's plane. He estimated the maximum size of the object as about half a nautical mile.

At around that time, with the two objects still in sight, Bowyer had to descend into his landing pattern. The Trislander put its nose down, and as it flew through the hazy cloud layer at two thousand feet, he and his passengers lost sight of the two objects.

For the UK Civil Aviation Authority (CAA), Bowyer filed the standard report for an unidentified aircraft in controlled airspace and without a transponder (the latter provides altitude and other information to air traffic control). Attached to the report, he enclosed a couple of drawings of the objects.

During his inspection of the first object through his binoculars, Captain Bowyer had observed quite a few details, and his summary of the implications of what he saw is sobering:

> "Due to my close proximity, the dark area on the right of the nearest one now took on a different appearance at the boundary between the brilliant yellow and the dark vertical band. There appeared to be a pulsating boundary layer between the two differences in colour, some sort of interface with sparkling blues, greens, and other hues strobing up and down about once every second or so. This was fascinating, but I was now well beyond our

descent point and, to be frank, I was not too displeased to be landing." [118]

Two pedestrians on Sark also reported the objects in a phone call to BBC Radio Guernsey. Jersey ATC sent its radar recording to the CAA. It showed two faint objects moving slightly north and south for a period of about fifty-five minutes.

The explanation for Captain Bowyer's objects is impossible to pin down at present. A number of possible explanations were carefully examined by NARCAP in 2008. [119] The article is well worth reading as an example of the organisation's extremely detailed and careful investigation of a UFO sighting and the considered attempts to find a rational explanation. In the case of the Channel Islands sightings, the research came up with sixteen possible hypotheses but only two possible, moderate explanations at what it terms Rating 3 (on a five-point scale of plausibility), that is, "somewhat plausible". The investigation could find absolutely no possible explanations which would be classed as very plausible or definite. The first "somewhat plausible" was glasshouse reflections, and the second was "earthquake lights" which themselves are not well understood as a phenomenon. Researchers have also proposed that the faint radar returns might have been reflected surface targets (ships) – but why they would be stooging around for fifty-five minutes is not addressed.

Captain Bowyer says he saw distinct colours and bands and that the objects moved relative to each other. The 2008 NARCAP study is impressive both in its detail and its balance, but in its way, it is like nineteenth-century scientists concluding that rocks that fall from the sky are beyond consideration.

Bowyer, himself, believes he witnessed something "not originating on this planet". He considers that the authorities have their hands tied to

---

[118] Leslie Kean, 2010.

[119] Jean-Francois Baure, David Clarke, Paul Fuller, Martin Shough. "Unusual Atmospheric Phenomena Observed Near Channel Islands, UK, April 23, 2007." *Journal of Scientific Exploration*, 22, 3, 2008. The relevant extract can be seen at http://martinshough.com/aerialphenomena/jse.pdf

a certain extent where such sightings and reports are concerned for, he believes, if people were informed of the truth, the result could be recrimination against authority in many forms, resulting in civil unrest. His concerns reflect those of a number of other thoughtful insiders in wondering whether we should really be wanting to open Pandora's box.

CHAPTER 14

UFOs and Military Aircraft

STARTING HERE, WE'LL LOOK at some of the most credible cases over the past seventy years in which unidentified objects have been sighted by, or have interacted with, military aircraft. However, getting solid data from military sightings is virtually impossible these days. The sceptics would say that this is because such sightings don't happen, but there is a lot of circumstantial evidence that they do and that they haven't stopped simply because of official secrecy. In the United States, there are stories of encounters with military aircraft going back beyond the famous Mantell accident[120] and as far back as the foo-fighters. USAF fighter aircraft were apparently chasing UFOs over Washington in 1952 and were still chasing them over missile bases in the 1970s. An Iranian Phantom fighter over Tehran was the subject of one of the most detailed encounters of the 1970s, and F-16s were used to do the chasing in Belgium in the 1990s. The UK has its own stories of Tornado fighter-bombers chasing UFOs and even being lost in suspicious circumstances.

The problem for the researcher lies in the inevitable secrecy of any nation's armed services. The outsider rarely gets to hear of military encounters until years after the event – and possibly not even then.

---

[120] Captain Thomas Mantell was a USAF National Guard fighter pilot who, in January 1948, crashed and died after chasing an unknown object and apparently blacking out due to lack of oxygen at high altitude. The USAF said it was a Skyhook balloon but the UFO community believe he was trying to get close to a UFO.

I've selected three examples over the years which I consider to be good ones, but none are from the United States. There just aren't sufficiently open and evidenced examples from the latter nation. The first is a dual set of sightings from Britain in the 1950s, the second from France in the 1970s, and the third from Portugal in the 1980s.

Operations Mainbrace and Ardent 1952

Date: September and October 1952
Locations: USS Franklin D Roosevelt; RAF Topcliffe, Yorkshire; RAF Little Rissington, Gloucestershire
Type of Sighting: One visual sighting by an American photographer, two visual sightings by RAF pilots/crew; one radar and visual by a pilot instructor and his student.
Type of Prime Witness: RAF pilots
Other Witnesses: Ground crew

In September 1952 (compare with Exeter, NH, 1965), a NATO exercise was taking place which simulated a Soviet invasion of western Europe. Operation Mainbrace was a huge exercise. It involved somewhere between sixty thousand and eighty thousand personnel, a very large fleet of warships, which included two US aircraft carriers, the brand new Royal Navy aircraft carrier HMS Eagle, and amphibious landings in Denmark by US Marines. Large numbers of British Fleet Air Arm and RAF aircraft looked for simulated enemy submarines, "attacked" simulated enemy ships, or helped to cover the fleet and its landings. As an aside, on board the carrier HMS Eagle, the executive officer was one Commander Peter Hill-Norton who we will come across again in the next chapter (one wonders, also, whether he heard about what happened near the USS Franklin D Roosevelt).

At sea, an American press photographer, on board the USS Franklin D Roosevelt (then the largest aircraft carrier in the world) got a series of colour photos of an object which was white or silvery and circular or spherical, almost right above the carrier. Checks were made, and it was not a balloon.

Meanwhile, over Britain, there were a number of sightings of strange objects by service personnel, some of them (both the sightings and the personnel) very impressive.

On September 21, the British newspaper the *Sunday Dispatch* published a story which was headlined "Saucer chased RAF jet plane". It reported something that had happened on September 19, when two RAF Shackleton[121] pilots and some of their crew were standing on the flight lines at RAF Topcliffe in Yorkshire. They were watching a Meteor jet fighter as it was coming in to land at the next-door airfield, RAF Dishforth. The fighter was at about five thousand feet and descending towards the runway when those watching saw an object at about ten thousand feet, around five miles behind the jet.

The object descended. Its flight mode was described in Flight Lieutenant John Kilburn's report as being like a falling sycamore leaf. The RAF men at first thought it was a parachute or an engine cowling which had come loose from another aircraft. Soon, however, it moved towards the base as though it was following the Meteor. It then stopped dead in the air, and Kilburn said it started to rotate on its axis before racing off at very high speed to the west. Finally it turned again, this time onto a south-easterly course, and disappeared.

Kilburn, with over thirty-seven hundred flying hours, was clearly stunned by what he and the others had seen. He said it was faster than a shooting star with "unbelievable" acceleration. The sighting quickly became known to the press. Dr R V Jones, who was the Ministry of Defence's new director of scientific intelligence, was alleged to have been "distressed" by the amount of press coverage the sightings received. The MoD decided, after this, to covertly reform the British Flying Saucer Working Party, this time under the chairmanship of Dr Jones.

About a month after the sighting at RAF Topcliffe, a separate incident

---

[121] Shackletons were four-engined, long-range maritime surveillance aircraft. They saw service from 1951 right through to the 1990s.

occurred during a different exercise. Operation Ardent had been organised by RAF Bomber Command, but the sighting was by an RAF aircraft not directly involved in the exercise.

Flight Lieutenant Michael Swiney was a staff instructor based at the RAF's Central Flying School (CFS) at RAF Little Rissington, in Gloucestershire. The base was located in the Cotswolds, not far from Cheltenham. On the afternoon of October 21, 1952, Swiney took off in a Meteor trainer with a student, a Royal Navy lieutenant named David Crofts. The flight plan called for a south-westerly course, which would have seen them cross the coast between Exmouth and Weymouth after a journey of about a hundred miles, then turn and return to base.

The Meteor climbed after take-off and pushed through a layer of fairly solid cloud at about fifteen thousand feet. At this point, Swiney said

> "[I] got the fright of my life because there appeared to be, smack in front of the aeroplane, three white, or nearly white, circular objects. Two of them were on a level keel, and one of them was canted at a slight angle, to one side".[122]

At first, he took them for parachutes and thought that someone had been forced to bail out at altitude. He took command of the aircraft and tried to avoid the objects. He said they were circular "saucers" which appeared to be stationary.

In accordance with his flight plan, he continued to climb. By the time the Meteor had reached thirty thousand feet, Swiney said that the objects were sideways on and looked like flat plates. The objects moved from one side to the other of Swiney's flight path, a fact he checked by keeping a straight and level path for a while.

The two men in the Meteor's cockpit could see no engines, no portholes, or any other features which might identify the objects as conventional planes. As the flight commander, Swiney decided that discretion

---

[122] See Timothy Good, 2006.

was the better part of valour, and after calling the sighting in to base, he turned the fighter around and returned. He later said that he was too shaken by what he had seen for him to continue the exercise. But some sources say that Swiney may have been ordered to turn around and approach the objects. He said that he got to a point at which one object filled half his windscreen, but then it turned on its side and climbed away at great speed.

When Swiney touched down again at Little Rissington, the two men had logged between seventy and eighty minutes of flight time.

Contacts were also spotted on radar shortly after Swiney and Crofts encountered the objects. They were plotted by radar at RAF Sopley, and two quick-reaction Meteors were scrambled from RAF Tangmere in Sussex. The radar operators at RAF Box, which was the central control location, watched as an object disappeared off their screen. The two scrambled Meteors tried to find it but without success.

This was an event that the press did not get hold of at the time. It was kept top secret for many years in spite of the fact that the witnesses and others were told that the Air Ministry discounted an extraterrestrial explanation.

Swiney, who rose to air commodore rank in the RAF, always maintained that he was open-minded about the incident, but he stuck by his story. His old RAF logbook for that period contains an entry for October 21 in his own handwriting. It says, "Flying saucers sighted at height. Confirmed by GCI [Ground Controlled Interception]". The next day, he was up again, this time with Flying Officer Kemp, and the day after that, he flew with four different student pilots (including Lieutenant Crofts again).

Because this event was kept secret, there was never any announcement of whatever explanation the Air Ministry or the Ministry of Defence came up with. The incident is simply left in limbo, and the files on it, including the original reports and drawings by Flight Lieutenant Michael Swiney and Lieutenant David Crofts, are simply not available. Air Commodore Swiney evidently managed to see the files once when he was posted to the Air Ministry in London, but they do not appear to be available now.

Leslie Kean reports that a retired RAF signals officer called Terry Barefoot contacted her in 2002 to say that he remembered the call that the headquarters at Rudloe Manor had taken from a ground radar station. He reported that the station said that three objects had entered UK airspace travelling at around 3,000 mph.

Like the events at Farnborough, the Little Rissington sighting involved the sort of men who had not the slightest bit to gain from telling such outlandish tales. The descriptions were very detailed. They saw objects, not lights, and the objects moved in ways that aircraft could not duplicate. For the first two incidents, at Farnborough, the main witness was an RAF test pilot, for the other it was a Flying Instructor who went on to become an RAF Air Commodore (equivalent to a USAF Brigadier General). In both cases there were multiple witnesses.

These two cases are powerfully persuasive for the outsider.

Major Giroud, 1977

Date: March 7, 1977
Location: Near Chaumont, France
Type of Sighting: Visual
Type of Prime Witness: Supersonic bomber pilot
Other Witnesses: Navigator

On that day in March 1977, French Air Force Major (now Colonel) René Giroud[123] was flying a Mirage IV supersonic bomber between Dijon and Chaumont. He and his navigator, Captain Jean-Paul Abraham, had just completed a night navigation exercise and were returning to the French airbase at Luxeuil (east-north-east of Dijon) at about thirty thousand feet. It was then 8.34 p.m.

Suddenly, they noticed a white light coming straight at them from their right. They instantly thought it was another aircraft on a collision

---

[123] M Giraud is called both René and Hervé in the COMETA Report.

The Outsider's Guide to UFOs

course, but after querying control, there was nothing on ground radar, and no other aircraft were in their vicinity. The ground controller asked them to check their oxygen (standard practice when a controller thinks the crew may be hallucinating).

In order to understand what happened next, one has to get into the mind of a military combat pilot. The worst thing that can happen, particularly in those days when most air-to-air missiles were relatively short range and heat-seeking, is for an enemy aircraft to get behind you. From the rear, a missile can "see" a massive heat-bloom from your jet engines. From such a position, the missile's job is made extremely easy. So combat pilots always did their best to avoid an enemy getting on their tail. In fact, they still do but the distances involved are much greater..

Giraud was almost at supersonic speed when he made a sharp right turn to try to evade what he had to assume was a hostile aircraft. He was trying to avoid it getting onto his tail. By turning in this way, towards the oncoming object, he had the best chance of preventing it from getting behind him, but he was forced to tighten the turn to around 4G without success. The object got behind the French aircraft at a distance of about 1.5 kilometres (about a mile), and Giraud instantly threw his aircraft into an opposite bank to attempt to get it head-on and to keep it in sight.

The manoeuvre also enabled the pilot to check that he and his navigator were not simply seeing reflections on their canopies. Both men noticed that there was a dark object behind the light, and both light and object stayed behind them for a few more seconds. The major said that the shape was larger and much faster than his Mirage.

Just as the Mirage came around again to the left, and the crew had reacquired the object visually, it flashed away to their left and disappeared. Giraud estimated its speed at Mach 2 (about 1,500 mph).

About forty-five seconds later, the object, or another just like it, reappeared, this time at the aircraft's rear-right. Giraud must have sworn silently. He immediately banked sharp right again, this time pulling 6.5G, in order to keep the object on his right and not allow it to get behind, but again it managed to get behind the Mirage (about two kilometres back), and yet again, Giraud was forced to pull another sharp left turn.

- 233 -

The object did exactly the same thing and then flashed off in the same direction as the first time. Ground radar painted nothing except Giraud's Mirage during the entire event, and there was no sonic boom in the area.

Giraud and Abraham landed safely, although the major said they were shaken. The incident is described in the COMETA Report and is still recorded as an unknown with no current explanation.

Portugal, 1982

Date: November 2, 1982
Location: Alenquer, Portugal
Type of Sighting: Visual
Type of Prime Witness: Three pilots in two different aircraft
Other Witnesses: None

The last powered aircraft in which a pilot would wish to encounter an unidentified object would be a De Havilland Chipmunk (DHC-1). I've flown in these many times as an air cadet, and many air forces over the years have used them as basic twin-seat pilot trainers. They are lovely, gentle aircraft but they are incredibly slow by modern standards. They do, however, have great visibility from the all-over canopy, and they are agile, even capable of simple aerobatics.

Back in 1982, the Portuguese Air Force was still flying these useful trainers, and Julio Guerra was a flight instructor.

On the morning of November 2, he was flying alone to the training range at Alenquer, north of Lisbon, Portugal. At about ten minutes to eleven, he was at five thousand feet when he noticed an object below him and to his left, which he first took to be another aircraft. He says it was grey, metallic, and disc-shaped. It looked like two bowls placed on top of each other, with a band around the circumference (where have we heard that description before?). The top was reflective and the bottom darker, possibly red or brown with a dark spot in the centre (the red-brown colour was similar to that reported by Air France 3532 in 1994). The centre band may have had lights, but Guerra said the sun was so bright, he could not tell for sure.

He immediately banked completely around to his left to try to identify the object, which was headed south. At that point, the object climbed within ten seconds up to his height,. He said it wavered and wobbled a bit and then stayed still. It then paced his aircraft at first and then began circling in an elliptical orbit, which took it about a mile to his south – ahead of his new course – and then a couple of miles to the north, behind his aircraft. It travelled anti-clockwise and did this circuit several times, during which he called his control tower and told them about it. Other pilots came on the air to say it must be a weather balloon, and Guerra responded with understandable scorn. He said that they weren't the pilot seeing this thing and invited them to come and see it themselves.

Another Chipmunk accepted the invitation, and when Carlos Garces and Antonio Gomes arrived, the two watched with Guerra for about ten minutes as the object kept doing its circular orbits.

Guerra's aircraft was inside the orbit of the object, and the other aircraft was outside. As it flew between them, the pilots were able to estimate its size at between eight and ten feet in diameter. Guerra was clearly not a scaredy-cat, even in his old, slow Chippy. He told the other plane that he was going to try to intercept the object. He aimed for a point somewhere along the elliptical orbit. When he got to that point, the object whizzed up and then stopped dead, only about fifteen feet above his plane. It remained there a few seconds and then flew off at high speed south-westerly towards the Atlantic.

It is instructive – and refreshing – that the Portuguese treated the incident as a scientific problem not as something to write-off as an hallucination as might have been the case in America or Britain. A team of thirty scientists studied the entire event, including the reports of all three air force officers who had witnessed it. In 1984, the scientists released a 170-page report. In it they said the object must have been doing around 300 mph vertically. This implies inhuman G-forces. The average elevator/

lift travels between 5 mph and 20 mph. A few, in China, can achieve 45 mph. When the object circled Guerra's Chipmunk, it was probably doing around 1,500 mph.

The scientists could find no explanation for the object or the sighting and said that it must simply remain "unidentified". But at least they tried.

CHAPTER 15

UFOs and Landings

HAVE MYSTERIOUS UFOS EVER landed on planet Earth?

Cue spooky music, flashing lights, and brief glimpses of grey aliens with large black eyes. The answer, of course, is that we don't know for sure. There are lots of accounts of landings but no real proof as yet. Gordon Cooper, the famous astronaut, tells of one which landed in the desert, and abductee after abductee has testified to the fact that they were taken aboard UFOs as the sinister craft sat silently waiting for their human cargo.

If one agrees that a proportion of the 5 percent is genuinely not of this planet, if one remembers that the 5% amounts to a minimum of about 6,000 cases a year across the globe, then logic alone would support the idea that some of them must have landed. Arguing to the contrary would be akin to asserting that Christopher Columbus sailed all the way to the Caribbean and then stooged around all those islands for several months without actually setting foot on any of them.

The chances, therefore, are that if UFOs exist that are not of this world, then a few must have landed, and some may even have had contact with human beings. The logic chain could take you further, but that's scary enough for one chapter.

The problem with landed UFOs is that they have rarely been seen by officials like police officers. But "rarely" does not mean "never"; off the top of my head, I can name Lonnie Zamorra in the States and PC Alan

Godfrey in Yorkshire who say they have seen "landed" objects. For some reason, however, the French (sensible people that they are) take reports of landings much more seriously than the Americans and the British. The French investigate, but that does not mean their reports do not go missing, any more than those of the United States and the UK in such cases.

One such case in France concerns the famous 1954 Quarouble "visitation". On a night in September of that year, at about 10.30 p.m., a steelworker in the town of Quarouble, just to the east of Valenciennes and close to the Belgian border, reported a close encounter of the third kind (except the term had not then been invented).

Marius Dewilde claimed that a craft landed and that two small beings paralysed him before leaving. You will be forgiven, not only for that sigh of disbelief, but also for the thought that has just raced across your mind that, by 10.30 p.m. in the early 1950s, a steel worker in that region might perhaps have imbibed a couple of small glasses of beer.

But even in the hard-working, beer-drinking north of France, it cannot have been that common for workers – even after a few beers – to report small alien beings. There was an official investigation of M Dewilde's claims and the famous French ufologist, engineer, and head of GEPAN and SEPRA, Jean-Jacques Velasco,[124] tried for years to find the report on that investigation, but without success.

That could mean that the investigation revealed a fraud or showed that the sighting was a non-event, but in that case, why was the finding not simply released to the newspapers at the time? A somewhat similar event occurred a decade later, in a field at a place called Valensole, which lies north-east of Marseilles in southern France. The difference is that more details have survived of the Valensole affair.

[124] Velasco was head of GEPAN, the early investigative arm of CNES.

Valensole, 1965

Date: July 1, 1965
Location: Valensole, France
Type of sighting: Visual; effects on land and crops
Type of Prime Witness: Farmer
Other Witnesses: None

This is a very early incident but deserves to be included for its strangeness and the subtle sense of veracity which derives from the simplicity of the account. It occurred a full decade before the French investigative organisation GEPAN (predecessor to GEIPAN) was established in 1977, so there was no methodical or sustained scientific investigation of the claim. However, the gendarmerie conducted as good an investigation as they could, given the circumstances.

Valensole is a pretty hilltop village in the Alpes area of Haute-Provence, lying to the north-east of Marseilles. It has its fair share of vineyards, but its main claim to fame is its beautiful lavender fields with their long rows of colourful, fragrant bushes stretching across the countryside. In the summer time the bushes were in full bloom, and as is the case in any agricultural community, people started work early.

On the morning of July 1, 1965, a local farmer named Maurice Masse had risen with the sun, eaten his breakfast, and by about 5.45 a.m. was walking out to one of his lavender fields. It's not difficult to picture him trudging off in the cool of the early morning, his mind pretty full of the jobs he had to do that day.

But, as he approached the field he wanted to work in that morning, he was surprised to hear a faint whistling sound. When he looked closely at the field, he saw an object sitting in it. He told investigators that it was dark coloured with a matt finish and that it was shaped like a rugby football (same shape as an American football). It was, he said, standing on six legs, and there was a central "leg" which appeared to be stuck into the ground.

Okay, so not a normal day at the office. But what came next was quite incredible. Masse said that two small beings were standing in front of the object. At first, he thought they were children and was therefore probably going to ask them what they were doing in his field, along with that largish object which had crushed some of his lavender bushes.

He kept walking towards the pair and got pretty close before he realised that they were not children playing a game. Masse said he got within about fifteen feet (about five metres) before one of them pointed something at him, which looked like a pencil. He was immediately paralysed and could only watch as the beings boarded their craft and took off. Masse said it floated silently away towards the nearby town of Manosque. He estimated that the whole event took about five minutes.

Although it could not have investigated the incident, GEIPAN has come into possession of the records of the case. They say that Masse did not tell anyone else about the incident until he got home that night and related his experience to his daughter. That same evening, at about half past eight, he took her to the field to show her the star-shaped mark and the hole where the central leg had been. The central hole, he said, had been "soggy" when he'd first inspected it that morning. By the evening, the whole area had become as hard as cement. There is a black-and-white photograph in existence which clearly shows the bare circle of ground in his field where the lavender bushes had been crushed.

The next day, it appears that he told more people, and quite a few came to the field to see the circle and the marks. This was somewhat unfortunate, as the whole area soon became trampled. The gendarmerie were never informed by Masse himself of what had happened. Instead, it seems they learned of the affair at about 9.30 a.m. on July 2 via a rumour.

The farmer was interviewed twice: at about 8 p.m. on July 2 and again between 11 and 11.30 p.m. The final interview was held after, at about 10 p.m., Masse had shown the gendarmes the field where it was supposed to have happened.

On July 3, another group of gendarmes took photos and measurements, and Masse was interviewed yet again at length on August 18. The official reports rate Masse as being honest and credible, and the fact that he did not immediately inform newspapers and never saw anything strange again seems to underline a certain degree of credibility to the weird tale.

This somewhat unbelievable event was well-investigated, and there is the photograph of a circular patch of disturbed field and confirmation that the patch was incapable of growing crops for a "long time". Investigators also found what they called a "long trace" of damage in the direction which Masse said the craft took as it left.

The French UFO investigators, Pierre Guérin and Jacques Vallée, carried out their own research, but the case remains an unknown. GEIPAN's statement on the event's fiftieth anniversary, in 2015, says that it is unlikely that any further conclusions would have been possible, even if GEIPAN had existed at the time. The length of time which was allowed to elapse after the event, before it came to the notice of the authorities, and the spoiling of the site by curious local sightseers, would have made a robust scientific investigation impossible.

The sceptics would doubtless say that this incident was either an out-and-out hoax or the befuddled vision of a man who'd had too much wine the previous evening. It is far too late to be sure either way, but the French gendarmes took their role pretty seriously (two different brigades were involved in this investigation), so it seems unlikely that they would have failed to spot a hoaxer or a man whose visage indicated the strong possibility of a serious hangover. The fact that they did not leaves us, as outsiders, with a strange sense of unease.

It's easy to retreat under one's comfort blanket, the one under which such events simply cannot happen. UFOs do not exist ... do they? Little aliens are just plain silly ... aren't they? But if just a single UFO could be shown to be of some origin other than this beautiful Earth, we might well have to apologise, mentally at least, to Monsieur Masse.

Rendlesham Forest, 1980

Date: December 25 and 26, 1980
Locations: RAF Bentwaters; RAF Woodbridge (both were USAF bases at the time)
Type of Sighting: Visual (possibly British radar too)
Type of Prime Witness: USAF security men; USAF deputy base commander
Other Witnesses: Many of the base complement

The Rendlesham Forest incident attracts more emotion and debate than probably any other UFO sighting except Roswell.[125] Many of those who were there are still alive, and most have given TV and video accounts of themselves. All are credible and convincing people.

The eastern counties of England are not the most comfortable of places in winter, and East Anglia has never been a popular posting for US forces' personnel. The region used to be a difficult one to get to London from. It is damp and cold and, speaking as someone who has lived there, when the east wind sweeps in off the North Sea in winter, it cuts you in half. So in the deepest, darkest days of the year, the best place to be in East Anglia is indoors with a roaring fire and a glass of whatever pleases (and you wonder why British pubs are so popular).

But when you are guarding what was one of the largest and most powerful USAF air bases in Europe, the roaring fire is but a dream, the drink will get you in deep trouble, and the freezing cold hours on duty at the east gate of RAF Woodbridge drag interminably. It was just such a night, on December 25, 1980.

Christmas Day had slipped away, and what the British call "Boxing

---

[125] The events at Roswell, New Mexico, in 1947 are now so complex and confused by argument and hoaxes that it has not been included in this book. The event may or may not have happened, and there is plenty of "evidence" for both sides, but you will need a good year or so of dedicated study to evaluate it all and at the end will find that there is still not enough hard evidence for either side. Life is too short.

Day" was entering, teeth chattering, stage left. In the early hours, one of the security detail on the east gate spotted lights in the woods which separate the twin USAF bases of Bentwaters and Woodbridge. In most accounts, the lights were described as looking like an aircraft had crashed. So a three-man patrol from the 81st Security Police Squadron set out to see what had happened. The patrol consisted of Jim Penniston, John Burroughs, and Ed Cabansag.

Rendlesham Forest. (Jason Salmon/Shutterstock.com)

The location of the "crash" wasn't far away, but because it was in the forest,[126] they had to leave their vehicle and walk the last part of the logging track towards the lights.

According to the three men (and their accounts have not really varied over the years), they saw a small metallic "craft" settled in a confined clearing. The object was triangular or wedge-shaped, about three metres across

---

[126] The British call it a forest, but to Americans, it would just about qualify as a small wood or a softwood plantation.

and a couple high, and bright lights shone from it. It sat there reasonably quietly, so Penniston walked up to it and circled it, all the while making notes in his notebook. He noticed markings on the side which he could only liken to hieroglyphics. These he scrawled into the notebook too. The other two men took up more distant positions and did not see these markings.

Eventually, the machine's lights began to grow brighter, and the men say they backed off into "defensive" positions before it rose into the air and negotiated its way out of the trees, away from them. Then it shot off into the distance, and they saw it no more.

Their accounts, when they returned to the base, were passed to the deputy base commander, Lieutenant Colonel Charles Halt, who interviewed them together with a couple of what might have been intelligence officers. It is not much of a stretch of the imagination to see that Halt must have suspected that a bored set of security men, on a bleak and quiet Christmas night, had cooked up a little excitement. Nevertheless, he had the three men write up their official reports and attached to them their notes and drawings. It might be worth noting here that, if the men had invented the whole thing as a harmless prank, now was the time to come clean and tell everyone. The lieutenant colonel would be pretty mad at them wasting his and other officers' time, but once those reports got sent off to HQ and then to Washington or wherever the USAF sent its UFO reports in 1980, things were bound to get a whole lot more serious. It would have been clear to all three men that the seriousness of what they had reported would follow them for the rest of their service careers. Seeing UFOs, especially close up, is not something that would be overlooked when one's service record was being updated and when promotions were being considered.

The men did not retract their stories, though, and as a result, they took a lot of ribbing from their compatriots on the bases. But in many ways, their spectacular sighting was the least of what was to occur that fateful Christmas in the Forest of Rendlesham.

Two nights later, on December 28, Lieutenant Colonel Halt presumably thought the whole strange incident was behind him. The men had not tried to invent any other story, and their reports and drawings were safely delivered into the murky depths of headquarters.

That evening, he was at a social function (the accounts differ as to whether it was a delayed base Christmas party or a private affair) when an airman burst in and ran up to him, announcing that "it's back". Halt was naturally confused and asked the obvious question. "The UFO, sir," the man responded. "The UFO's back".

An artist's impression of the object encountered by the three-man USAF patrol on a cold winter's night in 1980. (Fortean/Topfoto.co.uk)

Cats were very quickly set amongst pigeons, and Halt's boss, who was also at the party, very wisely decided that his deputy should go out into the freezing night and see what on earth was going on. Rank has its privileges.

Lieutenant Colonel Halt says that he was determined to get to the bottom of what he thought was an extended practical joke, and he did it properly. He got a large team together and ordered portable lights (the USAF calls them Light-Alls) and ventured out, as we say in England, "mob-handed". He was sceptical and probably not a little peeved at those who had interrupted his nice, warm, convivial party. To use his own word, he said he wanted to "debunk" the whole thing. Doubtless he also wanted to get back to the party. And that's where this particular sighting gets really interesting because now we are talking about a full lieutenant colonel going out in the pitch-black, freezing East Anglian night, chasing a suspected UFO.

Life is never straightforward, especially where unidentified flying objects are concerned. Halt got to the forest with his men, but the transmissions on their hand-held radios were breaking up, and the Light-Alls wouldn't work properly either. Halt had to send back for more, and the effort to get them fuelled and working stirred the base up even more.

Halt did one thing, however, which has made this series of sightings unique. He took with him his handheld tape recorder, and he recorded voice notes as he went. The recording he made as he trudged across the muddy fields that night is available online.[127]

The lieutenant colonel and his men found the clearing and the marks which Penniston had said were where the UFO had landed. They took a Geiger counter which, depending on whose version you read, either recorded well over the natural background or was misread by the operator.

Then, about two-thirds of the way through the recording, Halt's men saw some lights, and the whole group trooped off in that direction. That is, they tried to get into a position where they could see the lights more clearly. They trekked out of the forest, across a field, past a farmhouse, and into another field, all the while trying to evaluate what the lights were. The group squelched across the bleak, soggy fields, and they seem to have closed in on the lights at one point, when they saw beams of white light shoot onto the ground below. The lights moved quickly, and at one point, Halt tells the tape-recorder, a beam of white light was shot down very close to where he and his men were standing.

Halt was truly baffled, and you can hear it in his voice:

> "I see it, too ... It's back again ... It's coming this way ...
> There's no doubt about it ... This is weird ... It looks like an
> eye winking at you ... It almost burns your eyes ... He's com-
> ing toward us now ... Now we're observing what appears to

---

[127] Halt's tape recording with subtitles: https://www.youtube.com/watch?v=7KChGKhJ4Ro

be a beam coming down to the ground ... one object still
hovering over Woodbridge base ... beaming down".[128]

Halt says that the objects (there were clearly more than one) had red,
green, and blue lights, and that they became several objects in the northern sky, moving very rapidly in sharp angles. He said that what concerned
him most was that one of the objects shot a beam of white light down into
the base's weapons storage area where, almost certainly, nuclear weapons
were being stored.

Eventually, the lights shot off and disappeared, and Halt and his men
made their weary way back to the base. It was after 4.00 a.m.

There were official reports to be written and debriefings to be under-
gone.[129] After some time (on January 13, 1981), Halt wrote a memo to the
Ministry of Defence in London. No one was at all sure whose responsibility the sightings were. The forest between the two bases was British
territory and there are a number of references in the source material sug-
gesting that the Americans would dearly have loved for the Brits to take
the matter under their control. The Brits for their part were clearly very
happy to leave the matter to their allies.

The lieutenant colonel's memo to the British Ministry of Defence
was entitled "Unexplained Lights"; he was not prepared to use the term
"UFO". In the memo, he said that the thing that was seen on the first
night was triangular and seemed metallic. He described it as having a
pulsing red light on top and a bank of blue lights underneath. He further
explained that animals on a nearby farm went into a frenzy, but what he
did not know was that the noises almost certainly came from Muntjac
deer in the forest itself. He told the MoD what the radiation readings had
been and, in the third paragraph, as though of much lesser import and
part and parcel of the first night's events, described his own sightings of
lights and white beams.

---

[128] Nick Pope. *Encounter in Rendlesham Forest.* 2014. His book provides a much more
detailed account of the entire affair.

[129] Some accounts say that many of the enlisted personnel were subjected to aggressive
interrogation and threatened if they revealed anything that had happened.

DEPARTMENT OF THE AIR FORCE
HEADQUARTERS 81ST COMBAT SUPPORT GROUP (USAFE)
APO NEW YORK 09755

REPLY TO
ATTN OF: CD

13 Jan 81

SUBJECT: Unexplained Lights

TO: RAF/CC

1. Early in the morning of 27 Dec 80 (approximately 0300L), two USAF security police patrolmen saw unusual lights outside the back gate at RAF Woodbridge. Thinking an aircraft might have crashed or been forced down, they called for permission to go outside the gate to investigate. The on-duty flight chief responded and allowed three patrolmen to proceed on foot. The individuals reported seeing a strange glowing object in the forest. The object was described as being metalic in appearance and triangular in shape, approximately two to three meters across the base and approximately two meters high. It illuminated the entire forest with a white light. The object itself had a pulsing red light on top and a bank(s) of blue lights underneath. The object was hovering or on legs. As the patrolmen approached the object, it maneuvered through the trees and disappeared. At this time the animals on a nearby farm went into a frenzy. The object was briefly sighted approximately an hour later near the back gate.

2. The next day, three depressions 1 1/2" deep and 7" in diameter were found where the object had been sighted on the ground. The following night (29 Dec 80) the area was checked for radiation. Beta/gamma readings of 0.1 milliroentgens were recorded with peak readings in the three depressions and near the center of the triangle formed by the depressions. A nearby tree had moderate (.05-.07) readings on the side of the tree toward the depressions.

3. Later in the night a red sun-like light was seen through the trees. It moved about and pulsed. At one point it appeared to throw off glowing particles and then broke into five separate white objects and then disappeared. Immediately thereafter, three star-like objects were noticed in the sky, two objects to the north and one to the south, all of which were about 10° off the horizon. The objects moved rapidly in sharp angular movements and displayed red, green and blue lights. The objects to the north appeared to be elliptical through an 8-12 power lens. They then turned to full circles. The objects to the north remained in the sky for an hour or more. The object to the south was visible for two or three hours and beamed down a stream of light from time to time. Numerous individuals, including the undersigned, witnessed the activities in paragraphs 2 and 3.

CHARLES I. HALT, Lt Col, USAF
Deputy Base Commander

The memo written by Lt Col Halt to the British Ministry of Defence concerning the events of Christmas, 1980. (Topfoto.co.uk/ Fortean)

The memo's three numbered paragraphs[130] informed the British government that:

1. When US security personnel investigated lights in Rendlesham Forest at about 3 a.m. on the morning of December 27, 1980, they'd found a triangular object roughly three metres across by two in height.
2. This eventually rose and disappeared but was seen again near the base's back gate about an hour later.
3. On the following day, security investigations found depressions about 1.5 inches deep and 7 inches across in the place where the object had been witnessed. Radiation tests were reported in the colonel's memo.
4. On December 29, red, blue, and green lights were seen and objects examined through binoculars. The objects were elliptical and moved in a sharp, angular manner. They were seen for several hours and sent beams of light to the ground at times.

Lieutenant Colonel Halt says in the memo that he was one of the witnesses to the later stages of the events, but he did not attempt to describe his reactions as revealed, later, by his recorded notes.

Ian Ridpath and other sceptics believe he and his men were mistaken. The sceptics' story is that the marks were rabbit scrapings, the radiation readings were insignificant, the majority of the lights were just those of the local lighthouse, the first night's lights were actually a fireball which descended that night on southern Britain, and the lights seen by Halt and his men were actually stars which "appeared" to send down beams of light. Sirius, says Ian Redpath, is an exceptionally bright star and was in the right position. Colonel Halt was misled, on the second night of sightings, by the lighthouse and by stars and other "nocturnal objects". However, Halt

---

[130] Note that Lt Col Halt got the date wrong, as the first incident occurred on the night of December 25/26. His memo was written more than two weeks after the event.

rebuts all this and says that he and his men could always see the lighthouse off to the right of the sightings on the night he was out. It would certainly be very strange if lights from a lighthouse or stars suddenly started moving rapidly and making sharp turns high in the sky. Even stranger if they were so distinct as to be perceived as elliptical by Halt and his men.

But perhaps the privilege of the last word should go to the late Admiral Lord Hill-Norton, ex-chief of the Defence Staff whom we last met on board HMS Eagle during Operation Mainbrace. He is on film stating, most emphatically, the following:

> "There are only two possibilities: either an intrusion into
> our airspace and a landing by unidentified craft took place
> at Rendlesham, as described; or the Deputy Commander
> of an operational, nuclear armed, U.S. Air Force Base in
> England, and a large number of his enlisted men, were
> either hallucinating or lying".[131]

We should note, however, that Lieutenant Colonel Halt and Messrs Penniston, Burroughs, and Cabansag have stuck, through some extremely vitriolic criticism, to the story they told on the nights in question. For me, the most convincing of them all is Lieutenant Colonel Halt. His statements on film, and his presentations on the subject to conferences, are delivered with a strong sense that he very much wishes he'd never gone out into the forest that night back in 1980. His eyes seem to reveal his bafflement that he was so unlucky, as well as his internal pain at the disbelief and scepticism with which his accounts have been greeted.

At the National Press Club conference of 2007, Colonel Halt gave a presentation. At the end of it, he said

> "I don't know what we saw that night. But I do know, with
> great certainty, that it was under intelligent control".

---

[131] I would recommend the two James Fox documentaries.

One of the things which sceptics rarely if ever acknowledge is the sheer courage it takes to stand up in public in front of an audience of sceptical journalists and explain a UFO sighting. The general assumption seems to be that all people who see UFOs are publicity-seekers or hoaxers. What we as outsiders need to ask ourselves is: a) does that apply to every single witness? And b) if some of them are honest and decent people trying to tell of something they genuinely experienced, what does that mean for our own approach to the subject?

Trans-en-Provence, 1981

Date: January 8, 1981
Location: Trans-en-Provence, France
Type of Sighting: Visual and physical effects
Type of Prime Witness: Farmer
Other Witnesses: None

Unlike the Valensole case, the sighting in Trans-en-Provence was very well investigated by the French authorities, over many years. Superficially, it was very similar to the 1965 incident, but the level of scientific analysis and research has turned it from what might have been just another "weird" and slightly unbelievable story into a very puzzling piece of scientific investigation. The case also shows up, very plainly, the difference between the American and British reaction to UFOs and the French approach. In the latter case there is no knee-jerk retreat to ridicule (although the French are not immune to that). Instead they investigate, if not completely thoroughly, at least to a far higher degree than the Anglo-Saxons over the water. More importantly the French accord the subject a modicum of respect and seriousness.

The area in which Trans-en-Provence is situated lies to the south-east of Valensole and slightly nearer the coast of southern France.

On January 8, 1981, about five o'clock in the evening, Renato Nicolai, a fifty-two-year-old technician, was working in his back garden. The land is steep in this area, so the garden had been structured into a number of terraces. It was on the upper terrace that he was constructing a small building to protect a pump.

While he was working, he heard a whistling sound to the east and saw an object, like two "bulging" saucers stuck together, float over some trees, descend, and then land in his garden, out of sight, about fifty metres away from him. Nicolai moved to where he could see the object and watched as, after just thirty or forty seconds, it took off again and flew off in the same direction from which it had arrived. As it sped away, Nicolai noticed two round protrusions on the underside and two circular markings that looked like trapdoors. He said the object was about two and a half metres in diameter and about 1.7 metres high. Naturally, he inspected the area where the object had set down. He found a two-metre circle with traces of other things on the circumference of the circle.

This event happened after GEPAN had been established as part of CNES, the French space agency, so unlike the earlier occurrences it was subjected to a fairly thorough investigation which, in the end, spread over several years.

The gendarmerie conducted the initial investigations before alerting GEPAN[132] During those early examinations, they found two concentric circles (2.2 metres diameter and 2.4 metres diameter). As required by the regulations, they also collected soil samples, including control samples. A month later, GEPAN investigators arrived and collected additional samples and cuttings from vegetation. The GEPAN people also assessed the witness himself and did all the usual checks with the relevant authorities for weather conditions, air traffic, and so on. The plant and soil samples were analysed by four different laboratories, each using different techniques. The plant samples were analysed at the prestigious INRA.[133]

The combined gendarmerie/GEPAN investigation took two years, and GEIPAN has returned to the site since the initial report was published.

---

[132] *Groupe d'Etude des Phenomenes Aerospatiaux Non-Identifies* (GEPAN), part of CNES, and now known as GEIPAN.

[133] The French National Institute for Agricultural Research.

Needless to say, Renato Nicolai was interviewed several times and, over the years, has given several interviews to other researchers.

The original report (GEPAN Technical Note 16) concluded:

1. Evidence indicates a strong mechanical pressure on the ground surface, probably due to a heavy weight, of about four to five tons.
2. At the same time or immediately after this pressure, the soil was heated up to between 300 and 600 degrees C.
3. Trace quantities were found of phosphate and zinc.
4. The chlorophyll content of the wild alfalfa leaves in the immediate vicinity of the ground traces was reduced 30 percent to 50 percent, inversely proportional to distance.
5. Young alfalfa leaves experienced the highest loss of chlorophyll and, moreover, exhibited "signs of premature senescence".
6. Biochemical analysis showed numerous differences between vegetation samples obtained close to the site and those more distant.

Its final words were:

> An unusual important phenomenon occurred that day,
> and the investigation did not determine its origin.

In 1988, seven years after the original event, Dr Jacques Vallée and Dr Michel Bounias revisited the site. Their goal was to reassess the evidence, but specifically to assess the evidence (or lack of it) for an explanation put forward by a neighbour of M Nicolai. The neighbour thought that a tractor, cement dust, and chemicals used on the tractor would have caused the hardening of the soil and the damage to plants. To introduce yet another level of scientific rigour and to avoid charges that perhaps French laboratories would be unwilling to contradict the findings of another French laboratory, they used a US laboratory to double-check the findings of the original investigations.[134] As an aside, it is interesting that, according to Dr Vallee, the US laboratory was so wary of the stigma associated with UFO studies in America that it would only perform the analyses if it were permitted to remain anonymous.

The report is detailed, and the conclusions were:

> "The results of our analysis of the soil samples from Trans-en-Provence are consistent with the statements by the witness and his wife regarding the history of the soil. In particular, careful microscopic and physical analysis failed to detect any of the substances, such as cement or other construction and drilling materials, that have been proposed to "explain" the traces. Our results tend to support the earlier findings of the French laboratories consulted by the CNES as well as the truthfulness of the witness' testimony."

The case remains one of the most thoroughly examined UFO cases in the world and one that has baffled scientists and sceptics alike. Nicolai and his wife have not invited publicity; in fact, quite the opposite. They appear to have cooperated fully with every investigation that has been mounted, in spite of being subjected to a degree of ridicule and scorn in their village. The assiduous outsider will find videos of M Nicolai on the Web. His frustration and bafflement are very evident.

For the outsider it is important not to overlook two things:

1. this was a case involving an unidentified object, the nature of which is still unknown. It is a UFO, or a UAP if you prefer.
2. it is an example of a UFO/UAP for which there is a good deal of physical evidence (even if we do not yet understand its meaning).

---

[134] Dr Jacques Vallee. *Return to Trans-en-Provence*. http://www.noufors.com/Documents/Books,%20Manuals%20and%20Published%20Papers/Specialty%20UFO%20Publications/Journal%20of%20Scientific%20Exploration/jse_04_1_vallee_1.pdf Dr Vallee's own website has the same document, but it seems incomplete: http://www.jacquesvallee.net/bookdocs/Return_to_Trans-en-Provence.pdf

CHAPTER 16

Mass Sightings, 1950—1989

UFO SIGHTINGS NEVER SEEM to fit neatly into a category. There are some objects which are seen by a single person in a single location, and one breathes a sigh of relief and stacks them quickly into a chapter on single-sighting UFOs. But then one finds out that other, similar objects were seen just the next day, or in the next county, or that there actually were other people who saw the same object but from different vantage points.

Ufologists seem to spend most of their time trying to pin down the category into which a sighting should be placed. Should it be a single sighting, should it be multiple sightings, or even, the excitement mounting, should it be a wave sighting? My own view is that, to the largest extent, none of it really matters. In some ways, one could categorise the whole UFO phenomenon as a wave sighting from 1945 onwards; looked at from another standpoint, one really ought to treat every single sighting as totally separate until one can prove beyond a shadow of a doubt that several of them are linked in some way.

But the bottom line is that ufologists over the years have labelled certain sets of sightings as "waves", each day's encounters being automatically linked in some way to the previous ones. And one can understand this tendency because – to put it bluntly – the sightings do seem to be connected in different ways, geographically or by the appearance of the objects or by the time frame or whatever.

Connecting the dots in this way is just one way of looking at a set of sightings which may or may not be connected in reality. The problem is that the word "wave" to me implies an intent to flood the area in question over a period of time, and there is not much proof that this intent exists. So for the purposes of the next two chapters, I have simply called them "mass sightings". They may be waves, they may be ripples, or they may simply be a set of unconnected sightings, most of which are part of the explicable 95 percent.

Read on and see what you think.

Washington National, 1952

Date: July 1952
Locations: All across the United States but main sightings in and around Washington, DC.
Type of Sighting: Visual and airborne radar
Type of Prime Witness: Airport radar controllers/civilians/airline pilots
Other Witnesses: Military pilots

One of the most famous mass sightings occurred at Washington National Airport and around the city of Washington DC in 1952. It's one of those early cases which, however dated, is valuable because it illustrates how consistent witnesses can be over very long periods of time.

It is also a good example of how incredibly complex a set of events can become once one starts to list every single sighting and the reports of every single witness. Read J Allen Hynek's account of the Hudson Valley sightings in *Night Siege,* and you'll see what this means in practice. Even with the sightings stripped down to the major ones, there are so many that one gets "UFO-fatigue" about halfway through the book. It is almost impossible to comprehend that the ones you are reading about are just a few of those which were reported.

For the author or researcher trying to make sense of the whole episode, it's a bit like developing constellations in the night sky. We all know that the Great Bear could be a score of other things depending on how you join the dots, but it helps all of us if we can look for a particular shape in order to be able to work with the immense complexity of the heavens. People who write books like *Night Siege* are also "joining the dots". The way in which they are joined up depends on the author, and you should always be aware that there are probably different ways of categorising multiple sightings. There could be sets of sightings which could be defined as not part of the group, and even a mass of other sightings which might be linked. Also, it's entirely likely that different groupings and categorisations might lead to different conclusions.

So that was a long way of saying that I've done my best with the Washington DC sightings of 1952, but who can really tell when the "Washington National Sightings" began and when they ended? For convenience, we tend to see them as a geographically constrained set of sightings centred on the National Airport (a bit like the Hudson Valley sightings, which were given that name but which actually encompassed a great deal more territory). But there were many sightings outside the strict DC area around that same time period, and many sightings within the DC area outside the accepted time frame of the Washington National affair!

Whatever authors do, the dots can be joined in many different ways, and the outsider should bear that in mind while reading all of the cases in this book.

Okay, let's begin with the Washington flap of 1952. The sightings of that year spooked an entire nation, intrigued the world, and paralleled similar sets of sightings in other countries. There were so many sighting reports that year that the US military became just as spooked as the general population. And the British had their own set of important sightings that year too. For the US government and the military, however, the extended sightings created a double whammy. On the one hand, they had to reassure the public that they were on the case and would defend them to the death. On the other hand, they themselves were just a little anxious that perhaps the Soviets had stolen a march on Uncle Sam and, with utter impunity, were stooging backwards and forwards across the Land of the Free.

Understandably, then, there was a very real sense that UFOs posed a threat, which is not, perhaps, the underlying feeling in the second decade of the twenty-first century. In the early 1950s, almost every member of the top brass was seriously concerned. These things were either extraterrestrial spacecraft or very sophisticated aircraft the like of which Uncle Sam could not match.

A 1952 photo of Captain Edward Ruppelt, head of Project Blue Book (standing), and Major General John Samford, USAF director of intelligence. (Fortean/Topfoto.co.uk)

It's not easy to think of a parallel situation in recent years, one in which the director of US Air Force Intelligence gives a televised press conference to calm the fears of an entire nation. But on July 29, 1952, Major General Samford, who occupied that exact position, held a huge press conference on the subject (attended by foreign as well as US press). Among other things about "flying saucers", he said

> "Air Force interest in the problem has been due to our feeling of an obligation to identify and analyze, to the best of our ability, anything in the air that has the possibility of [being] a threat or menace to the United States. In pursuit of this obligation, since 1947, we have received and analyzed between one and two thousand reports that have come to us from all kinds of sources. Of this great mass of reports, we have been able adequately to explain the great bulk of them— explain them to our own satisfaction. However, there are then a certain percentage of this volume of reports that have been made by credible observers of relatively incredible things. It is this group of observations that we now are attempting to resolve. We have, as of date, come to only one firm conclusion with respect to this remaining percentage. And that is that it does not contain any pattern of purpose or of consistency that we can relate to any conceivable threat to the United States".[135]

Samford's press conference came at the end of a whirlwind month of civilian and military sightings. Some of the most interesting are listed in Table 3, and one or two are discussed in more detail later. It's perhaps worth pointing out, right at the start, that the official explanation, after the sightings died down, was "temperature inversions in the atmosphere" or mistaken planets and stars.

The USAF's latest jet interceptor at the time was the Lockheed F-94 Starfire. It was equipped with an early form of gun-control radar which was reasonably effective at short range, and it was these fighters which were generally involved in the attempted air intercepts mentioned in the sightings.

On the first of July 1952, there were two separate sightings of silvery,

---

[135] Leslie Kean. UFOs: Generals, Pilots, and Government Officials Go on the Record.

cigar-shaped objects over the Boston area. It appears that two F-94s were scrambled, but a couple in Lynn, near Boston, saw the fighters searching well below the level at which two of the silvery objects were travelling. One of the objects was also seen separately by an Air Force captain on the ground.

Two similar objects were plotted by radar and seen visually by radar students from Fort Monmouth, New Jersey, at 9.30 a.m. that same day. They reported the objects at fifty thousand feet and said that they departed to the south-west at high speed.

Later that evening, an object was seen from the ground from central Washington. There were a number of notable sightings in the first half of July, but the most spectacular events began over Washington DC on the night of July 19/20. The following table provides a skeletal overview of what seem to be the most interesting sightings of what has become known as the "Washington DC Wave", even though sightings during July came from as far away as Boston, Chicago (in the middle of a heatwave), and California. The events include sightings by civil and military pilots, military officers on the ground, air traffic controllers, radar operators at a civilian airport and a military airbase, and, of course, civilians.

The shaded dates are those most often described under the title of the Washington National Sightings.

Table 3: The Washington National Incidents, July 1952[136]

Date	Time	Location	Event
July 10		National Airlines plane near Quantico, Virginia	While flying south at two thousand feet near Quantico, Virginia, just south of Washington, the aircraft reported a light "too bright to be a lighted balloon and too slow to be a big meteor".

[136] Developed from several sources but mainly from Edward Ruppelt.

Date	Time	Location	Event
July 12	9.42 p.m.	Montrose Beach near Chicago	On a sweltering Chicago night, around four hundred people saw, for five minutes, an object come from the west-northwest, make a 180-degree turn directly over their heads, and disappear over the horizon. It was described as a "large red light with small white lights on the side".
July 13		Airliner sixty miles southwest of Washington	At eleven thousand feet, the crew saw a light below them. It came up to their level, hovered off to the left for several minutes, and then took off in a fast, steep climb when the pilot turned on his landing lights.
July 14		Pan American airliner en route from New York to Miami	Reported eight unidentified objects near Newport News, Virginia, about 130 miles south of Washington.
July 16	9.00 p.m.	Near Newport News, Virginia	A civilian scientist (from the National Advisory Committee for Aeronautics Laboratory at Langley AFB) and another man were standing near the ocean looking south over Hampton Roads when they saw two amber lights, "much too large to be aircraft lights", off to their right, silently traveling north. Just before the two lights got abreast of the two men, they made a 180 degree turn and started back towards the spot where they had first been seen. As they turned, the two lights seemed to "jockey for position in the formation." Then a third light came out of the west and joined the first two. As the three objects climbed out of the area southwards, several more lights joined the formation. The entire episode lasted three minutes.

Date	Time	Location	Event
July 18	10.45 p.m.	Patrick AFB, Florida	Two officers were standing in front of base operations when they saw an amber-coloured light, "quite a bit brighter than a star", at about a 45 degree angle from the horizon off to the west. They thought it was a balloon. The light drifted over the base, stopped for about a minute, turned, and headed north. They checked, and it wasn't a weather balloon. A second amber light now appeared in the west, also headed north, but at a much greater speed. In a few seconds, the first light stopped and started moving back south over the base. Then a third light travelled at high speed, directly overhead, from west to east. In the next quarter of an hour, two more amber lights came in from the west, crossed the base, made a 180 degree turn over the ocean, and came back over the observers. Radar did not pick any of them up.
July 19	9.30 p.m.	Alexandria, Virginia	An Army artillery officer, Joseph Gigandet, was sitting on the front porch of his home in Alexandria, Virginia, across the Potomac River from Washington. At 9:30 p.m., he saw "a red cigar-shaped object" which sailed slowly over his house. Gigandet estimated the object's size as comparable to a DC-7 airplane[137] at about ten thousand feet altitude; he also said the object had a "series of lights very closely set together" on its sides. The object eventually flew back over his house a second time. When the object flew away a second time, it turned a deeper red colour and moved over the city of Washington itself; this occurred less than two hours before an operator named Edward Nugent spotted unknown objects on his radar at Washington National Airport.

---

[137] A DC-7 was a four-engine, piston-powered airliner.

Date	Time	Location	Event
	11.40 p.m.	Washington National Airport	Two radars at National Airport picked up eight unidentified targets east and south of Andrews AFB. The targets flew slowly at 100 to 130 mph then suddenly accelerated to "fantastically high speeds" and left the area. Radars were checked technically. ARTC radar[138] and local airport radar, plus radar at Andrews, picked up the same group. One target logged at 7,000 mph; some were in prohibited areas over White House and the Capitol.
		Airliners	During the night, the crews of several airliners saw mysterious lights in the same locations that the radars plotted targets. Staff in the control tower also saw lights visually; jet fighters were scrambled but without being able to catch anything.
July 20	c12.10 a.m.	Capital Airlines	After this aircraft took off from National just after midnight, the controller asked the pilot to keep watch for anything unusual. Just after the aircraft cleared the traffic pattern, the pilot radioed, "There's one—off to the right—and there it goes". The controller had been watching the scope, and a target that had been off to the right of the airliner was gone. During the next fourteen minutes, this pilot reported six more identical lights.
	c2.00 a.m.	Aircraft approaching National Airport from the south	The pilot reported that a light was following him at "eight o'clock level". The tower checked the radar, and there was a target behind and to the left of the airliner. The area radar also had the airliner and the target, which followed the airliner until it was within four miles of touchdown. Both the pilot and the radar agreed on when the object departed on final approach.

---

[138] ARTC = Air Route Traffic Control

Date	Time	Location	Event
			Once during the night, the two radars at Washington and the one at Andrews AFB picked up a target three miles north of the Riverdale Radio beacon, north of Washington. For thirty seconds, the three radar operators compared notes about the target, then, very suddenly, it was gone. It left all three radarscopes simultaneously.
			A little later, an area traffic controller at National called the control tower at Andrews AFB. He had a target just south of the Andrews tower. The tower operators at Andrews AFB looked, and there was a "huge fiery-orange sphere" hovering in the sky directly over their range station. When the tower operators were questioned later, they apparently changed their story and said that what they saw was merely a star. They said that on the night of the sighting, they "had been excited". Edward Ruppelt writes: "I heard from a good source that the tower men had been 'persuaded' a bit".
			Around daylight, an F-94 arrived over Washington National, but the targets were gone. The F-94 crew searched the area for a few minutes, but they couldn't find anything unusual, so they returned to their base.
July 26	10.30 p.m.	Washington National Airport	A number of USAF officers[139] watched and listened as radar operators at the airport tried to help USAF fighter aircraft intercept UFOs; the same slow-moving targets were spread out in an arc around Washington from Herndon, Virginia, to Andrews AFB.
	11.30 p.m.		Four or five of the targets were continually being tracked. Two F-94s from New Castle County AFB were scrambled.

[139] Al Chop (an officer who assisted Edward Ruppelt), Major Dewey Fournet, and Lieutenant Holcomb, a Navy electronics specialist assigned to the Air Force Directorate of Intelligence.

Date	Time	Location	Event
July 27	Midnight		All civilian air traffic was cleared out of the area. The radar targets disappeared just as the two F-94s arrived in the area. They searched for a while, and a few minutes after the fighters left the Washington area, the unidentified targets were back on the radarscopes in that same area.
			Just after the above, people near Langley AFB near Newport News, Virginia, began to call Langley Tower to report that they were looking at weird bright lights that were "rotating and giving off alternating colours."
		Langley AFB, Newport News	The tower operators saw a similar light, and they called for an F-94 which was patrolling in the area. The operators *visually* vectored the fighter onto the light. They watched as the F-94 turned towards the light, and the light went out "like somebody turning off a light bulb". The F-94 crew carried on in the same direction and got a radar lock-on, which was broken as the target sped away. The fighter got two more lock-ons, but each time, they were broken after a few seconds.
		Washington National Airport	Targets now reappeared back at Washington, and the controller again called Air Defense Command. Two F-94s arrived with the targets still on the radarscopes. The controllers vectored the jets towards group after group of targets, but each time, before the jets could get close enough to see anything more than just a light, the targets sped away. It seems that the closest any of the aircraft got was about two miles from the lights.

Date	Time	Location	Event
		California	On the same night as the second Washington visits, an Air Defense Command radar picked up an unidentified target, and an F-94C was scrambled. The fighter was radar vectored onto the target, and the radar operator in the back-seat of the F-94 locked on to it. As the aircraft closed on the target, it was seen to be a large, yellowish-orange light. The aircraft and the light jockeyed for position for a few minutes, but as soon as the airplane got almost within gunnery range, the object suddenly pulled away at high speed. Then it slowed down enough to let the F-94 catch it again. The pilot told Edward Ruppelt that it felt like a cat-and-mouse game – but he said it was he who felt like the mouse. After talking to the press and to Ruppelt, the pilot of the F-94C changed his mind. His official report says that he saw a ground light reflecting off a layer of haze.
July 29	4.00 p.m.	Washington	General Samford's famous press conference.
	9.40 p.m.	Michigan	An Air Defense Command radar station in central Michigan plotted an unidentified target coming straight south from Canada across Saginaw Bay on Lake Huron at 625 mph. The ground controller called one of three F-94s on patrol. At 30,000 feet, the pilot and radar operator in the F-94 saw a large bluish-white light, "many times larger than a star." In the next second or two, the light "took on a reddish tinge, and slowly began to get smaller, as if it were moving away". At that point, the controller said that the target had just turned 180 degrees. The target was now heading back north. At full power, the F-94 got close enough for the radar operator to get a good radar lock-on. Later he said, "It was just as solid a lock-on as you get from a B-36". At 4 miles, and for thirty seconds, the F-94 held the

Date	Time	Location	Event
			lock-on, but then the object pulled away and broke the lock. Sometimes, the unidentified target would slow down, and the F-94 would start to close the gap, but when the F-94 got almost within radar range, the target would accelerate (up to 1,400 mph) and pull away again. Ruppelt says that the F-94 was heading straight for the star Capella, which is low on the horizon and is very bright, but that would not explain the ground and air radar contacts.

In the Bettman Collection, there is a photograph of crew and men of the 142nd Fighter Interceptor Squadron, standing in front of their F-94s, supposedly discussing their flights over Washington chasing UFOs during their second appearance.[140] The photo is dated July 29, 1952.

The main focus for this set of UFO sightings was at the airport, or rather airports, for the radar contacts and sightings were made from three different airports in the Washington area: Washington National Airport, Bolling AFB (which lies across the wide Potomac, almost opposite National), and Andrews AFB, which lies a bit further to the east of Bolling.

One of the chaps in the control tower at Washington National Airport on July 19 that year was Howard Cocklin. It was his colleague who was called by the long range radar room (ARTC) and asked if he had anything on his scope. He responded yes and said that he could actually see the lighted object from his window. Cocklin was interviewed fifty years later by the *Washington Post* (in 2002). He told the reporter that he was still "convinced that he saw an object over Washington National ... I saw it on the [radar] screen and out the window ... it was a whitish-blue object. Not a light, a solid form ... a saucer-shaped object." (*Washington Post*, 2002).

On that evening, there was an important sighting at about 9.30 p.m. (the Gigandet report, see Table 3), and then, about two hours later, it all began in earnest. The other central character at the airport was no less than the chief air traffic controller, a chap named Harry Barnes.

---

[140] The men included Lt F Lamar Watson, Lt John Fagan, and Capt John C Casey.

Like a huge proportion of UFO witnesses, Barnes and Cocklin reported what happened and what they saw and subsequently came in for some very rough treatment at the hands of their colleagues, the newspapers, and the sceptics. The outsider needs to note, however, that like most witnesses to strange objects, they stuck doggedly to their story for the rest of their lives. They had nothing to gain from what they said they saw and, in fact, their statements cost them a great deal in personal anguish

At about 11.40 p.m. on the night of July 19, one of Washington National's area air traffic controllers, Edward Nugent, saw seven unexplained blips on his radarscope.[141] He logged them as being located about fifteen miles south-south-west of the airport (near Fort Belvoir or Mount Vernon). He called to his boss, Harry Barnes, who then stood behind Nugent, watching the blips and their very strange movements. Barnes told the author, Curtis Peebles:[142]

> "We knew immediately that a very strange situation existed ... their movements were completely radical compared to those of ordinary aircraft".

Barnes had the radar checked and then called the airport control tower. This was a separate control room which managed the air-space in the immediate vicinity of the airport (unlike Harry Barnes' control room, which monitored a much wider area). On that call, Barnes learned that two of the controllers, Howard Cocklin and Joe Zacko, had seen, through the tower's large windows, a whitish blue light "hovering". They said it left at incredible speed. In an interview with Peter Carlson for the *Washington Post* in 2002, Cocklin said that it was a solid object which looked like a saucer.[143]

Other objects began to appear on the radar screens, and when some of them entered sensitive airspace above the White House and the Capitol,

---

[141] The airport is now known as Ronald Reagan Washington National Airport.

[142] Curtis Peebles. *Watch the Skies!: A Chronicle of the Flying Saucer Myth*. Berkley Books, 1994.

[143] Peter Carlson. "50 Years Ago, Unidentified Flying Objects from Way Beyond the Beltway Seized the Capital's Imagination." *Washington Post*, July 21 2002.

Barnes decided that it was serious enough to call Andrews AFB. Later that night, the staff at that airbase also saw strange objects and lights (although the USAF subsequently denied those early reports).

It was at this point that the controllers enlisted the help of a commercial pilot. A Capital Airlines DC-4 (four-piston-engined passenger aircraft) was about to take off from Washington National. The pilot was asked if he could keep his eyes peeled and report back anything he saw.

Captain Pierman, in that DC-4, must have felt that this was a pretty strange request, but he agreed and motored into the warm night sky. Over the next quarter of an hour, he reported no less than six objects or lights ("white, tailless and fast moving"). Barnes was interested to know whether the objects that Pierman was seeing were the same ones he was looking at on the radarscopes. In every case, he confirmed that the objects witnessed by Pierman were also picked up on the radarscopes, and that when the objects being watched by Pierman left, they disappeared from radar too, at the same time. During the course of that long, hot night, there was one point at which the radars of both National and Andrews AFB plotted the same object over a tower at Andrews (again, this was later retracted by the USAF).

At about 3 a.m., a pair of F-94 Starfires arrived over the capital, and all of the objects disappeared from the radar sets almost simultaneously. When the fighters returned to base to refuel, some of the blips returned. The final blip disappeared from the radar screens at about 5.30 a.m.

Harry Barnes gave a newspaper interview shortly afterwards, which was quoted in the *Washington Post* fifty years later. He said about the objects they'd witnessed on the radar screens:

> "They acted like a bunch of small kids out playing ... It
> was helter-skelter, as if directed by some innate curiosity.
> At times, they moved as a group or cluster, at other times
> as individuals."

On July 28 1952, the *Washington Post* ran a front page headline reading "Saucer Outran Jet, Pilot Reveals". The article was written by Paul

Sampson, who quoted the pilot in question as saying that he was "unable to overtake the glowing lights". Because of this, Sampson estimated the speed with which the objects shifted position as being more than 600 mph. He also confirmed that between four and twelve objects stayed on up to three separate radar screens for six straight hours, from around 9 p.m. until 3 a.m.

Then there appears to have been an absence of sightings in and around Washington until, almost exactly a week later, the objects reappeared. It was the evening of July 26.

At about 8.15 p.m. that evening, the pilot and a flight attendant on a National Airlines flight coming into National Airport reported strange lights above their plane. These were seen on radar at National and at Andrews. By 9.30 p.m., the radarscopes were showing a lot of unidentified blips, and this time, the blips were witnessed by a number of USAF officers, including Albert Chop, the press spokesman for Project Blue Book.

The blips sometimes crossed the screens slowly, and at other times, they turned completely around and accelerated to an estimated 7,000 mph. Two F-94s tried to find the objects, but only one pilot actually chased four white glows. The pilot later bemoaned the fact that he just could not catch them. Around midnight, two more officers arrived in the radar room: Major Dewey Fournet (the Pentagon liaison officer for Blue Book) and Lieutenant John Holcomb (a Navy radar specialist). They watched the images, and they considered temperature inversions and other weather issues, but both men rejected them.

Fournet said that there had been weather targets on the scopes, but they were nothing like the blips from the UFOs. He stressed that everyone in the radar room, including the specialist Holcomb, agreed that the targets were solid objects, probably metallic. Two more F-94s conducted air searches, but only one pilot saw a strange light. Nevertheless, commercial flights in the area continued to report lights, and they corresponded with where the radar was showing unidentified blips.

The sightings, as before, ended at sunrise.

The USAF explanation for all of this was essentially that the visual sightings were caused by "misidentified aerial phenomena" or by stars or meteors. The radar sightings were, we were told, simply temperature inversions reflecting the radar signals. There were certainly inversions on the nights of the sightings, but Edward Ruppelt said that he'd checked, and there had been inversions on almost all of the nights during that period, many of which had been without sightings. However, the strange blips only occurred on certain nights. Several fighter aircraft saw nothing, even though they'd been vectored onto unidentified blips by National control.

The sceptics generally agreed with the idea that weather inversions disproved the radar operators' testimony as well as completely overturning the views of a couple of USAF experts that the objects were solid and probably metallic. Philip Klass was unnecessarily brutal in his dismissal of the control tower radar operators. He argued that radar technology was insufficiently developed at that time and that it would not filter out flocks of birds, weather balloons, or temperature inversions. That is true.

But he did not leave it at that. He went on to malign the controllers themselves by saying that "we had two dumb controllers at National Airport on those nights." This ignored the fact that more than two controllers witnessed the events but was, also, insulting to an experienced chief air traffic controller and the tower operators. The abuse came from someone who was not there, who was not a qualified radar operator, and who was totally ignoring the testimony of several other radar operators who were there, a number of USAF officers who were there, and a USAF radar expert. It also failed to take into account the fact that those same controllers managed to get hundreds of aircraft a week into and out of Washington National Airport in spite of the deficiencies of their radar sets. It does not take a radar expert to understand that they *must* have been able to distinguish between anomalies like flocks of birds, weather balloons and inversions, and real aircraft, sufficiently well to keep aircraft in the air and their crews and passengers safe.[144] So why would they only be fooled by weather, birds, and balloons on those two nights when others, too, were

---

[144] As an outsider, I would really like to see some recorded footage of a radar screen showing returns from a temperature inversion which look like solid blips from aircraft-sized objects. It seems from research that the normal return for an inversion is a vague line on the screen.

seeing things (including a couple of fighter pilots whose eyesight, we can be fairly sure, was pretty good)?

Klass may have been right that the fitting of digital filters to modern radars has reduced UFO sightings by radar, but that does not automatically mean that all blips on old-fashioned radar screens were weather or balloons or birds. In some ways the old radar sets were *better* at seeing whatever UFOs are. What he carefully overlooked was the fact that the modern digital filters also filter out anything travelling too fast or too slow to be a normal aircraft. The old radar sets were unfiltered and "saw" everything. The newer ones are deliberately blinded to certain types of target in order to make aircraft more clearly visible in today's crowded airspaces.

If there are UFOs which can fly incredibly fast and UFOs which can hover or fly as slow as a few miles per hour (and there are hundreds of witness testimonies which say that those things happen), it is not surprising that modern radars see fewer UFOs.

The tower and radar room staff at National always held to their account that the objects were solid and probably metallic. The men told the US Air Force, the Robertson Panel, and the Condon Committee exactly the same thing, and like many other similar witnesses, they have maintained their stories into and beyond retirement.

When the eighty-three-year-old Howard Cocklin was interviewed by Peter Carlson for that *Washington Post* article in 2002, he said he was still convinced that he saw an object over National that night.

He went on to say that, apart from that one occasion, he never saw anything like that saucer; not before, and not since. The outsider who looks into the UFO phenomenon comes across hundreds of such statements from witnesses, and it is that innocent, perplexed sense of utter honesty which impresses the neutral observer. If only Cocklin, alone, had seen a lighted object that night, we could possibly dismiss it as tiredness or a visual aberration. But Cocklin was not alone. Even in the limited account above, his experiences were mirrored and corroborated by an impressive number of other professionals. As far as can be found, none of the witnesses made any money out of the sightings; all they received was ridicule and, from Philip Klass, completely unjustified abuse.

Between 2010 and 2014, there was another series of UFO sightings over Washington DC over a lengthy period, but this time, without the inimitable Edward Ruppelt to investigate them. In fact, there was not much of an investigation at all.

The bottom line is that, even after almost seventy years, the Washington National events remain one of the most convincing and compelling sets of UFO sightings on record.

Hudson Valley, 1982-1984

Date: 1982-84 (but continued thereafter)
Locations: Hudson Valley, New York State, and Connecticut
Type of Sighting: Visual
Type of Prime Witness: Civilians (thousands)
Other Witnesses: Police

There was a bunch of sightings in the areas north and north-west of New York during an approximate three-year period in the early 1980s. In common with most "wave" or mass sightings, the incidents carried on and are still happening. But unlike the Washington DC sightings of 1952 and those over Belgium in 1989, there was never an official investigation of the Hudson Valley events – at least not one which was made public.

From an outsider's point of view, it is frustrating that there was nothing official done about the mass sightings. Back in the 1950s, Edward Ruppelt's Project Blue Book team was at least able to investigate and record the 1952 events, which has given us a bare minimum of data, but there was apparently no official US government examination of the Hudson Valley affair.

A number of private UFO groups recorded as much as they could, but their resources permitted almost no scientific analysis apart from the creation of databases of sightings and, eventually, the publication of a major book recounting the events and quoting the statements of witnesses.

The astronomer J Allen Hynek first came to our attention with his work for Projects Sign, Grudge and Blue Book, the UFO investigations by the US Air Force. In the course of his career, he underwent a gradual and fascinating metamorphosis – from outright scientific sceptic to thoughtful and constructive scientific neutrality.

It was he who made the painful "swamp gas" blunder, and it was he who set up the Center for UFO Studies (CUFOS). In the 1980s, it was people from CUFOS under his direction who carried out most of the investigations and interviews during the long Hudson Valley saga.

There is certainly no space to go into the scores, possibly hundreds, of Hudson Valley events in any detail here (you are advised to read the book which was published after the astronomer's death in 1986: Hynek, 1987). *Night Siege* is a very detailed, almost too detailed, account of what happened. It must be said that it is not easy reading; the sheer amount of detail – dates, times, names, places, sightings, possible connections, and so on – makes it extremely difficult to follow – virtually impossible for the reader to piece everything together into anything like a cohesive narrative. The book is a bit of an endurance test, but if one takes it in short chunks, it is very rewarding.

The estimate is that some five thousand people saw something un-usual during that period (the outsider, having read the book, might well wonder if that is not a massive underestimate). Residents of New York State and Connecticut witnessed myriad events, but we cannot ever know how many were simply not reported at all. Many people were involved in incidents during which large numbers of cars and trucks were stopped on the open roads by the presence of strange objects. This appears to have been particularly true of the Taconic State Parkway.

There were many sightings of what people said were very large, silent objects. Sometimes, they were seen in groups, hovering low over highways and houses and showing bright lights of various colours. Some of the witnesses saw the objects at close range; some stood underneath them, and at least one person is said to have actually jogged beneath one. There were many reports of "structures" being seen behind the bright lights, but in common with the Belgian sightings a decade later and the UK reports this century, a lot of witnesses saw very large black or grey objects, shaped like boomerangs or wedges or triangles, some as large as football fields, which could shoot off at very high speeds.

An artist's impression of the sort of large triangular object seen on several occasions during several UFO waves around the world. (Ursatii/Shutterstock.com)

The MUFON and NUFORC websites carry a huge number of reports about the Hudson Valley wave, and even looking at just a few sightings from that period, one gets a forceful impression of the events themselves and of the effect they had on individuals. The Hudson Valley wave is typified by large triangular craft, silent, sometimes very slow, and at other times very fast. A number of people saw the objects shining lights down into ponds and lakes. Two sample accounts – from many hundreds – have been quoted below, drawn from the two major UFO databases in the US:

those constructed by MUFON and NUFORC. The databases parallel and, to some extent, duplicate the reports contained in Hynek's 1987 book.

The text is exactly as the databases record the testimony of the witnesses or their relatives (except that occasionally, I have corrected a typo to make them easier to read). The tone and style of the accounts, again in common with a great proportion of UFO witness statements from other nations, places, and times, tend to lend weight to the utter bafflement of the witnesses and their fear of ridicule. Their words are tentative and modest, and as far as I am aware, none received financial reward for their statements.

Sceptics would probably express no surprise at this innocence and bafflement. They would simply argue that the witnesses were honestly misled. The problem with that solution is that many of the sightings were witnessed by several different people, in different locations, and from different angles. Due to the passage of time, some of the accounts are second-hand. The original witnesses may be unwilling to come forward (or may have passed away), but they confided their experiences to their families or to close friends. The first example epitomises such a situation.

June 1983: Carmel (MUFON)

"My mother told me that while travelling on Rt 84 near the exit for rt 52, all the cars on the highway stopped to look at the object in the sky ... the size of a football field, rectangular in shape ... one could see through the center and see the stars in the sky ... it just stayed above them making no sound whatsoever ... for about 10 minutes or so. Then left the area without making any noise."

August 1983: Bedford Hills, NY (NUFORC)

"Observed a huge black boomerang shaped UFO in the sky hovering over the women's prison in Bedford Hills.

The underside of this UFO had five round white lights (one at what seemed to be the front, one at each rear tip and one between the front and tail end of each side of the boomerang shaped UFO). It ... made no sound except for a very low vibrating hum."

The description is extremely detailed, and it tied in very closely with what other, completely separate and unconnected people saw during the period.

October 1983: North Syracuse, NY (MUFON)

"Back in 1983 I'm guessing, around 4 [to] 4:30 am, me and a friend were riding our bmx bikes ... we seen what we thought was a shooting star. followed it across the sky from east to west ... and out of nowhere this ball of fire comes down slowly right behind my house in this open field area in the woods. it was a huge ball of fire just hovering over the trees. it stayed there for what seemed like 15 minutes or so, then slowly started moving straight up and then shot off at an amazing speed and was gone ... I to this day have no idea what I saw, and think that people think I'm crazy when I bring it up."

This incident, witnessed by two young boys, is extremely similar to the Exeter incident of 1965, when the eighteen-year-old Norman Muscarello and two police officers saw a bright ball ascend and move towards them. It is noteworthy that the North Syracuse boys did not attempt to make anything of it at the time, and one of them waited many years before giving an account of what they had experienced.

The boy had no discernible ulterior motive for putting the account on the Web database. But the sceptics would probably argue that he and his friend misidentified a planet or a star. Because there were no formal investigations and interviews, what actually happened will always be a mystery. And yet a "huge ball of fire" doesn't sound like a star or planet.

Another person, in July 1984, was walking with a friend along Route 6 to a summer carnival near Mahopac Falls. The two were sitting on a roadside rock, waiting for another person, when a passing motorist pointed above them. When they turned around, they saw an enormous, noiseless "lighted object" floating directly above them. It was evidently triangular or boomerang shaped and showed many pulsing lights. One of the interesting things about the account is that the person reported the lights as not simply pulsing but "pulsing softly". The witness who left the report on the MUFON website explained that they and their family had experienced multiple sightings over the years but had never reported them because only nowadays does the technology exist to do so easily and confidentially. In response to official explanations, the witness explicitly ruled out ultralights or other aircraft. They lived near Mahopac Airfield and the Air National Guard bases at Newburgh and Stewart and were well used to aircraft of all descriptions. What they saw that day, the witness said, was too large, too quiet, and too slow to be an aircraft or a group of ultralights.

The wedge or boomerang shape cropped up in a great many sightings during the Hudson Valley wave, as did descriptions of slow movement and huge size. The shape has been seen many times since then – particularly in Belgium in the 1990s and in the UK during the 2000s and 2010s.

As you will find if you look into Hynek's *Night Siege* account, the hundreds of sightings were made not only by ordinary people across New York State and Connecticut, but by lots of police officers. However, apparently many of the police were told not to say too much about them.

At the time, the FAA and the police authorities (as opposed to some individual police officers) kept firmly to the story that all these sightings were caused by mischievous groups of people flying ultralight aircraft in formation, playing an extended practical joke on the inhabitants of the Hudson Valley. Some of the people who wrote the quotations, above, mention this explanation, and there are a number of reasons why it seems ludicrously unsound. The dangers of close formation flying, at very low altitude and at night, are just too numerous to list. Ultralights are extremely susceptible to wind gusts and updrafts, and the instability of the craft would have been obvious to witnesses, not to mention a constant danger to their pilots. In addition, the immense noise from a group of ultralights flying in formation would be more than enough to make the real source of the lights plain to anyone below. If you live in the country, you get used to ultralights, and anyone who does so knows that they can be heard from a mile away, never mind just five hundred to a thousand feet above you. They certainly do not sound like an almost silent object, humming gently in the sky over your head. Even if a group of expert ultralight pilots planned to fly in formation up and down the Hudson Valley, pretending to be a huge UFO, it beggars belief that hundreds of people on the ground would have been fooled by the noisy, unstable formation. Furthermore (as if more is needed) the lights from each microlight would, partially or wholly, illuminate the others.

The outsider should check out the video of the Roskilde Airshow of 2009 in the Netherlands. It is provided on matteam.com, the website of MAT, one of the world's few microlight display teams[145] The video shows how an expert group can fly in formation, but one can easily see the in-stability in the pattern, even from such excellent pilots. The idea of them trying this at night would have crowds of knowledgeable pilots rolling in the aisles.

The Hudson Valley sightings of the early 1980s constitute one of the most interesting wave sightings. The events involved thousands of ordi-nary people and a great number of police officers and, as was mentioned at the start, many of the sightings were witnessed by multiple individuals at the same time and from different standpoints. Browse through the NUFORC and MUFON database listings, and read *Night Siege*. While you read those accounts, consider that they probably represent the mer-est tip of the iceberg. Edward Ruppelt thought that possibly only one in ten people reported a UFO sighting. Where the Hudson Valley was con-cerned, that proportion might well have been one in a hundred.

---

[145] See http://matteam.com/videos.htm and especially the video of the Roskilde Airshow.

I'll leave you with this amusing quote from *Night Siege,* in which the authors repeat the answer a policeman gave to a puzzled caller who was reporting a UFO: "It can't be a UFO," the police officer asserted, "because UFOs don't exist."

CHAPTER 17

Mass Sightings, 1989—2017

PERHAPS DUE TO THE way in which modern sightings are recorded and the ease with which we can now see patterns and links between them, the last thirty years have seen their fair share of mass sightings. Because of the ever increasing power of the Internet and, recently, of social media, the identification of mass sightings over lengthy periods of time has become much easier.

Modern communications have permitted people to report more of what they see – and in ways which maintain at least a modicum of privacy. The ever-present sceptics would naturally argue that this means it is all too easy nowadays for people to spoof the system and make silly reports. This is absolutely true, and at some point in the future, we may be able to revise downwards my "magic 5 percent" rule but whatever the new proportion of inexplicable sightings is, it will be of a much larger number of reports.

I've elected to include brief details of four mass sightings in the late twentieth and early twenty-first centuries: Belgium, Phoenix, the UK Midlands, and Hessdalen in Norway.

Belgium, 1989—1991

Dates: 1989–1991
Locations: Many locations over Belgium
Type of Sighting: Visual and radar

Type of Prime Witness: Pilots and civilians
Other Witnesses: At least two separate radar centres

There are strong correlations between this set of sightings and those in the Hudson Valley, Phoenix, and England in terms of triangular, slow-moving, low-flying objects.

The Belgian sightings appear to have begun in November 1989, when a lot of people, including police and civilians, reported a very large triangular object, with lights underneath it, flying silently at low altitude.

A patrol of two officers of the gendarmerie came across a field which they said was illuminated like a floodlit football game. They stopped their patrol car by the side of the road and said that they then watched a large triangular "platform" with three white lights and an orange-red light at the centre. It was silent and stationary, hovering over the field.

The object flew off slowly, and the two policemen (in a flashback to the Devon Fiery Cross event of 1967[146]) followed it in their patrol car as it travelled slowly towards the town of Eupen in eastern Belgium. As they followed, they saw "laser beams" coming out at the sides and a "ball" leaving the object and moving around.

That same patrol then saw a second object rising into the sky to their right. Their dispatcher, who they'd contacted earlier, also saw a similar object as close as five hundred feet away from the window of his office in Eupen. This particular object was seen by around thirty different groups of people and three separate groups of police officers. It was apparently seen from Liege to the Dutch/German border.

A few months later, on March 20 and 31, 1990, several objects were tracked on radar and were apparently chased by two Belgian Air Force F-16s. At least one of the objects was photographed, although, like most UFO photos, the resulting image has come in for severe criticism. Some twenty-six hundred written statements were filed with the police (that's a

---

[146] Two British police officers saw and chased a UFO shaped like a glowing cross for about fourteen miles through the county of Devon.

stat worth noting: twenty-six hundred *written* statements), and although estimates vary, up to thirteen thousand people are thought to have witnessed the objects.

At 11 p.m. on March 30, three lights were seen to the south-east of Brussels. People reported the lights as being of different colours and triangular in appearance. The police from Wavre were sent to investigate, and they confirmed the sighting about half an hour after the first report. The radar control centre at Glons also confirmed the sighting on its radar. Several other lights were reported as moving erratically, and these were also seen on radar by a separate control centre at Semmerzake.[147] At that point, just before midnight, F-16s were scrambled from Beauvechain (east-south-east of Brussels). Evidently, the two F-16s attempted nine separate intercepts. They achieved radar lock-on on three occasions but only for a few seconds before the locks were broken. During these attempts, the objects accelerated extremely rapidly and descended equally quickly, but there was no sonic boom. Neither of the Belgian Air Force pilots were able to get a visual observation of the objects.

The final radar lock by the F-16s was at twenty to one in the morning. As usual, it was quickly broken by the object, which accelerated and then disappeared from both of the ground station radars. From the ground, at about 1.30 a.m., the gendarmes from Wavre saw four lights in a square formation, making short jerky movements. They said that the lights disappeared by losing luminosity steadily before they shot off in four different directions.

This short series of sightings also produced a couple of photos of lights in a triangular formation, but one was certainly a hoax, and the other is still the centre of much controversy. But from the outsider's point of view, the most interesting element in the Belgian wave was the involvement of the chief of the Belgian Air Staff, Major General de Brouwer, who was responsible for assessing the radar and aircraft reports from those evenings

---

[147] The objects were plotted by radar as performing some amazing feats: accelerating from 150 mph to over 1,100 mph while changing altitude from nine thousand feet to five thousand feet in two seconds, then up to eleven thousand feet and then back down to almost ground level.

(as well as others) and who, in his somewhat dour and serious manner, lent a good deal of authority to subsequent discussions of what occurred.

The sceptics have argued that the wave was the result of a mass delusion egged on by a Belgian UFO organisation called SOBEPS (now defunct): a modern-day version of the Klass theory. A number of scientists have proposed the mass delusion solution, although no one has yet either convincingly explained how this process works in practice with so many people or explained why mass delusion operates with UFOs but not with other reports of strange sightings and events which are aired by the tabloids (e.g. ghost and monster sightings).

A further problem about the way mass delusion theories might impact on the Belgian wave is that there were a lot of sightings, stretched over many months, with lulls in between. Are mass delusions which affect hundreds of people, including police officers, replicable weeks after the previous sightings have ended? And if so, what is the mechanism?

The radar locks have been disputed too. One sceptic, Brian Dunning, stated that the F-16s only reported three lock-ons and that all of those were on each other; this is somewhat unbelievable because a lock-on by another aircraft would sound an alarm in the other plane's cockpit. The pilots would know that they'd got a false lock-on and tell the controllers.

There is also the issue of how the objects, whatever they were, broke the lock-ons so easily and quickly. Modern fighter pilots train hard to achieve lock-ons, and they also train hard to break them. However, breaking a lock-on is extremely difficult if the other pilot is competent, and modern tracking radars are not easily fooled by a plane breaking hard left or right or down. If the two aircraft had locked onto each other, there would have been no need to break the lock-on. One pilot would simply have radioed the other and asked him, very politely, to stop tracking him.

Dunning also questioned the almost complete lack of photographic evidence. He argued that if thirteen thousand people saw a UFO, there should be more than a single photo. It's not a bad point, but we are speaking of mainly night-time sightings in the late 1980s and early 1990s – that is, well before cameras on cellphones became available. You might also like to watch the Robert Stack documentary on the event (from his series

"Unsolved Mysteries") and judge whether the police officers involved were deluded or hysterical or just the usual calm professionals we are generally used to.[148]

In spite of the flaws in the sceptics' arguments, all these frantic events might easily constitute just another wave of mass delusion (whatever that is) if it were not for Major General Wilfried de Brouwer, who was then chief of operations for the Belgian Air Staff, and we should not forget the aircraft radar lock-on pilots, and the ground radar officers who confirmed the traces. Lieutenant Colonel Pierre Billens of the Glons radar centre appeared in the Robert Stack documentary alongside Major General Brouwer.

The latter officer is a serious, experienced, and extremely professional person who is so convinced that there is something happening which needs further study and explanation that he has appeared at several conferences, including the 2007 National Press Club event in Washington. To my knowledge, however, he has not written a book about the events.

The Robert Stack documentary is somewhat sensational, and you have to try to endure the cheesy re-enactment scenes inside patently false studio police cars, but inside the whole sixteen-minute piece, there are some fascinating nuggets. The most impressive thing about this documentary is the calm, matter-of-fact, highly professional way in which police and military officers describe what they experienced. There is not a single sign of any sensationalism or over-egging of the events. They saw what they saw, take it or leave it.

---

[148] The out-take from the series "Unsolved Mysteries", with Robert Stack presenting it, is available at https://www.youtube.com/watch?v=UwAF7CglHlM

Phoenix Lights, 1997

Date: March 13, 1997
Location: Arizona
Type of Sighting: Visual and radar
Type of Prime Witness: Civilians (hundreds)
Other Witnesses: (estimates of up to ten thousand witnesses)

In the early 1950s, there were multiple sightings over Washington DC; a wave of sightings in the 1980s in the Hudson Valley, New York, and Connecticut; a similar wave in the early 1990s across Belgium; a large number of strange sightings in Arizona in March of 1997; and arguably a steady stream of similar sightings over Britain in the twenty-first century.

Are they *all* hoaxes and mass delusions? The sceptics would argue a hoax or mistake followed by mass delusion, but to make that argument stick they would have to show how the events were staged to fool the police and military, to fool fighter pilots, and to trick radar operators.

Could they all be the result of social pressure on easily led people? A great many people in the huge state of Arizona would say no.

The collection of sightings which eventually became known as the Phoenix lights comprises yet another contentious collective viewing of strange objects. Today, twenty years later, the events have spawned commercial enterprises in Arizona to match those in New Mexico around Roswell, numerous books and articles, a couple of documentaries, and a well-used website dedicated to the sightings and all of the subsequent developments and discoveries[149]. The website has an interesting "myths" page, which looks at all the various theories and sceptical explanations for the Arizona events in 1997. It is well worth visiting not only with respect to this particular event, but also because it looks at most of the explanations which have been put forward for other sightings.

What was it all about? The sightings involved hundreds, if not

---

[149] See http://www.thephoenixlights.net/.

thousands, of people seeing boomerang or triangular craft throughout the state. Many of the objects were said to be huge. One witness, who was told that what he saw could be a B-2 bomber, replied that the United States could land all forty of its then complement of B-2 bombers on the *wing* of what he saw.

On the evening of March 13, objects and lights were reported from many places on a two-hundred-mile line from Paulden in the north, through Phoenix, to Tucson in the south of the state.

It was a clear spring night, one when many Arizonians had stationed themselves outside in order to see Comet Hale-Bopp, which was appearing brightly in the night sky at that time.[150] What many hundreds of people saw, in addition to Hale-Bopp, was one or more objects of large size moving slowly, at low altitude, through the night sky, sometimes blanking out the stars as they passed. Those sightings extended in time from about 8.15 p.m. to 9.30 p.m. (local time), and there is evidence to support sightings of them through to the early morning of March 14.

Those who witnessed strange things were not shy in reporting them. They jammed police phone lines, did the same to the switchboard at the nearby Luke Air Force Base, and sent scores of messages to the National UFO Reporting Center (NUFORC) in Seattle.

None of the reported objects appear to have been recorded on radar (at least no such reports are on public record). Many of the accounts of the night treat the sightings as being of a single object which moved from north to south, but there does not seem to be any way of being certain of the "one object" theory. Descriptions varied, although most specified a large, dark or grey object of triangular or boomerang shape. It, or they, were silent, and when they did decide to leave, they disappeared at very high speed.

The first recorded sighting was by a man in Nevada, to the north of the Arizona line, who reported a large V-shaped object above Henderson, moving from north-west to south-east. It was said to have had six lights

---

[150] Comet Hale-Bopp was only discovered in 1995, and its appearance in 1997 was one of the brightest and longest in recorded history. On March 13, it was within a week or so of its closest approach to Earth.

on its leading edge. At about 8.15 p.m., an anonymous police officer in the town of Paulden in northern Arizona saw four reddish orange lights with a fifth trailing light moving south through the sky.

Sightings of a V-shaped object with lights were then reported from areas between Paulden and Phoenix until the main events occurred at between 9.30 p.m. and 10 p.m. It was around those times that a series of lights were seen over the latter city. One witness said that he watched the lights hover for up to twenty minutes, but the only video of the Phoenix lights shows a row of lights, with one outlier, existing for only a minute or two (on the video tape). Further sightings were made of V-shaped craft, flying low and slow, down towards Tucson later that evening.

There was virtually no national coverage of the events at the time, although the local media did cover the sightings pretty thoroughly and with varying degrees of scepticism. The only investigation at the time was launched by a local councilwoman called Frances Barwood. She took great pains to speak to eyewitnesses, but she was generally derided by her political colleagues and by the media.

Minimal coverage, together with large doses of ridicule, worked as they always will, to dampen down subsequent investigation, specu- lation, and discussion. But for some reason, the newspaper USA Today decided to cover the events of March in its June 18 issue. In fact, it gave the Phoenix lights a front-page spot. The networks ABC and NBC also covered the events in brief. As an outsider I would very much like to know what prompted the media to become interested more than two months after the events.

These fresh airings opened the floodgates again, and the next day, the governor of Arizona, Fife Symington, ordered a full local investigation. He also held a separate press conference at which he revealed the "truth" about the events by having marched onto the stage one of his aides dressed as an alien. It caused great hilarity among the assembled press but made many of the electorate extremely angry. They saw his spoof as being insult- ing and patronising. "I know what I saw" was a very common cry.

Much later, at that famous National Press Club presentation in 2007, Symington apologised publicly for his spoof. He explained that he himself had seen an object, but that he felt the atmosphere of hysteria surrounding the events required lightening a little. What he also revealed was that his official investigation never arrived at a satisfactory explanation.

Part of the official explanation of the sightings involved USAF A-10 Warthog aircraft dropping a line of flares near Phoenix at 10 p.m. on the night of March 13. You should remember, however, that the first witnesses saw lights over Phoenix at about 9.30 p.m.

The V-shaped objects have been explained by sceptics as planes or helicopters flying in formation, but witnesses reject those explanations for a silent, single-mass object which blocked out the stars. There's also the very inconvenient fact that planes and helicopters do not fly in close formation at night; not even the elite USAF or RAF jet display teams would dare to try such a foolhardy stunt.

But of all the sightings, it is the videoed one over Phoenix which has attracted the most controversy. There is a famous video on record which shows a series of lights in a slanting line, hanging over the city of Phoenix. The military has pretty much stuck to the explanation that what people saw in that video were flares dropped by aircraft on exercise over the nearby Barry Goldwater military range. Witnesses, and others, question this explanation because the lights appeared to be steady and at a constant height during the sightings. They argue that a flare, when launched, trails a plume of smoke (which is illuminated by the flare itself), and the flares tend to drift and swing on their parachutes in different ways (whereas the Phoenix lights on the video appear to be extremely stable). Others have queried why highly dangerous phosphorus flares would be dropped so near to a densely inhabited area.

The argument reverberates to this day, and interested outsiders can get a more rounded appreciation by perusing the fairly balanced Wikipedia article, as well as the Phoenix lights network website (complete with rebuttals of sceptics' criticisms), and the famous video mentioned above.[151]

---

[151] The Wikipedia article on the subject presents a fairly balanced accounting by both the UFO proponents and the sceptics: https://en.wikipedia.org/wiki/Phoenix_Lights

England, 2007–Present

Dates: 2007–Present
Locations: All across the United Kingdom, but main reported sightings in the Midlands of England
Type of Sighting: Visual
Type of Prime Witness: Civilians
Other Witnesses: Unknown

The English wave was a difficult choice for inclusion in this book, primarily because it consists mainly of civilian eyewitness accounts, with no apparent corroboration by radar or official personnel. There are quite a few photographs, but none appear to have been authenticated in any way, and the outsider's understandable reaction is to suspect a series of hoaxes.

In some cases, hoaxes may, indeed, be the most plausible explanation, but the wave has been included on the grounds that it has been going on for a very long time; that many of the sightings are of objects very similar to those seen during the Hudson Valley incidents, the Phoenix lights, and in Belgium – that is, triangular or wedge-shaped craft with lights; and that there are now a great many videos and photos on record.

The main problem for anyone attempting analysis is that the only evidence is eyewitness statements to the press or UFO organisations. The British press, in its own inimitable fashion, has not made detached consideration any easier by naming the whole set of sightings "the Dudley Dorito" (after the triangular chip or crisp and the Midland town over which some of the early sightings were made).

What follows is a straight reporting of a tiny proportion of the witnesses and the dates and places. Because the British Ministry of Defence is no longer investigating anything which is not clearly a potential threat, official corroboration is sparse to non-existent.

- November 2007: A lighted triangular object seen over Halesowen.

- April 4, 2009: Two bright-orange objects shaped like Cornish pastries (in other words, a curved wedge) reported over Sedgley.
- April 16, 2009: A group of builders at the West Midlands Safari Park reported seeing an object in the sky above them.
- October 2010: Object reported in Nottingham.
- November 4, 2010: Triangular object seen over Sutton Coldfield, reported as being four or five times the size of an airliner.
- November 2010: Two witnesses, Manesh Mistry and Neil Martin, reported a triangular object with corner lights and a central light over Dudley. They said it was fast moving and totally silent.
- June 21, 2016: A shiny, lit, tubular-shaped object filmed very high over Manchester. Its lights appeared to change from white to blue to purple.
- September 2016: A teacher named Darren Martin was walking his dogs in the Wrekin Hills in Shropshire at 7.30 a.m. when he saw a triangular object in the sky. He took a blurry photo on his cellphone and told the press that the object moved "so slowly, it almost hung in the sky".[152]
- In April 2017 a bus driver who was waiting for the bus on which he was due to take a shift videoed and photographed a triangular set of lights over Exmouth in Devon at about twenty to ten in the evening. The lights were later joined by a fourth light and took on an asymmetrical shape. The frustration of the chap at the fact that he did not have a decent camera with him was all too evident.[153]

A glance at BEAMS, the website of the British Earth & Aerial Mysteries Society, one of the UK's more active UFO organisations, will underline just how many claimed sightings there are and, these days, how many photos and videos. This is perhaps the best example of the problems faced by outsiders. On the surface, the website seems to be a hive of UFO nuts who propose that aliens are with us and much more. This is probably

---

[152] *Shropshire Star*, October 1, 2016.
[153] The report was made to MUFON and BEAMS re-published it. It is dated April 17th 2017

what it was like for Edward Ruppelt back in the 1950s in the United States: a mass of "sightings", a goodly bunch of hoaxers, a core of UFO nutters, a lot of honestly mistaken people, and just perhaps a few very puzzling and inexplicable events.[154] The difference is that in the UK today, as in the United States, there are only private UFO organisations to undertake the necessary investigations, and due to vanishingly small budgets, those get completed to a reasonable standard all too infrequently.

The Hessdalen Lights, Norway, 1981–Present

Date: 1981–Present
Locations: Mainly in the valley of the Hess
Type of Sighting: Visual, radar, instruments
Type of Prime Witness: Civilians
Other Witnesses: More civilians

The Hessdalen events are probably unique in the world, both for having lasted so long (from 1981 to date) and for being so carefully documented and recorded. What we mean by "lasted so long" of course is simply that they have been linked together over a very long period by geography and by a dedicated scientific team of observers. Take any area in the world – in the United States, in England, in France, or anywhere else – and it would almost certainly be possible to link events together in the same way over long periods of time. The difference with Hessdalen is merely that they have already done this and with a good deal of associated scientific investigation.

About ninety miles south-east of the city of Trondheim on the west coast of Norway lies the remote valley of the river Hesja, which flows north and west to become the River Gaula, which enters the sea near Trondheim.

---

[154] Take a look at the British Earth & Aerial Mysteries Society's page: http://www. beamsinvestigations.org/ufo-reports.html

The people of Hessdalen, as the area is called, began to see strange lights around the end of 1981. Although the main sightings occurred in the period to 1984, there are still about twenty sightings a year, right up to the present time. In the early days, there were up to twenty sightings of these strange lights each week. An investigation was launched for a month during 1984, which recorded over fifty observations. During that early period, some 85 percent of sightings were of lights of very different types and colours and mainly at night. There were, however, daylight sightings, and many were described not as lights but as "objects". The lights move and flash. Some are seen for very brief periods of time, while others appear to move around and to ascend and descend for much longer periods.[155]

The website of the Hessdalen Project is professional and scientific. For example, lights are divided into four different types, and the various sightings are described in great detail. The reader might like to visit the website and read an intriguing account from September 2016 of lights which "hovered" over a small lake and a white light like a flashlight which was shone towards the observers for a long time.[156]

In 1998, an automatic detection station was set up which records pictures and other data whenever an alarm is triggered. The automatic system is fairly sophisticated, comprising two time-stamped video cameras roughly 170 metres apart, two black-and-white video cameras, a motorised still camera, a magnetometer, a fluxgate magnetometer, plus automated weather feeds. The camera inputs are analysed by a computer, and an alarm is triggered only when *both* cameras are showing an unusual light in the frame and when the light is moving. These cameras are also connected to a separate still camera with a motorised pan-tilt system. The video cameras provide directional information which causes the still camera to move towards the light and take one or more photos.

There are many theories as to what is causing these phenomena. Some believe there are unknown geological causes, although that raises the questions as to why they are seen only in this region and why only since

---

[155] http://www.hessdalen.org/pictures/description.shtml
[156] http://www.hessdalen.org/observations/2016/

1981. Others have attributed the lights to "plasmas" and to other mete-orological events. Some have proposed psychological causes and have questioned the perceptions of the witnesses. But the photos and movies are fascinating, and the fact that the phenomena are being recorded auto-matically would seem to rule out human frailty in most cases.

PART 3

CHAPTER 18

Elusive Answers

THROUGHOUT THIS BOOK I have tried to stick to the "simple" question of UFOs and UAP because they keep on coming no matter what government reports, sceptics, and scientific review panels say. Whether one calls them flying saucers, UFOs or Unidentified Aerial Phenomena, large numbers of them come with high degrees of credibility (at least fifteen hundred every year across the world). Their credibility is derived from the seniority and professionalism of many of the witnesses, from the persuasiveness of the visual or radar evidence, from the fact that sceptics have failed to convincingly explain them, and sometimes from all three.

In order to see which way we must go from here we need first to consider the issue of cover-ups and conspiracies. Are they real and do they make a difference to the effort to scientifically examine UFOs and UAP? Furthermore what does the disclosure movement bring to the party?

Cover Ups & Conspiracies

The UFO phenomena is surrounded by swamp-lands in which lurk many monsters, including missing time accounts, abductions, alien visitations, cover-ups, and conspiracy theories. In chapter 2 we took a very superficial stroll through perhaps the grand-daddy of them all: the morass that is Roswell. In doing so we demonstrated that it constitutes a hopelessly entangled and impenetrable knot of proven fact, rumour, allegations, suspicion, and (not to put too fine a point on it) total fantasy. Today, the complex elements of Roswell as an incident (and we know that *something* happened because Colonel Blanchard issued a press release about it) are probably incapable of being disentangled. Was Major Marcel genuinely fooled by a few bits of weather balloon, were the officers and men of the 509th Bombardment Group ignorant of what a balloon's remnants looked like, why was Jesse Marcel so angry about the whole thing that he made what amounted to a death-bed attempt to have his say, why have so many other "witnesses" come forward, having seen the remnants why did Colonel Blanchard issue such a provocative press release? And so on into infinitely.

In the red corner we have ravening hordes of ufologists – some of them very well respected – who claim that it was about a crash of a flying saucer complete with the bodies of its crew. All of which was subsequently covered-up by the American government. Muddled amongst them is a huddle of researchers like Nick Redfern who are convinced that it was really about a very nasty set of experiments which went wrong and for which the US government used the flying saucer rumours as a cover. The armed might of the US government is massed in the blue corner supporting their claim that it was simply a balloon. Both sides have a great deal of "evidence" to throw into the pot.

There have also been alleged UFO crashes in other countries. Dorothy Kilgallen famously alleged that there had been such a crash in the UK prior to 1955, in 1964 a number of people alleged a crash of part of something near Penkridge in the English Midlands, in 1974 there was a suspected UFO landing or crash on the Berwyn Mountains in North Wales, more recently groups have accused the UK government of covering up a crash of a UFO into a windfarm. Crashes and landings are regularly reported from just about every nation from Mexico to China. Few are professionally corroborated but all add grist to the conspiracy mill. Yet one has to wonder why such supposedly advanced alien space ships crash quite so often and why their colleagues tend to leave the wreckage and the bodies lying around for anyone to stumble across.

Meanwhile the authorities sit on the sidelines giving every appearance of goading both sides by dropping into the arena just enough provocative information to keep the fight going in all its colourful splendour. Trying to make sense of it all is worse than finding a needle in a haystack – partly because someone keeps disguising the needle and then, just when one is getting warm, they move it to places which have just been searched.

Roswell is a powerful metaphor for the cover-up and conspiracy theories which characterise the "weird" side of the UFO business. The idea that governments are covering up knowledge about UFOs and conspiring to keep us all in the dark has been around since at least 1947. And of course the US government has not helped matters by changing its Roswell story on several occasions. Why did it feel the need? In Britain similar things have happened especially where the authorities have nailed patently silly explanations to sightings by very professional people.

That there have been "cover-ups" is probably unarguable. In a sense it's been proven by commentators such as Edward Ruppelt who told us that the public were given explanations of mistaken stars or weather phenomena in the 1940s and early 1950s when, behind the scenes, the US government was desperately trying to find out what the UFOs really were. This is the problem about cover-ups: sometimes they are eminently justifiable. The Manhattan Project kept the development of nuclear weapons pretty secret until they were used; and during the Second World War there were numerous cover ups of military disasters which would have severely damaged public morale if they had been revealed (e.g. the loss of HMS Dasher in 1943 and the Slapton Sands debacle in 1944). But sometimes cover-ups transgress the rule of law. Examples include Watergate in the US, the complicity of the British government in CIA "rendition" flights, and many others. The practice of covering things up for unethical reasons is not limited to government agencies. Large companies also step over the line from time to time (for example when, on separate occasions, they tried to cover up the effects of asbestos, tobacco, and diesel emissions). The problem for modern society is, perhaps, to acquire a firmer grasp of what is ethical and what is not in various situations. A cover-up to protect a nation's long-term interests can *perhaps* be justified. A cover up for the personal gain of individuals, financial or otherwise, is certainly not justifiable.

But, the "evidence" with respect to UFO cover-ups is not consistent between various authors. For example, some accuse the US or UK governments themselves of covering things up, some say it is a cabal within the governments, some that it is a global conspiracy within a secret society. And for every set of theories the authors have "evidence" of a kind.

But, if governments are covering up the fact that they know all about UFOs and have small alien bodies in their possession, why have the US and UK governments constantly returned to study the subject. And this behind closed doors and even when previous research has ruled them out as figments of people's fevered imaginations? Why bother to hold top-secret investigations like the Flying Saucer Working Party, the Robertson Panel, the Condon study, and the Condign investigation? The UFO community would probably respond by arguing:

a) none of those studies were robust investigations; they were too brief, too restricted in the things they examined, possibly too biased at the start, and anyway, they were focused primarily on whether UFOs were of defence significance; and,

b) they were for internal show as much as external consumption. That is, 99.9 percent of the government is working in the dark while only those in a secret "cabal" know the real truth.[157]

The credibility of some of the people claiming that governments are covering something up is unquestionable. The question therefore is: Why? What would be the rationale for not telling the public? The following come to mind:

1. **Panic**: fear of mass hysteria. This is the theory that people will run around screaming, waving their hands in the air. Could be, but

---

[157] This is the heart of what many committed UFO buffs believe. Others simply believe that there is an orchestrated government cover-up for unknown reasons. The latter include people like Robert Salas, astronauts Dr Edgar Mitchell and Gordon Cooper, and a former Canadian defence minister, Paul Hellyer.

    the American and British publics have faced some pretty terrible things without descending into abject panic.

2. **Social decay**: the knowledge of superior civilisations might act to undermine mankind's ambition and drive. If someone is so far ahead in the race, why bother?

3. **Shame**: having to admit that our governments cannot defend us. Not really likely one would think since many European nations have lived with that knowledge for decades.

4. **New weapons**: keeping the "secret" and learning new ways to kill your enemies.

5. **New technologies**: keeping the secret in order to learn lucrative new technologies.

There are two broad forms to the conspiracy theory: the evil government one and the good government one. The guys in the black hats are there to keep UFOs secret and make money and weapons with their jealously-guarded knowledge. They hoard the wealth, assassinate their opponents, and use knowledge to amass power. The chaps in the white hats, on the other hand, while still keeping things secret, have not been covering up so much as slowly revealing things. This is the "acclimatising" theory; that UFOs, and their implications, are so complex and frightening that humanity needs a long period of acclimatisation before the full reality can be revealed.

Not for the first time in this book ... you pays your money ...

Yet, somehow, the first two on our list seem much more probable than the last three.

"The Loch Ness Monster is of no defence significance."

If that was a statement by the British government to support its decision not to continue studies into the existence of such a creature (which it isn't) we'd be entitled to raise an eyebrow or two. It's almost certainly true. The British armed forces should be able to cope with such a creature if it decided to get uppity. But why focus on *defence*? Why ignore all the other things which the possibility of the Monster portends; the immense scientific value of finding a living prehistoric creature, the economic potential for Scotland if the creature were real, even the value to the social sciences of being able to study how society reacts to such news?

Yet this highly specific statement is how the US and British governments have consistently justified not studying UAP (even while doing so in secret).

"UFOs are of no defence significance."

Therefore, we will no longer be monitoring sightings and will close Project Blue Book/the Ministry of Defence UFO desk.

Three questions ...

- How can they be so certain that there is no defence significance?
- Why not leave the subject more open and say UAP are a phenomenon which exists but we will leave it to the academics to study because they do not appear to be of defence significance?
- Why such a carefully selected set of words which is virtually identical between the two governments and is never embellished by such additions as "but the phenomenon may be of scientific, economic, or social significance"?

And the shenanigans perpetrated by the FAA and the CAA add fuel to the conspiracy theorists fire. The way the FAA handled the Japan Airlines sighting in 1986 and the Chicago O'Hare events twenty years later (as well as several others in recent years) is typical. In 2017 the British Civil Aviation Authority (CAA) refused to release its files from 2011 to 2017 containing reports of flight occurrences from pilots. The organisation has managed to avoid the requirements of the UK Freedom of Information Act by invoking an EU regulation from 2014 which reportedly says

> "Occurrence information can only be used for the purpose of maintaining or improving aviation safety, and the release of occurrence information to the general public or the media, including in response to Freedom of Information Act (FOIA) requests, is not permitted."

They will allow occurrence information to be released only for the purpose of maintaining or improving aviation safety.[158] One can only guess at the hoops one would have to negotiate.

The answers to the three questions above are much more likely to be about ineptitude and poor decision-making as about devilish plots and efficiently guarded secrets.

From the outsider's point of view, one of the most surprising things about these cover-up theories is the number of credible, senior figures who allege that the cover-up is real. People like the astronauts Gordon Cooper and Edgar Mitchell, the very senior FAA executive John Callahan, the ex-White House Chief of Staff John Podesta, and even the ex-Admiral of the Fleet Lord Hill-Norton. These and numerous others have alleged that the American and British governments have been covering up UFO activities and associated events for decades. One has to admit that there are too many well-documented pieces of evidence to completely ignore the cover-up idea, but it is also important to remember that there could be a great many justifiable reasons behind it.

Disclosure

Openness and transparency sound like great ideas where the UFO matter is concerned but, even assuming that there are things which could be revealed, we perhaps need to be careful what we wish for.

In the United States, the Disclosure movement has a principal proponent in the shape of Dr Stephen Greer, a serious and down-to-earth medic, who believes passionately in the need for disclosure. Disclosure will occur, he argues, when the US government (or one or more other governments) steps into the limelight and admits to a cover-up and to the reality of UFOs and some (or all) of the associated phenomena. There are a number

---

[158] https://www.caa.co.uk/Our-work/Make-a-report-or-complaint/MOR/Mandatory-occurrence-reporting/ The EU has regulated Mandatory Occurrence Reporting under CAP382. For pilots they must report a range of things including Flight approach and take-off area incursions but – interestingly there is no requirement to report in-flight "strange object" occurrences.

of experienced ufologists who believe that disclosure is not far off. In his 2014 book, Richard Dolan, for one, states unequivocally that disclosure is close and that this will change the world profoundly. This is typical of much of the rhetoric about disclosure. It focuses on what it will mean for us to be told that aliens and UFOs actually exist and have been visiting our planet for many years. From there, the prognostications flow on into rivers of possible futures, but mainly towards a brand-new world, bright with promise, in which humanity changes beyond all recognition and the race joins a galactic community. The messages are almost messianic.

However, what if what could be disclosed is the story that aliens are scheduled to invade and conquer an indefensible Earth within the next fifty years and that the few humans who remain after the conquest will be enslaved and sent to work themselves to death in the uranium mines of Alpha-Centauri? Would the disclosure movement be so keen to know that an end for which there is no conceivable defence is all that is waiting for us?

Cover up is taken for granted. But what if the government should step forward and say "apart from a few memos and some military reports, there's actually nothing to disclose. And we haven't got any flying saucers or bodies." You get just one guess what the response of the UFO community would be.

It's a win-win situation for the Disclosure movement: No news means that the cover-up is ongoing. Any government official who steps up to a microphone and informs the world that there is *no* cover-up is simply disbelieved. If someone reveals all then the Disclosure movement is triumphantly vindicated.

The expectation of what I call the disciples of disclosure is a generally positive and beneficial set of revelations; of aliens as neutral but largely beneficent mentors. To me, even if there are aliens and they turn out not to be evil reptilian monsters, this seems a little like waiting for a fairy-godmother to solve all our problems. Disclosure comes across as a free-pass. By revealing all about UFOs and aliens, governments will be ushering humanity into galactic civilisation and we'll receive high-tech knowledge without us doing anything for ourselves. It boils down to a sort of comfort blanket designed to wrap humanity in the protection of advanced species. Within its folds we'll be able to live happily and peacefully ever after.

Dolan, for example, speaks of hidden research which may save the world from its current descent into the "underculture", and of revelations which will essentially elevate humanity into new capabilities. It may turn out to be so, but relying on such free gifts is a little like leaving it to one's big brother to do one's homework.

There is some logic in the thought that perhaps all these very visible UFOs are trying to teach us something and are prodding us to move forward in some way. But if that is the case, surely disclosure is the last thing the UFOs would wish. If they have any agenda beyond tourism, surely it could only be to get us to help ourselves, to stimulate us to push on and sort out our many problems.

So my take on all this is that, if we are to learn about UFOs and whatever is behind them, we must do the job ourselves by whatever science and original thought we can deploy. We should be seeking not disclosure but investigation and learning. If they exist, the unexplained UFOs have given us plenty of hints over the past seventy years. The teacher has written enough stuff on the blackboard. Now we have to do the research and learn the lessons for ourselves.

CHAPTER 19

The Way Forward

ANSWERS ARE ELUSIVE BECAUSE the whole UFO/UAP arena is chaotic and confused. There are compelling reasons for wanting greater confidence and certainty but the nature of the evidence is like the proverbial parson's egg – only good in parts.

Sometimes I get the impression that elusive answers are precisely what the ufologists themselves subconsciously want. The study of the phenomenon and the money to be made from books, DVDs and such like have become ends in themselves. For the unpaid volunteers who work hard to uncover the facts behind sightings all over the world the task itself becomes a defining part of their lives. So why do anything to bring all that to an end?

As with any other area of human endeavour one will find among ufologists the greedy, the avaricious, the hoaxers and the conmen (is there a word for con-persons?), but most people in the UFO field are simply ordinary Joes trying to do the best they can for constructive reasons. From the outsider's standpoint the main problem is that nothing has really happened. Seventy years of such well-intentioned endeavours have produced virtually no progress. Far from destroying the work of local enthusiasts and national study groups, a more organised, cooperative, and scientific future would actually create a greater sense of fulfilment and, hopefully, more substantial and robust results.

A Science of UFOs

Over the past seventy years there have been sporadic scientific evaluations of existing sightings or even fairly detailed attempts, such as the Condign study, to assess possible causes. But *sustained* scientific investigation of the phenomenon itself has not been attempted (at least, not in public). A phenomenon which forms a pervasive, ongoing theme in the culture of the modern world, and looks set to continue in undiminished numbers, deserves far more intensive treatment.

There is some reason to believe that groups such as those in France (UFO-Science, GEIPAN, Sigma 2) and the United States (UFOData, NICAP, NARCAP, CUFOS) may be beginning to nibble at the issue, but progress is painfully slow, and there have been few genuinely scientific outputs to date.

All of the American studies since the Robertson Panel, and both of the British studies (the Flying Saucer Working Party and the Condign report), reached conclusions that UFOs are simply the result of natural phenomena and human suggestibility. Yet, in spite of seventy years of ridicule and abuse, the great American and British publics continue to report what they see. And a surprising number of UFO reports keep coming in from professional and other highly credible observers. People can be wrong, but are we really trying to say that *all* these reports over such a long period of time are wrong? The reports of the thousands of witnesses deserve to be treated respectfully and with due diligence; not with disdain and insolence.

While a few people have attempted to establish proper scientific research processes with decent equipment (particularly in the United States in the early days – see below – and by private groups in France and Norway in more recent years), for the most part, such scientific work as has been done by Condon, by Condign, and even by the COMETA Group has simply been the review of secondary data from already recorded cases, usually with scant evidence, and set firmly against current scientific knowledge and conjecture. It's a little like studying volcanoes by only looking at whatever information one can glean from witness statements and photos about past eruptions. Instead, of course, volcanologists study the *current* state of volcanoes; they measure vibrations in the earth with seismometers, they measure heat, they watch the movement of the ground, and they measure electromagnetic anomalies in the surrounding areas. In other words, they really *study* the phenomenon.

One of the earliest attempts at a proper scientific study of the UFO phenomenon is worth reviewing here in the final chapter of this book. It was established in the United States back in 1950 and was the first study which proved that UFOs do *not* exist. It was also the first which, it seems, proved that the phenomenon most certainly *does* exist. But more on that in a moment.

As we've already seen, the sightings of strange objects in the skies of America between about 1945 and 1949 gave the powers-that-be a serious scare. In public, the explanations were of natural phenomena or misidentified objects, but in private, it seems a battle was fought between those who were sure the things were Soviet aircraft of advanced design and those who had reluctantly come to the conclusion that they might be extraterrestrial. In those years, the region around the White Sands facility was regarded as being of the utmost secrecy and sensitivity. It also experienced multiple UFO sightings. Between 1947 and 1949, a number of unexplained objects had been seen near and over the range, most of which were described as "fireballs".

A hovering object photographed by Ella Fortune over the White Sands rocket testing ground in October 1957. (Charles Walker/Topfoto.co.uk)

As the data on sightings flowed in, especially from military personnel and from locations near sensitive bases, the top brass realised that there was really only one way to be sure. There needed to be a serious research programme established, with scientific-grade equipment and instruments. It needed to be properly operated and designed to record as many UFO events as possible.

Such a programme, named Project Twinkle, was established (it's a name which stands with the British Flying Saucer Working Party as evidence that governments sometimes do express a sense of humour – even if unwittingly).

The idea was to use an existing database of sightings, maintained by a Colonel Rees at Kirtland AFB, to identify the best places from which flying saucers might be photographed and measured. The initial $20,000, half-year project to set up a scientific watch was awarded to a company called Land-Air Inc.[159] It began March 23, 1950, equipped with photo-theodolites, spectrographic cameras, and radio spectrum analysers. The instruments were manned twenty-four hours a day, and the plan was to have them in at least three locations so that sightings might be triangulated. If two highly accurate cine-theodolites could track the same object, it would be possible to calculate speed, height, direction, course, and size. And if that could be achieved, the objects would be confirmed as real, and the authorities would gain a good idea of size and capabilities.[160]

Project Twinkle ran through two six-month contracts ending in March 1951 with, as the project head Dr Louis Elterman put it in his final report in November 1951, "no information gained". On the surface, therefore, that would seem to be a pretty decisive outcome. A decent scientific study of a supposedly UFO-infested area turns up zilch.

For his 2014 book, however, Bruce Maccabee unearthed a number

---

[159] That six-month contract would be worth around $250,000 these days. Land-Air Inc. – along with many other companies – was subsumed into what is now DynCorp International, a major US government contractor which still holds maintenance contracts for White Sands and nearby bases.

[160] There's a photo of a photo-theodolite and more explanation here: http://www.nicap. org/ncp/ncp-brumac.htm

of interesting things about Project Twinkle. Firstly, for some unknown reason, the visual sightings of unidentified objects dropped off to almost nothing as soon as the project began. In 1949, there had been seventy-five UFO sightings in the New Mexico area around the key US bases and research establishments of Holloman, Los Alamos, Sandia, Alamogordo, and White Sands. A high proportion of these sightings of strange objects were by US military personnel. This rate of sightings was exceeded in 1950, so it was eminently sensible to set up the research around these sensitive bases. But the rate of sightings dropped off remarkably once the equipment of Project Twinkle had been installed and its crews were avidly scanning the skies.

It's an interesting finding in itself. If UFOs are just natural phenomena or due to human frailty, there really should be no reason why the frequency of events should drop off so abruptly simply because a research project had been set up. It's almost as if either something like Heisenberg's uncertainty principle has some impact on UFO sightings (that is, the very presence of instrumented observers affects the frequency of the events) or, and this is the weirdest possibility, the UFOs somehow knew that there was a research project with reasonably accurate instruments and decided to massively reduce their appearances in the area. Sceptics might argue that everyone knew the research was going on and therefore held back on their hysterical hallucinations. There's something in this point but it assumes that virtually everyone – military and civilian – knew all about the project.

The second interesting thing pointed out by Bruce Maccabee is that the project might have been designed and operated in a less-than-sensible way. Maccabee says that the project's choice of locations was flawed. One of the areas covered by a team of technicians was Vaughn AFB which, according to Rees' database, did not have a history of lots of UFO sightings. It could have been designed as a "control" area but the whole idea of Twinkle was to try to triangulate and that would be difficult-to-impossible if one of the tracking stations was in an area where few UFOs were being seen.

Thirdly, there is evidence, according to Maccabee, that Project

Twinkle actually *did* succeed. Dr Elterman, it seems, did not notice the report, thought it too slender a case, or deliberately ignored it. Maccabee says that a single corroborated sighting by the technical teams was, in fact, acquired and partially triangulated. Maccabee found evidence for this in the National Archives in the papers of Dr Anthony Mirarchi, who had been the first head of Project Twinkle[161]. The report says that on April 27, 1950, the cameras recorded objects travelling at high speed at one hundred fifty thousand feet over Holloman AFB. The theodolites measured the objects as being about thirty feet across.

As Maccabee accurately states, these were not meteors and there were absolutely no human-made aircraft at that time which could fly at that altitude[162]. There were also no satellites in existence. So, if that report is correct, and we have no reason to doubt it, we are left asking what those high-flying, fast-moving, thirty-foot objects were.[163]

In spite of the scale of the UFO phenomenon, in over seventy years no one has taken a long-term, purely scientific approach by establishing hypotheses, conducting research and experiments, setting up control areas, measuring sightings, considering findings, discounting certain hypotheses, narrowing down the research, and so on. None that we know of.

The long-term monitoring of sightings by civilian UFO groups has been incredibly valuable but has never been sufficiently well-funded to be effective in a scientific sense. Photos and videos are uncalibrated and from amateur equipment, visual sightings lack detail and are insufficiently well investigated and documented, and other issues, including alleged physical evidence, are inconsistently investigated and recorded over the years.

We do have some pretty good witness testimony from professional pilots and some of it is well supported by radar. If these reports relate to

---

[161] The report in question, which was sent to him by Holloman AFB personnel, survived in the National Archives.

[162] One hundred fifty thousand feet is over twenty-eight miles high, almost three times as high as Concorde used to fly and almost four times higher than a modern airliner flies.

[163] Bruce Maccabee. *The FBI-CIA-UFO Connection: The Hidden UFO Activities of USA Intelligence Agencies*. Richard Dolan Press, 2014.

real objects, then why are the authorities dismissing them as being of no concern? And if the UFOs are imaginary, surely there should be a major scientific study into why pilots of aircraft carrying hundreds of people are seeing non-existent things which cause them to imagine that their aircraft are in danger. A further, not-unimportant, question might be: Why do other crew members experience these hallucinations at the same time?

To paraphrase Philip Klass: If they exist we should be investigating them; and if they don't exist we should be psycho-analysing a lot of pilots, air traffic controllers and police officers.

Most aviation authorities will go ballistic if a tiny drone strays into protected airspace[164], they will tear strips off microlight pilots who do the same, and they will bring down the full majesty of the law on the lunatics who endanger aircraft by shining lasers into the sky. Yet an object seen by multiple witnesses *within* the perimeter and airspace of Chicago O'Hare Airport is ignored, and UFO near-misses or UFOs with very bright lights are rarely given anything but a cursory look to see if they were drones, microlights, and such like. If not, then they go down as "unexplained" and we all get back to our day jobs.

The official response might well be that the authorities are 100 percent certain that UFOs are of no danger to either people or aircraft, that every single sighting is just a misinterpretation or mirage. But if so, why not say so? Why not explain to us why they are so certain and ask the aviation authorities to tell pilots not to worry about UFOs. If they see something, just ignore it, because it definitely – provably – doesn't exist. We'd just have to hope that all pilots would be able to tell immediately whether what was appearing in front of them was an hallucination or a microlight slap bang in the middle of the approach path.

In the late 1990s, alongside (but entirely unconnected with) the British Condign study and the French COMETA group, a senior academic at a top-class academic institution rolled up his metaphorical sleeves and got his hands dirty (as well as those of a number of other academics).

---

[164] In 2017 the British and American governments were considering changing the law to permit lethal force against drones which stray into protected airspace.

In 1997, Dr Peter Sturrock of Stamford University directed a small scientific inquiry into the UFO phenomenon. In scientific terms, it was the first since the Condon study (he would have been unaware of the Condign research). The idea was to see what a new group of scientists would conclude about UFOs. A four-day conference was convened in upstate New York to rigorously review evidence associated with UFO reports. Seven investigators presented well-researched cases with photographic evidence, ground traces and injuries to vegetation, analysis of debris allegedly from crashed UFOs, radar evidence, interference with automobile functioning and aircraft equipment, apparent gravitational or inertial effects, and physiological effects on witnesses. A review panel of nine scientists from diverse fields reviewed the presentations. Most of the panel members were "decidedly sceptical agnostics" who did not have prior involvement with UFOs.

They said that they were unable to conclude anything specific in such a short time but they made a number of recommendations:

- that there should be continued careful evaluation of UFO reports;
- that the Condon study was out of date (one wonders what they would have thought of the 400-plus page Condign Report);
- that whenever there are unexplained phenomena, they should be investigated; and,
- that further investigation and study of UFO data could contribute to the resolution of the UFO problem.

Occasional reviews by panels of scientists seem to be the norm in the UFO debate over the decades, and the Sturrock group was, unfortunately, just another in a long line of forgotten studies.

Yet there are a few private bodies which attempt an explicitly scientific approach on a longer term basis. Dr Haines's National Aviation Reporting Center on Anomalous Phenomena (NARCAP) has done its best to make it safe for pilots and other aviation people to report sightings of unidentified aerial phenomena. But NARCAP, in common with many private national UFO bodies, can only undertake analysis of mainly secondary data;

that is, witness reports and sometimes primary radar data where it is made available. Encouragingly, the organisation now works with other like-minded organisations overseas such as the Chilean *Comision de Estudio de Fenomeno Aerospaciales* (CEFAA) and the *Association Aeronautique Astronautique de France Commission Sigma 2* (3AF Sigma 2). One would hope to see that web of scientific cooperation expanded in the years to come.

Sigma 2 was formed in 2008 and works with GEIPAN to study aerospace anomalies; in particular those which fall into GEIPAN category D. Its website says that the reality of unidentified objects is indisputable, although their origin – artificial or natural – is not yet fully understood:

> "These strange behaviours", it says "defy the laws of physics, especially of mechanics."

There are also a few private bodies which are trying very hard to develop ways of acquiring primary data. They are the twenty-first-century descendants of Project Twinkle. UFO-Science, in France, is doing its best to develop a scientific approach through some pretty nifty equipment. It takes a detached, scientific approach and has developed a variety of UFO-spotting technologies which may or may not work but which look promising. Among them is a system for tracking apparent UFOs and another system for registering the spectrum of any lights which are spotted in the sky.[165]

A more established scientific organisation is that set up by Dr Mark Rodeghier and Dr Alexander Wendt. UFOData is backed by an impressive array of scientists and consultants, and is looking to use donations and crowdsourcing to establish a network of scientific instruments to monitor the skies on a 24/7 basis. The effort to create an automated tracking station appears to be in the proof of concept stage at the time of writing.[166]

The US group NICAP is one of the very oldest UFO organisations. It

---

[165] Take a look at the recordings: http://www.ufo-science.com/recherches/stations-de-detection/liste-des-detections-des-stations-ufo-science/
[166] http://www.ufodata.net/

was regarded as utterly defunct in the late 1980s but has somehow clung on to life and was still operating as of 2016. The organisation's top man, Francis Ridge, is active in the development and promotion of a scientific instrument which they have christened MADAR. This machine, which sounds like something out of a 1950s science fiction movie, is a UFO detector. It has gone through several versions but is now apparently available again.

There have been reasonably large private resources given to a few organisations (e.g. the now apparently defunct FUFOR in the United States), but still the best that the combined forces of ufologists worldwide can come up with is a few databases, some detailed analyses of historic cases, and the results (such as they are, as yet) from the long-term study in Hessdalen, Norway, the French UFO-Science instruments, and the MADAR instrument.

But still, very little cooperation, few joint endeavours, and only the tiniest shoots of long-term, truly scientific research.

A Shift in the Paradigm

As the astute reader will have noticed; the one thing we have certainly been able to do in more recent times is to begin to string-together long series of sightings and events. Flaps and waves have now become streams that are only rarely totally restricted to a single geographic location. In addition, we have begun to understand that, whatever these strange objects and lights are, they can exist not only in the atmosphere, but perhaps even under the water and in space.

It's not much after seventy years but we can conclude that

1. there are certainly such things as UAP/UFOs;
2. huge numbers of sightings are reported across the world every year; upwards of 60,000 and probably far more;
3. there is a small proportion of all reported sightings which is totally inexplicable within our current scientific paradigm (the 5 percent rule);

4. UAP/UFOs remain a persistent anomaly in scientific terms;

5. they occur all the time but can also focus or concentrate on a specific area for a period;

6. they occur worldwide and are not therefore a "national" issue but a global one;

7. their characteristics are fairly consistent over time – particularly those discussed in Chapter 9;

8. whether we like it or not the phenomena are linked with claims of people being temporarily paralysed, abducted, suffering periods of "missing time", and sometimes feeling a mental "link" with UAP;

9. whether we like it or not they are also associated with claims of conspiracies and government cover-ups; and,

10. finding the solution to the persistent anomaly of UFOs/UAP is important in scientific terms whatever they turn out to be.

Furthermore, the question of what these strange sightings, objects and events really are is still nowhere near being answered. The ufologists argue this is because governments and their agencies are covering everything up; the sceptics respond that there's nothing there to be explained.

Where the UFO phenomenon is concerned, the most difficult thing for an outsider is working out what can be done about it. After all, thousands of people have been researching it for well over seventy years without significant progress. Large numbers have written books about it and given lectures and presentations on the subject (some of them to the Pentagon, FBI, CIA, British government, and more), and a good many have presented high-profile experiences and arguments at prestigious conferences such as those at the National Press Club.

And virtually nothing has happened.

It sounds cruel, but let's be brutally honest: After all that time and with all that publicity, after all those books, articles, lectures, conferences, government research projects, and privately-sponsored reviews, almost nothing has changed. Sure, we have several million more words in print and a great deal of "evidence", but no genuine understanding and only the most tenuous shreds of proof.

It's taken us seventy years to get to the point at which we know that rocks fall from the skies. It's just that we have not yet even begun to search scientifically for the reasons why.

We collect "sightings", we are brilliant at amassing historical and qualitative data, and we argue interminably about causes, but very few are studying the phenomenon itself, and certainly no one is doing so on a well-resourced, long-term basis. Yet the outsider might justifiably consider that the UFO phenomenon (if you prefer you can call it the UAP anomaly) is now sufficiently important for it to enter the mainstream of scientific research. It may turn out to be entirely explicable in conventional psychological, social, and physical terms but there are convincing and compelling reasons why it needs to be researched.

In the same way as rocks from the sky, there needs to be a paradigm shift. In his 1962 book, the philosopher Thomas Kuhn mapped out what happens when a new idea comes up against established ideas in science:[167]

1. Something which Kuhn called a "persistent anomaly" is argued to exist which cannot be explained by existing scientific knowledge.
2. By its very existence, the anomaly challenges the prevailing truth, the accepted rules of science.
3. At first, it is dismissed entirely by the establishment of science.
4. Sometimes, it is ridiculed, and anyone who treats it seriously may endanger their careers.
5. Slowly, evidence mounts, and a few brave scientists try to study and define it.
6. This does not help because the scientific establishment closes ranks and further ridicules the idea.
7. Gradually, as the evidence mounts, more senior scientists agree to study it.

---

[167] Thomas S. Kuhn. *The Structure of Scientific Revolutions*. University of Chicago Press, 1962.

8. Eventually, the extra impetus in research produces results, and a new paradigm results.

9. The new reality becomes an accepted part of scientific understanding (until the next paradigm shift comes along).

The road which Kuhn identified has been travelled by hundreds of scientists whose ideas were at first ridiculed and derided by the scientific establishment. Einstein's theories from the early twentieth century are one example. In this century String theory is another. Today it is almost decent. Even prestigious universities are relatively happy for their name to be associated with it. But it wasn't always thus.

The UFO phenomenon is still firmly locked at stage five or six. What is needed is for more senior scientists from the physical and social sciences to give the subject house room. It is most certainly a persistent anomaly. Indeed, the topic is probably the most persistent and pervasive of all modern anomalies. In addition, there are arguably some potentially valuable insights to be gained from its study. So why not mount a proper study into an anomaly which results in upwards of sixty-thousand sightings of UAP and affects people all over the world every year?

The effort to explain it comprehensively would be more than worth the scientific and financial resources. Who knows what significant scientific advances in physics, psychology, aeronautics, meteorology, biology, engineering and sociology may result from such a study?

We need a new and systematic science of UAP/UFOs, on the basis of which we might eventually be able to make informed judgments as opposed to simply reiterating dogmas which have been constructed by sceptics and ufologists from very incomplete data over three-quarters of a century of "things" in the sky.

Such a science will have to do four things:

1. Look to acquire new, objective evidence and data by using current and new scientific instruments and clever experimentation;

2. Examine existing cases and reports only where there are substantial data in them and where they contribute to aggregate patterns and characteristics;
3. Test the data against a wide range of hypotheses;
4. Follow up promising lines of enquiry to advance science and knowledge.

The world is arguably accumulating more than fifteen hundred inexplicable UFO sightings a year. Over the next decade that will deliver a massive base of study material to a well-funded scientific study.[168] That's going to take concerted effort by some heavyweight scientists and engineers over a lengthy period. The next questions, therefore, are: who would do it? where would the cash come from? and how much would it take?

I would argue that the global nature of the phenomenon, national rivalries, and in-group jealousies probably preclude any national group organising or leading such an effort. The need for a highly credible international group of senior people to lead it would also tend to discount those with too much baggage from existing bodies. No, it would take a new international, non-profit body formed for purely scientific purposes. Its funds would be used to support university-level research and to help private UFO-group efforts wherever possible. It would need to be neutral and English-speaking but probably not headquartered in the USA (too much baggage) It could for example be headquartered somewhere like Edinburgh with offices in the USA, England, France, and representatives in most of the world's nations. It should be a totally transparent body with regular reports to its members and only the most reasonable licence fees for any science outcomes.

The cost? It would need to raise a lot of cash – enough to fund several decades of ongoing research (we are probably talking $50 million to $60 million per year). Some, to get it all started, might come from scientifically-minded billionaires and multi-millionaires. There are over

---

[168] That's based on conservative estimates of total sightings and my "5 percent rule". In 2017 the GEIPAN percentage was nine percent and others say anything from ten to thirty.

2,000 billionaires in the world today (according to Forbes magazine's annual tally) and no one knows how many people who are close to that level of wealth.

Once the new organisation attracted enough initial funding for (say) three years of operation it might launch a global crowd sourcing effort and open its doors to membership across the planet. Those sources would potentially provide a large amount of money for the central fund – enough to enable the body to conduct research and to deliver scientific insights for decades to come.

A global UAP Research body run on commercial lines but with a scientific purpose would attract massive public support and – due to the primacy of science and the distance from existing UFO organisations – many top university scientists might find it possible to lend their names to such a venture.

There are lots of people out there who will smile indulgently and say that none of this will ever happen because "they" will not permit it. Even asking for such a research project will seem, to them, incredibly naïve in the face of the global conspiracy which they take for granted. The actual nature of the cover-up and conspiracy differs subtly from author to author but they are certain it exists. But, such cover-ups as have existed and may still exist may not be quite as sinister as the prophets of doom have made out. There may be a whole host of fairly mundane and sensible reasons why things have been swept under carpets.

Shifting the paradigm to Kuhn's levels seven and eight is, amazingly, a win-win situation. If some of the UFOs/UAP turn out to be from some-where other than this planet or time we'll have changed humanity's future profoundly and for ever (hopefully for the better). If, on the other hand, they are hitherto unknown physical, social or psychological phenomena, the answers will have a similarly profound and lasting impact on science and technology across the board; on future engineering and propulsion technologies, Earth-sciences, the social sciences, and much more.

UAP, whatever they are, constitute an anomaly with considerable scientific promise. Perhaps the most successful scientific investigation of recent years has been the Cassini-Huygens mission. In thirteen years it astounded almost everyone with the sheer amount and variety of scientific data it gathered about the Saturn system. The total cost was probably around $5bn – around $385m per year. One would think it would be worth $60m a year to solve a significant, seventy year old anomaly here on Earth.

Make It Happen

This book was intended to make you consider the UFO phenomenon in a new way: not as a fringe interest of geeks and weirdos, but as something which, at its core, raises a great many unanswered scientific questions, the solutions to which might help us to expand our knowledge and understanding of the world and, possibly, of things that are a lot more distant. The effort might also enhance international cooperation.

So, forget the aliens, forget the abductions, forget the conspiracies and cover-ups. This whole subject needs to be taken one step at a time, and the first step is to find the answers to a very simple question:

What are the phenomena which make up the 5 percent?

As an outsider one has to say that there is simply far too much in the way of evidence of an anomaly for the scientists to continue their "there's no such thing" act. I challenge any open minded scientist to read this book and then say that there is nothing at all to be gained in scientific terms from deeper study and serious evaluation.

Unexplained UFOs exist in large numbers and are being experienced by people all over the world all the time. At present, we have only theories and conjectures. Are they unknown atmospheric and electromagnetic phenomena, little-understood social or psychological forces, extraterrestrial visitors, interdimensional tourists, fantastic mental projections? Who knows ... yet?

Whatever they are, we need to know. And there is only one person who can make that happen: you.

Glossary of Terms, Acronyms, and Organisations

3AF Sigma 2
Association Aeronautique Astronautique de France Commission Sigma 2.

APRO
Aerial Phenomena Research Organization (US); no longer exists.

BST
British Summer Time – one hour ahead of GMT and Zulu time.

BUFORA
British UFO Research Association; established in 1962 and still going. Its website is, unfortunately, not a good shop window to an organisation which does good work and tries its best to be scientific in its approach.

CAA
Civil Aviation Authority: the UK body responsible for aviation safety and control.

CEFAA
Chile's Committee for the Study of Anomalous Aerial Phenomena, founded in 1997 and directed by General Ricardo Bermúdez.

CENAP
German UFO investigative body.

CIA
Central Intelligence Agency (US).

CNES
French national space agency: *Centre National d'Etudes Spatiales.*

COBEPS
Belgian UFO investigative body.

COMETA
French group of scientists and ex-military who investigated and wrote the COMETA Report in 1999.

CSETI
Center for the Study of Extraterrestrial Intelligence: Dr Stephen Greer's organisation, founded in 1990 (US).

CSICOP
Committee for the Scientific Investigation of Claims of the Paranormal (Klass): launched in 1976 and now called the Committee for Skeptical Enquiry, but still widely referred to as CSICOP.

CIAAP
In 1985, the Soviet Union established the Commission for the Investigation of Anomalous Atmospheric Phenomena within and under the ultimate control of the Academy of Sciences. After the demise of the USSR, a number of Russian UFO organisations were represented by SoyuzUFOsentr (the Unified UFO Centre).

CUFOS
Center for UFO Studies, established in 1973 by J Allen Hynek.

CUFORS
China UFO Research Society: established in 1980 within the Chinese Academy of Social Sciences.

ELINT
Electronic intelligence gathered by the use of electronic sensors.

FAA
Federal Aviation Administration: the US body responsible for aviation safety and control.

FBI
Federal Bureau of Investigation (US).

FUFOR
Fund for UFO Research.

GEIPAN
Groupe d'Etudes et d'Informations sur les Phénomène Aerospatiaux Non-indentifies: from 2005, the current organisation responsible for receiving, investigating, and providing information on UFO sightings in France. It is part of CNES. Launched in 1977, it was originally called GEPAN.

GEPAN
See GEIPAN.

GMT
Greenwich Mean Time: equivalent to UTC and military Zulu time

IMINT
Imagery intelligence collects information via satellite and aerial photography.

MoD

UK Ministry of Defence (a variety of military-related departments within the MoD looked at UFO reports through to about 2009).

MUFON

Mutual UFO Network (US).

NARCAP

Richard Haines's National Aviation Reporting Center on Anomalous Phenomena: established in 2001 (US).

NASA

National Aeronautics and Space Administration (US).

NICAP

National Investigations Committee on Aerial Phenomena: was thought to be extinct by the 1980s but, apparently, is still going.

NORAD

North American Aerospace Defense Command

NUFORC (US)

Peter Davenport's National UFO Reporting Center: still going strong but, unfortunately for those with poor eyesight, still uses the outdated, white-on-black website display.

Project 1947 (US)

Valuable Web-based resources on much of the early days of the phenomenon.

SEPRA

Service d'Etude des Phénomènes de Rentrées Atmosphériques (Department for the Study of Atmospheric Re-entry Phenomena): GEPAN became SEPRA in 1988, moving decisively away from any mention of UFOs.

UFO-Science (France)

French UFO organisation dedicated to scientific investigations and the development of tracking devices.

SIGINT

Intelligence from electronic signals and systems used by foreign targets, such as communications systems, radars, and weapons systems.

UAP

Unidentified/Unknown aerial phenomenon (or phenomena).

UFO

Unidentified flying object.

UTC

Universal Coordinated Time = GMT = military Zulu time

Zulu

Universal military time. Used particularly by the USA and NATO to ensure exact coordination. It is equal to GMT and UTC.

Bibliography (Chronological)

1948   USAF. *Analysis of Flying Object Incidents in the US*. Air Intelligence Report No. 100-203-79, December 1948 (see http://www.nicap. org/docs/airintelrpt100-203-79.pdf)

1950   Skully, Frank. *Behind the Flying Saucers: The Truth about the Aztec UFO Crash*. The first book about UFO crashes, reprinted August 1, 2008.

1950   Keyhoe, Donald. *The Flying Saucers Are Real*. CreateSpace.

1952   Arnold, Kenneth, and Palmer, Raymond. *The Coming of the Saucers*. Createspace Publishers.

1953   Keyhoe, Donald. *Flying Saucers from Outer Space*. Henry Holt.

1956   Ruppelt, Edward J. (former head of Project Blue Book). *The Report on Unidentified Flying Objects*. Ace Books, Doubleday, 1956; revised edition 1959.

1962   Kuhn, Thomas S. *The Structure of Scientific Revolutions*. University of Chicago Press.

1964   Hall, Richard H. (ed.). *The UFO Evidence*. NICAP.

1965   Quintanilla, Hector, Jr. *Letter*. Reprinted in Hynek, *The Hynek UFO Report*. Dell Publishers, 1977.

1966   Fuller, John G. *Incident at Exeter*. New York: G.P. Putnam's Sons.

Klass, Philip J. "Plasma theory may explain many UFOs." *Aviation Week & Space Technology*. August 22.

Vallée, Jacques, and Vallée, Janine. *Challenge to Science: The UFO Enigma*. NTC/Contemporary Publishing.

1968   Jones, Dr R V. "The Natural Philosophy of Flying Saucers." *Physics Bulletin, 19, 7*.

Däniken, Erich von. *Chariots of the Gods*; currently Souvenir Press.

Klass, Philip J. *UFOs: Identified*. Random House.

1969   Condon, Edward U. *Scientific Study of Unidentified Flying Objects*. Bantam Books.

1972   Hynek, J Allen. *The UFO Experience: A Scientific Enquiry*. Marlowe & Company.

1974   Klass, Philip J. *UFOs Explained*. Random House and Vintage (1976).

1975   Jacobs, David. *The UFO Controversy in America*. Indiana University Press.

1977   Hynek, J Allen. *The Hynek UFO Report*. Dell Publishers.

1979   Hendry, Allan. *The UFO Handbook: A Guide to Investigating, Evaluating, and Reporting UFO Sightings*. Doubleday.

1980   Story, Ronald D. *The Encyclopedia of UFOs*. Garden City, New York: Doubleday.

1981   Sachs, Margaret. *The UFO Encyclopedia*. Putnam.

1983   Klass, Philip J. *UFOs: The Public Deceived*. Prometheus.

1984   Fawcett, Lawrence, and Greenwood, Barry J. *Clear Intent*. Prentice-Hall.

1985   Hynek, J Allen. *The Roots of Complacency*.

1986   Sheaffer, Robert. *The UFO Verdict*. Amherst, New York: Prometheus Books.

1987   Hynek, J Allen, Imbrogno, Philip J, and Pratt, Bob. *Night Siege: The Hudson Valley Sightings*. Llewellyn Publishers.

        Vallée, Jacques. *UFOs in Space: Anatomy of a Phenomenon*. Mass Market Paperback.

1988   Good, Timothy. *Above Top Secret*. William Morrow.

1989   Klass, Philip J. *UFO Abductions: A Dangerous Game*. Prometheus.

1991   Spencer, John. *UFO Encyclopedia*. Headline Books.

1994   Peebles, Curtis. *Watch the Skies!: A Chronicle of the Flying Saucer Myth*. Berkley Books.

1995   Berliner, Don. *UFO Briefing Document*. Dell.

US Air Force. *The Roswell Report: Fact versus Fiction in the New Mexico Desert.*

1996   Hopkins, Budd. *Witnessed.* Pocket Books, Simon & Schuster.

Friedman, Stanton T. *Top Secret/Majic.* Marlowe & Co.

Pope, Nick. *Open Skies, Closed Minds.* Pocket Books.

1997   Corso, Lt Col Philip J. *The Day after Roswell.* Simon & Schuster.

Stone, Clifford E. *UFOs Are Real.* SPI Books.

Klass, Philip J. *The Real Roswell Crashed-saucer Coverup.* Prometheus.

Spencer, John. *The New UFO Encyclopedia.* Revised 2nd ed.

1998   Clark, Jerome. *The UFO Encyclopedia*, 2nd ed., vols. 1 and 2. Omnigraphics, Inc.

1999   COMETA Report.

Sturrock, Peter A. *The UFO Enigma: A New Review of the Physical Evidence.* Warner Books.

Maccabee, Dr Bruce. "Optical Power Output of an Unidentified High Altitude Light Source." *Journal of Scientific Exploration, 13,* 2, p. 199.

Truman, Harry S. *Memoirs.* 1945. Konecky & Konecky, reprinted, 1999.

2000   Dolan, Richard M. *UFOs and the National Security State*. Keyhole Publishing Co.

Maccabee, Bruce. *UFO/ FBI Connection*. Llewellyn Publications.

Condign. *Unidentified Aerial Phenomena in the UK Defence Region*. UK Condign Report (researched 1996–2000; released 2006).

Hall, Michael David. *UFOs: A Century of Sightings*. Galde Press.

2001   Hall, Richard H. *The UFO Evidence: A Thirty-Year Report*, vol. 2. The Scarecrow Press.

Weinstein, Dominique F. *Unidentified Aerial Phenomena: Eighty Years of Pilot Sightings*. National Aviation Reporting Center on Anomalous Phenomena (www.narcap.org), Technical Report 4.

Davenport, Peter B, and Geremia, Peter. "Exeter (New Hampshire) sightings." In *Story*, 170–72.

Storey, Ronald D. *The Encyclopedia of Extraterrestrial Encounters*. New York: New American Library.

2002   Carlson, Peter. "50 Years Ago, Unidentified Flying Objects From Way Beyond the Beltway Seized the Capital's Imagination." *Washington Post*, July 21.

Story, Ronald. *The Mammoth Encyclopedia of Extraterrestrial Encounters*. Mammoth Books, Robinson.

2003   Druffel, Ann. *Firestorm: Dr. James E. McDonald's Fight for UFO Science*.

Hallion, Richard P. *Taking Flight: Inventing the Aerial Age, from Antiquity through the First World War*. OUP USA.

2004   Parmentier, François, and Vélasco, Jean-Jacques. *OVNI. 60 ans de désinformation (UFOs: 60 Years of Disinformation)*. Editions Rocher.

Vélasco, Jean-Jacques. *OVNIS: L'évidence (UFOs: The Evidence)*. April.

2005   Salas, Robert, and Klotz, James. *Faded Giant*. Booksurge Publishing.

2006   Good, Timothy. *A Need to Know: UFOs, the Military and Intelligence*. Sidgwick & Jackson.

2007   Sillard, Yves. *Phénomènes spatiaux non identifies - Un défi à la science (Unidentified Aerospatial Phenomena. A Challenge to Science)*. Le Cherche Midi. April.

2008   Baure, Jean-François, Clarke, David, Fuller, Paul, and Shough, Martin. *Report on Aerial Phenomena Observed Near the Channel Islands, UK, April 23 2007*. February. http:// www.guernsey.uk-ufo.org/.

Wendt, Alexander, Ohio State University, and Raymond Duvall, University of Minnesota. "Sovereignty and the UFO." *Political Theory*, 36, 4.

2009   Fox, James. *I Know What I Saw*. DVD documentary. Break-Thru Films.

Clarke, David. *The UFO Files: The Inside Story of Real Life Sightings*. National Archives (UK).

2010   Kean, Leslie. *UFOs: Generals, Pilots, and Government Officials Go On the Record.* Crown/Archetype.

Bennett, Colin. *Flying Saucers over the White House.* Cosimo.

Spaulding, Richard E. "An Atmospheric Electrical Hypothesis for Spherical Luminosities Occurring at Aircraft Altitudes." January 2010 in Richard Haines, et al. *Spherical UAP and Aviation Safety: A Critical Review.* April. NARCAP.

2011   Jacobsen, Annie. *Area 51: An Uncensored History of America's Top Secret Military Base.* Orion.

2012   Weinstein, Dominique, F. *Aviation Safety and Unidentified Aerial Phenomena: A Preliminary Study of 600 Cases of Unidentified Aerial Phenomena (UAP) Reported by Military & Civilian Pilots.* NARCAP.

Fox, James (Director). *Out of the Blue: Definitive Investigation of the UFO Phenomenon.* DVD documentary.

Swords, Michael, and Powell, Robert. *UFOs and Government: A Historical Inquiry.* Anomalous Books.

2014   Pope, Nick. *Encounter in Rendlesham Forest.* Thistle Publishing, St Martin's Griffin.

Salas, Robert. *Unidentified: The UFO Phenomenon.* Career Press.

Maccabee, Dr Bruce. *The FBI-CIA-UFO Connection: The Hidden UFO Activities of USA Intelligence Agencies.* CreateSpace Publishing.

Dolan, Richard. *UFOs for the 21ˢᵗ Century Mind: A Fresh Guide to an Ancient Mystery*. Richard Dolan Press.

2015   Basterfield, Keith, and Dean, Paul. *Near-miss between an Australia [sic] Airplane and an "Unknown Object" near Perth, Western Australia, on 19ᵗʰ March 2014*. NARCAP IR-7; January.

Clarke, David. *How UFOs Conquered the World: The History of a Modern Myth*. Aurum Press Ltd.

2016   Friedman, Stanton T, and Marden, Kathleen. *Fact, Fiction, and Flying Saucers*. New Page Books.

2017   Redfern, Nick; *The Roswell UFO Conspiracy: Exposing A Shocking And Sinister Secret*; Lisa Hagan Books. 2017.

Bibliography (By Author)

Arnold, Kenneth, and Palmer, Raymond
  The Coming of the Saucers. Createspace
  Publishers, 1952.

Basterfield, Keith, and Dean, Paul
  *Near-miss between an Australia [sic] Airplane
  and an "Unknown Object" near Perth, Western
  Australia, on 19th March 2014.* NARCAP IR-7,
  January 2015.

Baure, Jean-François, Clarke, David, Fuller, Paul, and Shough, Martin
  *Report on Aerial Phenomena Observed Near
  the Channel Islands, UK, April 23 2007.*
  February 2008. http://www.martinshough.
  com/aerialphenomena/Report%20on%20
  Channel%20Islands%20UAPs%2023.04.07.pdf

Bennett, Colin *Flying Saucers over the White House.* Cosimo,
  2010.

Berliner, Don *UFO Briefing Document.* Dell, 1995.

Clark, Jerome *The UFO Encyclopedia,* 2nd ed., vols. 1 and 2.
  Omnigraphics, Inc., 1998.

Clarke, David	*The UFO Files: The Inside Story of Real Life Sightings.* National Archives (UK), 2009. *How UFOs Conquered the World: The History of a Modern Myth.* Aurum Press Ltd., 2014.
COMETA	COMETA Report, 1999.
Condign	*Unidentified Aerial Phenomena in the UK Defence Region.* UK Condign Report (researched 1996-2000; released 2006).
Condon, Edward U	*Scientific Study of Unidentified Flying Objects.* Bantam Books, 1969.
Corso, Lt Col Philip J	*The Day after Roswell.* Simon & Schuster, 1997.
Däniken, Erich von	*Chariots of the Gods.* Souvenir Press. 1968.
Davenport, Peter B, and Geremia, Peter	"Exeter (New Hampshire) sightings." In *Story,* 2001, 170–72.
Dolan, Richard M	*UFOs and the National Security State.* Keyhole Publishing Co. 2000. *UFOs for the 21st Century Mind: A Fresh Guide to an Ancient Mystery.* Richard Dolan Press. 2014.
Fawcett, Lawrence, and Greenwood, Barry J	*Clear Intent.* Prentice-Hall, 1984.
Druffel, Ann	*Firestorm: Dr. James E. McDonald's Fight for UFO Science.* Granite Publishing, 2003 (2nd ed. 2006).

Friedman, Stanton T   *Top Secret/ Majic.* Marlowe & Co., 1996.

Friedman, Stanton T, and Marden, Kathleen
     Fact, Fiction, and Flying Saucers. New Page
     Books, 2016.

Fox, James (Director)   *Out of the Blue: Definitive Investigation of the
UFO Phenomenon.* DVD documentary.
I Know What I Saw. DVD documentary. Break-
Thru Films, 2009.

Fuller, John G   *Incident at Exeter.* New York: G.P. Putnam's
Sons, 1966.

Good, Timothy   *Above Top Secret.* William Morrow, 1988.
*A Need to Know: UFOs, the Military and
Intelligence.* Sidgwick & Jackson, 2006.

Hall, Michael David   *UFOs: A Century of Sightings,* Galde Press, 2000.

Hall, Richard H (ed.)   *The UFO Evidence.* NICAP, 1964.
The UFO Evidence: A Thirty-Year Report, Vol. 2.
The Scarecrow Press, 2001.

Hallion, Richard P   *Taking Flight: Inventing the Aerial Age, from
Antiquity through the First World War.* OUP
USA, 2003.

Hendry, Allan   *The UFO Handbook: A Guide to Investigating,
Evaluating, and Reporting UFO Sightings.*
Doubleday, 1979.

Hopkins, Budd   *Witnessed.* Pocket Books, Simon & Schuster,
1996.

Hynek, J Allen   *The UFO Experience: A Scientific Enquiry.*
                        Marlowe & Company, 1972.
                        The Hynek UFO Report. Dell Publishers, 1977.
                        The Roots of Complacency. 1985.

Hynek, J Allen, Imbrogno, Philip J, and Pratt, Bob
                        Night Siege: The Hudson Valley Sightings.
                        Llewellyn Publishers, 1987.

Jacobs, David   *The UFO Controversy in America.* Indiana
                        University Press, 1975.

Jacobsen, Annie   *Area 51: An Uncensored History of America's Top
                        Secret Military Base.* Orion. 2011.

Jones, Dr R V   "The Natural Philosophy of Flying Saucers."
                        Physics Bulletin, 19, 7, 1968.

Kean, Leslie   *UFOs: Generals, Pilots, and Government Officials
                        Go on the Record.* Crown/Archetype, 2010.

Keyhoe, Donald   *The Flying Saucers Are Real.* CreateSpace, 1950.

                        Flying Saucers from Outer Space. Henry Holt,
                        1953.

Klass, Philip J   "Plasma theory may explain many UFOs."
                        Aviation Week & Space Technology. August 22,
                        1966.
                        UFOs: Identified. Random House, 1968.
                        UFOs Explained. Random House and Vintage,
                        1974.
                        UFOs: The Public Deceived. Prometheus, 1983.

UFO Abductions: A Dangerous Game.
Prometheus, 1989.
The Real Roswell Crashed-saucer Coverup.
Prometheus, 1997.

Kuhn, Thomas S   *The Structure of Scientific Revolutions.* University of Chicago Press. 1962.

Maccabee, Dr Bruce   "Optical Power Output of an Unidentified High Altitude Light Source." *Journal of Scientific Exploration, 13,* 2, p. 199, 1999.
UFO/FBI Connection. Llewellyn Publications, 2000.
The FBI-CIA-UFO Connection: The Hidden UFO Activities of USA Intelligence Agencies.
CreateSpace Publishing, 2014.

Parmentier, François, and Vélasco, Jean-Jacques
OVNI. 60 ans de désinformation (UFOs: 60 Years of Disinformation). Editions Rocher, 2004.

Peebles, Curtis   Watch the Skies!: A Chronicle of the Flying Saucer Myth. Berkley Books, 1994

Pope, Nick   *Open Skies, Closed Minds.* Pocket Books, 1996.
Encounter in Rendlesham Forest. Thistle Publishing, St Martin's Griffin, 2014.

Quintanilla, Hector, Jr.   *Letter,* 1965 reprinted in Hynek, *The Hynek UFO Report.* Dell Publishers, 1977.

Redfern, Nick   *The Roswell UFO Conspiracy: Exposing A Shocking And Sinister Secret;* Lisa Hagan Books. 2017.

Ruppelt, Edward J   *The Report on Unidentified Flying Objects.* Ace
                     Books, Doubleday, 1956; revised edition, 1959.

Sachs, Margaret   *The UFO Encyclopedia.* Putnam, 1981.

Salas, Robert   *Unidentified: The UFO Phenomenon.* Career
                     Press, 2014.

Sheaffer, Robert   *The UFO Verdict.* Amherst, New York:
                     Prometheus Books, 1986.

Sillard, Yves   *Phénomènes spatiaux non identifies - Un défi à la
                     science (Unidentified Aerospatial Phenomena. A
                     Challenge to Science).* Le Cherche Midi, April
                     2007.

Skully, Frank   *Behind the Flying Saucers: The Truth about the
                     Aztec UFO Crash.* 1950; reprinted 2008.

Spaulding, Richard E "An Atmospheric Electrical Hypothesis for
                     Spherical Luminosities Occurring at Aircraft
                     Altitudes." January 2010 in *Spherical UAP and
                     Aviation Safety – A Critical Review.* NARCAP,
                     April 2010.

Spencer, John   *UFO Encyclopedia.* Headline Books. 1991.
                     The New UFO Encyclopedia. Headline, Revised
                     2nd ed., 1997.

Story, Ronald D   *The Encyclopedia of UFOs.* Garden City, New
                     York: Doubleday. 1980.
                     The Encyclopedia of Extraterrestrial Encounters.
                     New York: New American Library, 2001.

The *Mammoth Encyclopedia of Extraterrestrial Encounters*. Mammoth Books, Robinson, 2002.

Stone, Clifford E   *UFOs Are Real*. SPI Books, 1997.

Sturrock, Peter A   *The UFO Enigma: A New Review of the Physical Evidence*. Warner Books, 1999.

Swords, Michael, and Powell, Robert
                           UFOs and Government: A Historical Inquiry. Anomalous Books, 2012

Truman, Harry S   *Memoirs, Vol. 1. 1945: Year of Decisions*. Konecky & Konecky, reprinted 1999.

US Air Force   Air Force. *Analysis of Flying Object Incidents in the US*. Air Intelligence Report No. 100-203-79, December 1948 (see http://www.nicap.org/docs/airintelrpt100-203-79.pdf)
                           The Roswell Report: Fact versus Fiction in the New Mexico Desert. 1995.

Vallée, Jacques, and Vallée, Janine
                           Challenge to Science: The UFO Enigma. NTC/ Contemporary Publishing, 1966.

Vallée, Jacques   *UFOs in Space: Anatomy of a Phenomenon*. Mass Market Paperback, 1987.

Vélasco, Jean-Jacques   *OVNIS: L'évidence (UFOs: The Evidence)*. April 2004, Salas, Robert, and Klotz, James. *Faded Giant*. Booksurge Publishing; 2005.

Washington Post   "50 Years Ago, Unidentified Flying Objects from Way Beyond the Beltway Seized the Capital's Imagination." Peter Carlson, *Washington Post*. July 21, 2002.

Weinstein, Dominique F *Unidentified Aerial Phenomena: Eighty Years of Pilot Sightings*. National Aviation Reporting Center on Anomalous Phenomena (www. narcap.org), Technical Report 4, 2001. *Aviation Safety and Unidentified Aerial Phenomena: A Preliminary Study of 600 Cases of Unidentified Aerial Phenomena (UAP) Reported by Military & Civilian Pilots*. NARCAP, NARCAP IR-4; 2012.

Wendt, Alexander, and Duvall, Raymond
          "Sovereignty and the UFO." *Political Theory*, 36, 4, 2008.

Index

Duboc, Jean Charles 220, 221
Dudley Dorito 290

E

East Anglia 242
Echo-Flight 196, 198
Edgeworth, Richard Lovell 18
Edwards, AFB 119, 120
Einstein 140, 141, 159
Einstein, Albert 11
Electro-magnetic interference 147
ELINT 82, 325
Elmendorf AFB 215, 216, 218
Elterman, Dr Louis 310
Engen, Vice-Admiral Donald 217
England (1909) 23
Esterle, Alain 88
Estimate of the Situation (1948) 62
European Union 160
Exercise Big Blast 171
Exeter, 1965 170

F

F-16s 147, 282, 283, 284
F-86 50
F-94 115, 259, 264, 265, 266, 269
F-106 205, 206
FAA 89, 207, 208, 210, 212, 213, 215,
    216, 217, 218, 219, 220, 278,
    303, 325
Farnborough (1950) 47
FBI 4, 38, 51, 62, 65, 217, 312, 317, 325,
    333, 335, 341
fire balloons 174
Flash Gordon 148
flying saucer 2, 5, 33, 37, 38, 45, 61, 98,
    110, 134, 135, 153
Flying Saucer Working Party 47, 49,
    58, 75, 229, 300, 308

Foo-fighters 30, 32
Fort, Charles 163
Fournet, Major Dewey 270
Fox, James 44, 109, 121, 217
France 96
Freedom of Information and Privacy
    Act (FOIPA) 4, 69, 208, 217
FUFOR 316, 325

G

GEIPAN (France) 88, 89, 90, 94, 95,
    96, 100, 102, 103, 104, 132,
    151, 221, 240, 241, 252, 308,
    315, 325
Gendarmerie 88, 221, 239, 240, 252
GEPAN (France) 88, 89, 94, 221, 238,
    239, 252, 325, 326
Ghost rockets 36
Giroud, Major 232
Good, Timothy 23
Gross, Patrick 23, 222
Guérin, Pierre 241
Guerra, Julio 144, 234, 235
Guerra, Portugal 1982 234

H

Haines, Richard ix, 123, 199, 208, 209,
    210, 212, 213, 314, 326, 335
Haisch, Dr Bernard 133
Halifax (WWII RAF Bomber) 30, 31
Halt, Lt Col Charles 150, 244, 245,
    246, 247, 249, 250
Hartman, William 74
Hatton Gardens, London 19, 20, 21
Heisenberg's Uncertainty
    Principle 311
Hellyer, Paul 104, 300
Hessdalen, Norway 292
H G Wells 3, 4

MADAR 316

Magneto-Hydrodynamics 88

Mahopac Falls, 1984 278

Malmstrom 195, 196, 197, 198, 199,
203, 205

Malmstrom AFB 195, 198, 199, 203

Mannor, Frank 180

Marcel, Jesse 43, 44, 45, 46

Marcel, Maj. Jesse A. 42

Marcel, Major Jesse 41

Mars 22

mass delusion 284

Masse, Maurice 239, 240, 241

McMinnville 74, 110

McRoberts, Hannah 123

Menzel, Donald 13

Meteor jet fighter 229

Meteors 9, 19, 20, 21, 115, 136,
137, 271

MI6 v, 4

Michigan, 1966 179

micro-lights 128

Milner, Yuri 129

Ministry of Defence (MoD) 49, 56, 75,
76, 94, 99, 100, 101, 132, 183,
184, 185, 186, 190, 229, 247, 326

Mirage IV (Bomber) 232

Mirarchi, Dr Anthony 312

Mitchell, Dr Edgar 300

M&M theory 163

M&M thesis (Hynek) 97

Mosquito (RAF Fighter) 37

MUFON 101, 276, 277, 279, 326

Muscarello, Norman 171, 172, 173,
174, 175, 177, 179, 277

Mutually-assured destruction 195

N

NARCAP 54, 102, 208, 209, 225, 308,
326, 335, 336, 337, 342, 344

NASA 7, 88, 143, 186, 187, 212, 326

National Academy of Sciences 73

Near field effects 83

Newhouse, Delbert 111, 116, 117

Newton, Sir Isaac ix

New York State, 2015 209

NICAP 71, 204, 308, 315, 326,
329, 339

Nicolai, Renato 251, 253, 254

NORAD 144, 171, 173, 200, 201, 203,
204, 206

North Syracuse, 1983 277

NUFORC 100, 276, 279, 287, 326

Nugent, Edward 262, 268

Nuremburg, Battle of 14

O

O'Hare (Chicago Airport) 155,
206, 207

Operation Ardent 230

Operation Mainbrace 228

Orson Welles 3, 67

Oscar Flight 197, 198

P

Paulden 287, 288

Pease AFB 170, 171, 174, 175, 178, 203

Penniston, James 243, 244, 246, 250

Phoenix Lights 111, 286, 288, 289

Plasma(s) 51, 77, 79, 80, 83, 127, 133,
140, 147, 294

Podesta, John 109

Poher, Claude 88

Poher, Dr Claude 88

police 169

Vandenberg, General Hoyt 56
Velasco, Jean-Jacques 88, 89, 90, 238
Venom (RAF fighter) 194, 195
Venus 20, 22, 137
Verne, Jules 23

W

War of the Worlds 67, 132
Washington National 211, 256,
        257, 260, 262, 264, 265, 267,
        268, 271
Washington National, 1952 256
Washington Post 129, 267, 268, 269,
        272, 344
Washington Press Club 217, 250,
        285, 317
Washington Press Conference
        109, 220
Water 151
Weapons Storage Area 201, 202
Weather balloons 138
wedge shape 37, 38, 57, 84, 133, 148,
        184, 278, 290, 291
Weinstein, Dominique 102
Welles, Orson 67
Wells, H G 22, 23, 67
Wendt, Dr Alexander 315
White, Henry 27
White Sands 40, 309, 310, 311
Windsor Castle (1783) 15, 16, 18, 19
Wobbling 152
Wormholes 141, 159
WSA (Weapons Storage Area) 203
Wurtsmith 199, 203, 204
Wurtsmith AFB 199, 203

Y

YouTube 199, 208, 220

Z

Zamora, Lonnie 51
Zeppelin(s) 26, 110

About the Author

Following a short scholarship to Trinity College in Hartford, Connecticut, he completed a Bachelor's degree in Politics and Economics at the University of York and later researched a Master's thesis at the University of Cambridge on global trade in the aerospace industry.

His career has encompassed time in the aerospace sector, in marketing, in education, and in commercial research. He's written and contributed to around a dozen academic books, and countless lengthy reports. His greatest professional love is research; having the view that there aren't that many jobs in which you get paid for having fun, but that's what research is like.

So why UFOs of all things? The answer is a long one, but it boils down to this: Like almost everyone else, the author gets hooked by a good mystery, and UFOs are perhaps the greatest mystery of all; one which is in desperate need of being properly investigated.

He lives with his wife in Yorkshire, England, where rabbits are the only alien menace. Or so he believes!

UFOs may or may not be of this Earth and time, but the huge job of trying to nail them down is incredibly fascinating.

Printed in the United States
By Bookmasters